D1062302

African American Dance

African American Dance

An Illustrated History

BARBARA S. GLASS

McFarland & Company, Inc., Publishers
Jefferson, North Carolina, and London

LIBRARY OF CONGRESS CATALOGUING-IN-PUBLICATION DATA

Glass, Barbara S., 1946–
African American dance : an illustrated history / Barbara S. Glass.
p.   cm.
Includes bibliographical references and index.

ISBN 13: 978-0-7864-2816-8
ISBN 10: 0-7864-2816-3
(illustrated case binding : 50# alkaline paper)∞

1. African American dance—History.
2. African Americans—Social life and customs.
I. Title.
GV1624.7.A34G53   2007   792.8'08996073—dc22   2006028783

British Library cataloguing data are available

On the cover: dancer ©2006 Comstock; *background*
Red set-girls and Jack in the Green
(artwork by Isaac Mendes Belisario in Belisario's *Sketches
of Character of the Negro Population on the Island of Jamaica* in 1837

Manufactured in the United States of America

*McFarland & Company, Inc., Publishers
Box 611, Jefferson, North Carolina 28640
www.mcfarlandpub.com*

For Terry, Grace, John, and Sarah

Acknowledgments

This book began as an introductory essay in an exhibit catalogue, and I appreciate the help of all who read it and commented on it at that stage of its existence—Vernon Courtney, Director of the National Afro-American Museum and Cultural Center; Floyd Thomas, Curator of Art; and the other members of the exhibit team. In its current longer form, the manuscript received a careful reading and an extensive and thoughtful commentary from John Fleming, Vice President of Cincinnati Museum Center and lifelong black history scholar. His responses were critically important in the revision that followed.

I am grateful to the librarians at the Ohio State University Libraries and at the Greene County Library, without whose patience and help I could not have obtained the resources I needed for this study.

Finally, my family members have been supportive beyond all expectation. My husband Terry, my daughter Grace, and my son John encouraged me throughout the long development of the manuscript and the obtaining of images. My daughter Sarah went with me to step shows and other dance events, photographed dancers, and worked tirelessly to help me organize and assemble all the images. Her computer expertise has been especially valuable and has saved me many hours of frustration. To my family members go my heartfelt thanks.

Contents

Preface

My interest in African American history goes back more than twenty years and has been nurtured in a number of scholarly and educational projects, including exhibits, videos and documentaries, articles, presentations, and classroom materials. In the mid 1990s, the National Afro-American Museum and Cultural Center in Wilberforce, Ohio, invited me to participate in an exhibit project on African American dance. It was a large effort, including companion art and history exhibits, the commissioning of a new dance performance piece to be co-choreographed by Donald McKayle and Ron K. Brown, a print educational package, extensive programming, more than ten monitors of moving film in the galleries, and a color catalogue.

After opening in Dayton and Springfield, Ohio, *When the Spirit Moves: African American Dance in History and Art* traveled to Detroit, Atlanta, and Washington, D.C., implementing an innovative partnership structure in which a mainstream and an African American museum hosted the exhibits and collaborated on programming in each venue city. The concept was created by then-director Dr. John Fleming, whose knowledgeable and wise leadership of the project guaranteed its prospects for success. After the travel in this country was complete, the U.S. State Department worked with the museum team to revise and reformat the exhibit for international travel.

During the eight years of development, my role included the work of project manager as well as significant curatorial duties such as exhaustive research, involvement in collecting exhibition materials, and the writing of concept statements, labels, and the introductory essay in the catalogue. In this work, I was guided first by John Fleming and then by current director Vernon Courtney, and had the pleasure of working with a wonderful exhibit team. Throughout the process, I recognized within myself a growing passion for the subject and a deepening sense of its historical complexity, Africanist characteristics, and profound beauty.

After the project was completed, I continued to research the subject, a task I now see as lifelong. I began and continue to add to a large collection of photographs, prints, drawings, memorabilia, and other materials, all focused on African American dance history. This book is an expression of that work and a reflection of my deep love for the subject as well as my awed respect for the thousands of ordinary people and entertainers, including many who never achieved fame, who faced hardship and danger to practice the Africanist art of dance in its myriad forms.

The topic of this book is black vernacular dance—including the Ring Shout, Buzzard Lope, Cakewalk, Shimmy, Charleston, Black Bottom, Big Apple, Lindy Hop, and more. Vernacular dance is street corner dance, living room dance, nightclub dance, party and ballroom dance, some vaudeville dance, and all the forms and contexts in which the dance of ordinary people, rooted in ancient African traits, reveals itself.

These forms crossed back and forth over the footlights in an endlessly intricate cross-fertilization among vaudeville entertainers of many kinds, children on the sidewalk, minstrel and circus acts, teens in living rooms, chorus lines in clubs and musicals, aficionados in ballrooms, buskers in saloons, tap dancers in movies and on television, teachers and coaches helping clients improve their steps, and countless other practitioners in seemingly endless performance situations. These dancers have been animated by the energy of originality, the joy of improvisation, the sharing of community, and the wellspring of ancient West African sources.

What I have presented here is a history that has constant reference to a set of Africanist dance characteristics and is consistently illustrated by period prints, paintings, photos, and other images. The dance forms surface through, and gain representation in, the ephemera and advertisements of every generation—the store displays, trade cards, magazine illustrations, postcards, newspaper articles, clothing packaging, how-to booklets, and other consumables that document our popular culture. Simultaneously, in larger terms the dance history shapes and is shaped by the socioeconomic realities of black life in American society, always shadowed by racism and its ever-present threat of violence. Through the tangible remains of the past, we can see a pattern, the pattern of a dance tradition that began in Africa, changed and remade itself in ever new ways during slavery and the following eras, and ultimately took possession of our national vernacular dance culture.

The story is enormous, so large that an overview of this sort is simply a good starting point for readers who want to learn more. If you enjoy this book, I urge you to keep reading and also to explore the many films and other audio-visual or digital resources available on the subject of black dance. As a continuing learner myself, I welcome you to this book. Please join me in an overwhelmingly interesting and exciting exploration of a vast and beautiful subject.

Barbara Glass
Ohio State University

1

Two Dance Traditions Meet in the New World

When captive Africans were brought to North America, beginning in the 1600s, they came without possessions, but not without culture. In their memories, their customs, and their worldviews, they carried their cultural arts. These would enrich the New World as Africans, Europeans, and Native Americans together created a new way of life. African dance, rooted in a distinctive musical tradition, was one of the most important of the cultural arts carried across the Middle Passage.

This dance tradition proved remarkably resilient and flexible. It was so vital in binding together and nurturing communities of Africans that it did not decline and die out in its new land, as the arts of oppressed minorities have often done, but instead retained its power as Africans became African Americans. Despite the discrimination and marginalization endured by African Americans, their dance survived and became increasingly important in American culture. Slowly, African-based dance began to reshape, and take ground from, European dance forms that dominated American social dance. By the early 1900s, a turning point had been reached and African American dances were becoming popular in mainstream culture.

As the twentieth century unfolded, this stream of influence became a tidal wave, giving America some of its most memorable dance crazes, as well as shaping theatrical dance in a variety of genres. Dances that we think of as quintessentially American, such as the Cakewalk, Charleston, Shimmy, Black Bottom, Lindy Hop, and many of the rock 'n' roll dances of the 1950s and 1960s, came from the black community out of the bedrock of African-based dance movement.

Theatrical dance yielded to African-derived movement most visibly after the Civil War. From the late nineteenth century through the middle of the twentieth century, African American dance greats such as Bill Robinson, the Whitman Sisters, Josephine Baker, Sammy Davis, Jr., the Berry Brothers, Ethel Waters, John Bubbles, the Nicholas Brothers, Florence Mills, Coles and Atkins, and a host of others took the dance forms they had grown up with, reworked this material, and from it made song and dance careers. In so doing, they brought African-based dance to the Broadway and vaudeville stage, to cinema, and to the new medium of television. Their work helped transform the American concept of social and theatrical dance.

Key characteristics of African-derived dance became fundamental to American vernacular dance, playing a major role in shaping it and giving it its unique appeal. These characteristics, described and discussed later in this chapter, will help us trace the development of African American dance and see how it grew from within American society to Africanize mainstream dance.

African captives being taken into slavery. The illustration is from *Heroes of the Dark Continent*, by J. W. Buel, published in 1889.

Anyone who doubts the capacity of culture to survive in alien surroundings should consider the story of the Black Seminoles—runaway slaves who took refuge with the Seminole Indians in Florida beginning in the late 1700s. The blacks built their own villages near Seminole towns and kept alive their cultural arts, including dancing the Ring Shout and speaking Gullah. Side by side with their Seminole allies, they fought two wars against the U.S., in 1817–1818 and in 1835–1842. At the end of the second Seminole War, many, perhaps most, of them were taken to Indian Territory, where they were declared slaves again. A few barely escaped the military to cross the Rio Grande into Mexico in 1850. Some came back to Texas around 1870 to help the American army fight Apaches and Comanches. In the 1940s, researcher Kenneth Porter found a group of Black Seminoles in Brackettville, Texas, and reported that they still spoke Gullah among themselves and still performed the Ring Shout in their worship. Their relatives in Mexico were still practicing the Ring Shout, too.[1] Customs that were two centuries old had clearly survived, despite changes of nation of residence. Culture may be sometimes intangible, but it is not insubstantial. The art of African dance may have been invisible when newly arrived Africans stood on the auction block, but it has shown incredible vitality.

Africa

Africa is a large and complex continent more than three times the size of the United States. Today, there are nearly a thousand African cultural groups. Thus, there is no mono-

This illustration, usually dated 1836, shows black dancers in a variety of poses. From "Negro Figurante," published in London by R. Jennings.

lithic African language, perspective, or way of life. Instead, there is enormous variety in speech, art, customs, and beliefs from the Mediterranean to the Cape of Good Hope, and from Senegal to Somalia.

The vast majority of African Americans can trace their ancestry to captives taken in West Africa and brought as slaves to the Western Hemisphere. Some black Americans are descendants of peoples of Central Africa. By the time U.S. law made it illegal to bring Africans to be sold in America, in 1808, the tentacles of the slave trade had reached deep into the center of the continent, with some prisoners marching more than a thousand miles to the western coast. Prisoners came from groups such as the Igbo, Dogon, Bamana, Mende, Ewe, Asante, Fon, Fante, Bakongo, Wolof, Yoruba, Mandinka, and many others. All of these captives brought the treasure of culture from their far-flung homelands, including Islamic worship and Arabic writing. It was yet to be seen, however, which of the customs and art forms would survive over the long term, and how.

Most of the cultural groups had little or no written history, making it difficult for many scholars and traditional Western oral historians to understand and analyze the intricacies of their histories, their religions, and their arts. Still, as Mechal Sobel points out, despite these acknowledged difficulties, it is not impossible to see into that distant time:

> Although the data now available on eighteenth-century Africa are far richer than what was known in the past, they remain problematic. They are, in part, based upon the records of slave traders

who visited the continent, the memories of slaves taken from there who recorded their recollections years later after exposure to other values, and accounts by missionaries and random travelers. However, in greater part, our ideas of eighteenth-century Africa are based on the works of twentieth-century anthropologists, who have often extrapolated past realities from later developments and/or relied on oral history. Notwithstanding these limitations, there are by now myriad studies of African cultures and languages and extensive data on their traditions that, with the above caveats in mind, can and should be utilized for comparative purposes.[2]

The multiplicity of African tribes is a problem in itself. Enslaved Africans were taken from cultural groups with as many as fifty different languages, arts traditions, and religions. Nevertheless, as John Thornton notes, "the degree of diversity in Africa can easily be exaggerated." Examining sources of commonalities among African nations, he cites cultural exchange, commercial interconnectedness, shared philosophical concepts, and linguistic similarities that allowed communication among peoples speaking distinct languages.[3]

In America, these commonalities among enslaved Africans tended to facilitate the formation of an African American culture. Peter Kolchin writes, "The existence of this common cultural background—which shared some notable characteristics with the premodern background of the English settlers but in other respects was strikingly different—meant that even as specific ethnic attributes faded in America, a general African approach or style survived."[4] Furthermore, blacks' ability to develop a blended culture helped them endure the harsh circumstances of slavery. Despite their diversity, then, African cultural groups of the time shared characteristics that served as a basis for the development of a common way of life.

In practice, this meant that Africans who were new to enslavement in America tended, in free time on large plantations during the slavery period, or in festivals such as Pinkster in Albany, New York, during the late 1700s and early 1800s, or in Congo Square in New Orleans during the first half of the nineteenth century, to gather together according to tribal affinity. With time, though, these allegiances became less important than solidarity with other blacks, regardless of tribal background or geographic origin. Neither the circumstances of slavery nor the culture of the enslaved were ever static, and ongoing change could be seen in black dance. From the amalgamation of the dance customs of individual groups came a new dance aesthetic, still based on African ways of dancing, but now accommodating itself to American conditions.

Crucial similarities in the ways these Africans viewed and practiced dance made this amalgamation possible. Chief among these was the extraordinary value placed on dance. It held a position of such importance in the societies from which they came that many contemporary Americans have difficulty understanding it. It was, at different times, a form of recreation and an avenue of religious worship, and always a principal artistic, religious, and recreational expression in any African group. As Lee Warren writes, "Dance is intermeshed in every aspect of day-to-day traditional African life."[5] Because of its power to bind slaves together as a community, to give them spiritual sustenance, to link them to a cherished African past, and to serve as a release and escape from oppression, it was a deeply nurturing experience that blacks kept alive.

In the African societies from which the enslaved people came, dance in both ritual and nonritual forms was extraordinarily significant in community life. Ritual dance, as Warren notes, was "the bone and blood of African culture with deep psychological and religious roots."[6] It commemorated the important events in the lives of the people, provided a means of self-expression, gave rise to arts such as mask and costume making, and

A dancer photographed in Sierra Leone, probably in the 1930s or 1940s, wears an elaborately carved crocodile mask with a human face.

connected them to God. Through dance, communities and individuals negotiated virtually every important experience in life. There were dances to increase crop harvests, to initiate the young into adulthood, to celebrate marriage and birth, to help the recently deceased move into the spirit world, and to protect against evil. There were dances to educate the young in proper behavior, to heal the sick, and to help the newborn become settled and stay healthy in the mortal world. There were dances to celebrate puberty, to represent the essence of male and female roles, and to satirize misbehavior. Some dances honored the living, and some honored the ancestors.

Dance provided much of the excitement and entertainment at local festivals and celebrations, as well as in everyday life. Individuals competed with each other in the dance arena, and simultaneously dance brought people together. Particular dances and the making of related masks and costumes were a major focus of secret and nonsecret societies and associations. Dances reflected the rich complexity of African musical traditions, and dancers built on familiar drum rhythms to create new variations on familiar moves.

Some dances dramatized community history or religious beliefs, and many ritual dances evoked the spirit world. In these, masking was often important. By putting on a mask and costume, the dancer set aside his human identity and portrayed a spiritual power. Such dancers looked at themselves differently, and the audience felt the difference as well. The dancer became a vehicle for an otherworldly being to appear to the community. In this possession experience, the dance was a meeting point between the human and supernatural worlds, so that people could communicate with ancestors and deities. Performance of a dance, with its particular movements, drum rhythms, masks, costumes, and associ-

Postcard ca. 1900, showing young girls being initiated into the Sande Society of the Mende. In this society, the girls learn the responsibilities of adulthood, as well as the art of dance. The society's masks are shown on the far right and far left, representing the ideal of beauty, with elaborately styled hair and folds of flesh around the neck as a symbol of prosperity. The mask shown here is perhaps the only one in Africa made to be worn by women. Most African masks are worn by men, even if they represent women.

ated customs, could literally evoke the presence of a deity, and the deity could wield his or her spiritual power to benefit and protect the community.

These ritual dances are staggering in their number, complexity, variety, long tradition, aesthetic power, and symbolism. Three well-known examples from distinct cultural groups amply illustrate this point.

Gelede. Among the Yoruba (YOR uh bah), who today dwell mostly in western Nigeria, the Republic of Benin, Sierra Leone, and Togo, the dance masquerade called Gelede (GELL eh day) dominates a lavish, colorful three-day festival. The festival is exciting and entertaining, but even more important, it has been widely felt to be efficacious in protecting and aiding the community. Through Gelede, the people access the enormous power of Iyanla, The Great Mother. She represents both living and ancestral women, especially their all-encompassing ability to create life. The incalculable potency of this spiritual force is clear from a statement made by a participant: "The Great Mother has power in many things … [she] is the owner of everything in the world. She owns you."[7] Coupled with the nighttime Efe performance, Gelede honors and placates the spirits of "the mothers," beings who can enhance or destroy the fertility of the land and the society that lives on it. The spectacle also protects against witchcraft, a negative female force.

Gelede dancers perform, vividly costumed. Peter Arnold Photography.

Gelede is danced exclusively by men, but the figures represented in the masquerade can be either male or female. Dancers wear masks that embody tradition and yet can incorporate new ideas. Costumes are mostly a collection of head ties, skirts, and baby wrappers borrowed from women in the community, and this connects the ritual to the contemporary and the ordinary. Drum rhythms are distinctive, and dancers practice long hours to make sure their leg rattles are precisely synchronized with the drum speech. Special Gelede societies train the dancers and safeguard the masks. Objectives include soliciting "the mothers" to bring prosperity to the community, enacting and examining male and female roles in society, and satirizing any anti-social behavior of individuals.

Dama. Another extraordinary ritual dance is the Dogon Dama, an event performed not so much for community members as for the dead who have been laid to rest in the high reaches of the Bandiagara Cliffs in Mali. Dogon villages nestle into the base of the cliffs, a little above the stretches of semi-arid farmland from which the people wrest their sustenance. As Stephen Pern notes, there is no concept of a distant heaven or underworld among the Dogon:

> A Dogon soul is not destined for some faraway paradise. In death, as in life, a persona remains indissolubly attached to its home village. As a man grows older and gains seniority, he tends to move from house to house, each one higher up the village slope, until he reaches the traditional abode of a clan or lineage head at the foot of the cliffs. What happens at death is little more than an extension of this upward progress: his spirit rises up the cliff. The rim of the cliff is the abode of the ancestors, who wander freely on the sheer rock face.[8]

The Dogon believe that these spirits can be harmful to the crops struggling for life in the poor soil, so it is important to keep the spirits at bay, to entice them to remain in

Dogon Kanaga dancers move together in a line. The Kanaga mask has been interpreted various ways. Many say it represents a mythical bird. ©Wolfgang Kaehler, www.wkaehlerphoto.com

the clefts of rock far up the cliffside. The spirits, however, still yearn for the life of the villages, and unless coaxed to the area of their gravesites, may haunt the living.

The Dogon dance drama averts catastrophe by cajoling the recently dead, giving them a last exciting taste of the world of the living, and finally, establishing them in their new role as ancestors. The dance drama presents a final spectacle of the living world as a

While a Dogon Kanaga dancer performs solo, other dancers rest in the background, some on stilts. Photograph © www.danheller.com.

In this postcard from about 1900, a group of Bamana dancers and drummers prepare to conduct a dance ceremony in the fields.

farewell to the dead, who then are content to keep their distance. So each dancer masquer-ades as some part of the material world—a bull, a lizard, a hare, a hunter, a young maiden, an enemy warrior—or another figure less easy to understand.

Each kind of mask—stylized and yet recognizable—dictates its own steps, but all the men who dance wear short skirts of black and red fibers. Performers move rapidly in cir-cles and lines, singing together as drummers keep up a polyrhythmic beat. At key moments, the muscular dancers sweep the ground rapidly with their tall, heavy masks or leap high in perfect synchrony. More masqueraders balance on high stilts, and the living audience cheers as the drama unfolds.[9] The other audience, the honored dead, is consoled by the performance for loss of participation in physical life. When the dance ends, the period of danger—a time when unsettled spirits could wander through the village—is over until the next death.

Chi Wara. Perhaps the best known of all African dance is the Chi Wara (CHEE WAH rah) dance of the Bamana of Mali, for the antelope mask used in Chi Wara became the symbol of Mali and of the airline Air Afrique. The dance reenacts a creation myth, com-memorating and celebrating the beginnings of the Bamana, when they learned to farm and thus to produce the food that ensured their survival. The Chi Wara was a supernatural crea-ture, half antelope and half human, who brought the knowledge of farming and taught it to the people. Traditionally, the dance was held in the fields to help ensure the germina-tion of the plants. The ritual also exhorted all members of the community to work together to raise and harvest food.

Dancers wear beautifully carved headdresses of antelopes, male and female. The female supports her young on her back as evidence of her fertility. The wooden figures are attached to basketry caps that in turn are attached to long vegetable fibers covering the dancers' bodies. The figures dance bent toward the earth, evoking the shape of the antelope as well as the posture of a farmer tilling the soil. A recent exhibit of African Art at the Metropolitan Museum of Art included Chi Wara masks and commented on the symbolism in the dance:

> In performance, the pair evokes the elements essential to sustain life. The male is associated with the sun, his female companion—who supports a miniature fawn on her back—has been described as a metaphor for the earth, and long fibers that are attached to the headdresses and cascade over the body of the dancers are interpreted as rivulets of water.[10]

Today, the Bamana no longer confine themselves to farming as a livelihood, and the dance performance has been secularized. Chi Wara now comments on and reflects a broad range of occupations.

These dances exemplify cultural concepts that were not left behind, but came to the New World, where they went underground for a time, then transformed themselves and resurfaced in new shapes. Furthermore, African-derived dance continued to be central to African Americans' lives and the lives of their children and grandchildren. As John Blassingame has pointed out, "There is overwhelming evidence of the survival of African song and dance forms in the United States in the nineteenth century."[11] In the brutal conditions of slavery, dance helped Africans and African Americans retain and reshape their sense of who they were, find emotional release, express individual creativity, and have fun.

CONTRASTING TRADITIONS

In the New World, Africans found themselves among Europeans. It soon became apparent that both Africans and Europeans valued dance, but that their dance forms, their dance aesthetics, and their movement vocabularies were dramatically different. As we examine the African and European dance traditions in greater detail, we will see how they were different and how their differences allow us to trace the impact they had on each other.

AFRICAN-DERIVED DANCE CHARACTERISTICS

Through the centuries of slavery, Africans molded a new way of life, adapting themselves to the new conditions imposed upon them. During the same period, additional arrivals of Africans helped keep ancient customs alive. This African influence did not stop at 1808, when the United States officially banned importation of slaves, for despite heavy penalties, slave smugglers did a brisk business right up until the eve of the Civil War.

In fact, the U.S. Navy intercepted three slave ships destined for Cuba (the *Wildfire*, the *William*, and the *Bogata*) off Key West in 1860 alone. All three had departed from New York at various times during the previous year. The *Wildfire* had taken 615 captives from the vicinity of the Congo River in Africa, but by the time the ship reached Key West, only 510 were still alive.[12] The other ships had comparable numbers of slaves. All told, the three ships had brought more than fourteen hundred contraband humans, mostly teens and children, and nearly three hundred were so ill that they died in the days after landing. The market value of the blacks was so great, moreover, that a group of opportunists tried to steal them and met instead with the deadly force of the U.S. Marshal.[13] Over the years of the antebellum period, the relatively low success of the American Navy in halting the

A masked Ebo dancer of the Ovra or Ovia Society wears an enormous hat of parrot feathers.

This drawing, from an April 25, 1874, *Harper's Weekly* magazine, shows a slave vessel endeavoring to escape capture by a British cruiser in the Mediterranean off the coast of Africa. The British attempted to capture slave vessels on the high seas to suppress the slave trade.

smuggling made for a steady stream of illegal Africans into the South. These newly arrived slaves continuously reinvigorated African culture among African Americans.

As a result, African dance and music continued to influence the formation of African American arts. Dances from various African nations blended into new, shared forms. The new dances were still based on African movement vocabulary and the African concept of how and why people dance.

In the U.S., African-style masking and ritual dance virtually disappeared during much of the slavery era, perhaps not discontinued but simply unseen. Masking later re-emerged in a few places, such as the Mardi Gras in Mobile and New Orleans, beginning long before the Civil War and combining white and black traditions, and vestiges of masking customs survived for a time in John Canoe dance in North Carolina. Possession dance, in which a dancer gives over his/her consciousness and body to be animated by a deity, continued in isolated, usually secret, pockets of African worship under the name Voodoo or Voudun. In the Caribbean islands, possession dance was practiced more widely by the descendants of Africans who had labored on plantations there. The great African American dancer and choreographer Katherine Dunham encountered it and participated in it in Haiti in 1936, when she was doing anthropological fieldwork as part of her doctoral studies. The three-day initiation ceremony she underwent marked a turning point in her life, as she changed her professional career from anthropology to dance. Returning to the U.S., she became a choreographer and dancer, emphasizing

Afro-Caribbean themes and movement vocabulary, as well as stressing their African roots.[14]

In the U.S., African ritual dance, which was viewed as idolatrous by European Americans, was in some places vigorously repressed. Some of this dance, however, reappeared in a new form during the slavery period, the Ring Shout, which will be discussed in the next chapter. African religious dance also continued as funeral ceremonies during the slavery era and later as rhythmic movement in Christian services in African American churches.

By and large, African Americans retained African-based dance movement by incorporating it into secular, social dances that subsequently became part of American mainstream dance.[15] These dances consisted of very old dance material recombined to make new forms. Their underlying characteristics, however, continued to define them as African. Among the most important of these characteristics are the following:

1. African Movement Vocabulary. African dance moves all parts of the body, in contrast to many European forms that rely mostly on arm and leg movement. Angular bending[16] of arms, legs, and torso; shoulder and hip movement; scuffing, stamping, and hopping steps; asymmetrical use of the body; and fluid movement are all part of African dance.

For Africans, torso movement and freedom of limb movement were not hampered by tight, formal clothing, as they were in many European venues, where people in the sixteenth through the eighteenth centuries might be burdened with stiff ruffs at the neck, high heels, or top-heavy pompadours of hair stretched over wire frames. In many traditional West African societies, both men and women wore minimal clothing and were nude from the waist up. Pelvic movement and shaking of the hips, which horrified eighteenth century Europeans, resonated with the deeply felt African interest in the fertility of both people and land.

Dance props and instruments reflected this value. Gelede dancers impersonating females sometimes wear wooden breastplates with rounded bellies and boldly colored, pointed breasts. Futhermore, similar impersonations can also be found among the Dogon and other cultural groups. Gelede dancers may also fit various kinds of improvised structures under their clothing to shape large, protruding buttocks. This portrayal of the female focuses on the critically important characteristics of sexuality and ability to bear children. In Benin, Sato drums are made in male and female pairs. In some cases, the drums carry large, realistic carvings of male and female genitalia. For the African dancer, the torso was not to be hidden, or held stiffly as a single unit of the body. It was to be celebrated and articulated. Its sexual characteristics were not to be ignored, but emphasized, for sexuality was part of fertility, and fertility was basic to survival.

2. Orientation to the Earth. The African dancer often bends slightly toward the earth, flattens the feet against it in a wide, solid stance, and flexes the knees. Compare this to traditional European ballet's upright posture, with arms lifted skyward and feet raised up onto the toes. The African stance also reflects work postures, especially agricultural labors.

Omofolabo Ajayi emphasizes this characteristic when he points out "the standard posture of Yoruba dances": "The upper torso" he writes, "is held forward at an angle of about 120 degrees to the rest of the body, while the lower torso is flexed forward at the knees."[17] From Yoruba dance to the Vai hunter's dance to Akan court dance to the African American Ring Shout to twentieth century tap dance, the forward carriage of the dancer is part of a loose, elastic bearing that radiates energy and total body involvement.

A Dogon dancer impersonates a woman, wearing a costume including carved breasts and a rounded belly. © www.danheller.com.

An Egungun dancer travels from one village to another. The men who walk with him carry sticks to keep his costume from touching them, for tradition says a touch from the costume could mean death. Peter Arnold photography.

3. Improvisation. Within the patterns and traditions of age-old dance forms, an African felt free to be creative. A dancer could make an individual statement or give a new interpretation to a familiar gesture. Ajayi explains how this trait surfaces in Yoruba dance:

> There is ample room for spontaneous and personal improvised movements, as long as the improvisations are in rhythm with the music and in consonance with the overall content of the dance. In fact, the dancer displays her or his virtuosity in the richness of improvised movements and the smooth subtlety with which they are blended into the main form of the dance.[18]

In fact, innovation in the dance is not a break with tradition, but rather a continuation of the tradition of improvisation.[19]

African dance is not static, but continuously changes and reshapes itself as dancers find ways to incorporate new insights and contemporary elements into old forms. Today, African dancers may incorporate European garments into their dance costumes and wear masks carved to look like European faces, so as to comment satirically on foreigners. A Gelede mask pictured in Henry and Margaret Drewel's 1990 book includes a carved airplane.[20] Ritual dance stretches in new ways to offer dynamic and ever-changing commentary on its community and world.

Furthermore, the dance's fundamental capacity to accept modification, to adapt to new surroundings and attitudes, and to respond to new musical sounds, while continuing to claim the admiration of onlookers, is the key feature that guaranteed its survival.

4. Circle and Line Formations. Many African dances are performed by lines or circles of dancers, as with the vigorous, fast-moving circles and sinuous lines of Dogon

In this Asante circle dance, some of the dancers carry pieces of cloth. Titled "The Handkerchief Dance," the illustration is from an 1897 engraving.

dancers in the Dama as well as the slow procession of Egungun dancers in Yorubaland. In North America, some of these traditions coalesced in the Ring Shout, in which Christian worshippers move around and around a counterclockwise circle to the singing of a hymn.

Traditional European dance also incorporated lines and circles. They were found in reels, cotillions, minuets, and other forms. During the slavery era, blacks adopted some of these forms, especially the cotillion, adding African movement, polyrhythmic music, and the calling of figures to make it their own. Dance influence, that is, could flow both ways, but African Americans nearly always put the stamp of African movement and sound on any dances they adopted. The common use of lines and circles tended to facilitate dance exchange between whites and blacks, and this dance characteristic was resilient. Black dancers in the twentieth century were still dancing in circles and lines with the Big Apple and the Madison, performed to the accompaniment of jazz and rock 'n' roll music.

5. Importance of the Community. Traditional African culture values individuality much less than stratified European society. To live in an African village is to let go of much of the need for privacy and the focus on the self that we find everywhere in western society. Pern's comment on the Dogon village is illuminating. "The layout of this cliff village [Tireli] made any concept of privacy laughable."[21] Rather, there is an emphasis on conformity, harmony, openness, and sociability. "Nobody," Pern writes of the Dogon he knew, "ever did anything that required solitude or concentration. No one crept off into the bush to work by himself. Such things would have been seen as anti-social and perhaps

A Dogon village rises up the cliffside. ©Wolfgang Kaehler, www.wkaehlerphoto.com.

even dangerous."[22] One of the purposes of the Yoruba Efe celebration is to identify and issue a reproof to anti-social individuals, and many Efe songs ridicule anti-social behavior. Unity with one's cultural group is important, and in many West African communities the sense of unity is internalized so deeply as to assure perfect unison in complex, polyrhythmic song and dance.

As Sana Reynolds points out, collective cultures in Africa and Asia have distinctively different ways of expressing the need for privacy than individualist cultures.[23] Collective cultures are comfortable with a great deal of physical closeness and tend to value cohesiveness. They protect individual privacy through personal restraint and avoidance of direct eye contact, as well as in other ways. In the American South, these habits were often misinterpreted by whites, who equated lack of eye contact with untrustworthiness, and who could not comprehend the depth of cohesiveness in Africanist cultures.

Africanist dance reflects this emphasis on the group. Africans danced mainly for and with the community. Solo dancers were supported and affirmed by the group through singing, hand clapping, and shouted encouragement. The tradition continued in America, where African American audiences actively communicated with dancers on the plantation and later onstage, ministers in the pulpit, and musicians in the bandstand. A participatory communion was implicit and important wherever people came together. Separation and individuality were less valued and even considered negative when they threatened the solidarity that protected against punishment.

Thus couple dancing was uncommon on the plantation. It did not become widely acceptable until the old slave communities began to be dissolved by emancipation and people moved into urban areas, where the African American couple then stood on its own as an economic and social unit, albeit with the substantial support of the extended family.

6. Polyrhythms. African music included several rhythms at the same time, and Africans could dance to more than one beat at once, often to the amazement of white onlookers. Dancers could move their shoulders to one beat, hips to another, and knees to yet another.[24] Dogon dance is an excellent example of this polyrhythmic movement. As Lomax comments, "Dogon dancing displays an orchestral use of the body where the upper and lower halves develop different supporting but complementary rhythms. It is with this polyrhythmic handling of the body, combined with dramatic bursts of strength and speed, that the African dancers produce an effect...."[25] In African American music, this rhythmic complexity, with a basic ground beat and counter beats played against it, formed the basis for ragtime, jazz, and rock 'n' roll.

7. Percussion. In much of Africa, percussion dominates the music, and in many cases the drum is the leading instrument. Often, a master drummer sets a central beat, and other drummers interpolate additional rhythms around that beat. In America, enslaved Africans used a broad range of percussive instruments, including drums.

Wherever drums were banned in the colonies, other forms of percussion were used and perpetuated. Body percussion, such as hand clapping, foot tapping, and patting became important. Tap dance, as it developed in the late nineteenth and early twentieth centuries, created its own percussive sound, with the stage or platform as a drum and the shoe taps beating out a rhythm.

8. Pantomime. Many African dances reflect the motions of life. Dance movement may, in a stylized fashion, imitate animal behavior like the flight of the egret, reenact human tasks like pounding rice, or express the power of spirits in whirling and strong movements.

Consider the example of Gelede. Dancers masquerading as male figures take large steps and exhibit great energy and physical power. The male Gelede figure moves with tremendous vigor, sometimes rushing violently at the audience and forcing onlookers to give way. Dancers masquerading as female figures are much more controlled, taking smaller, slower, less aggressive steps. In spite of this mimesis, the dance is not intended to be realistic, but rather to portray symbolically the deep, inner natures of men and women.

The pantomime can be also much more abstract, capturing the qualities of unseen beings. The Bwa people of Burkina Faso masquerade and dance to represent bush spirits who otherwise have no visible shapes. The power of these spirits is expressed in energetic spins, whirling, hops, stamps, and head and shoulder jerks.

9. Something in Hand. African ritual dance makes use of special objects, including masks and costumes, staffs, whisks, pieces of cloth, and other items. The Ntimi dancer of the Efik people, for example, holds a red parrot's feather between her lips and twirls a decorated gourd in her hands. In the New World, African Americans continued to use sticks or staffs, cloth, and other objects in dance. There are accounts of slaves dancing with containers of water on their heads. In black vaudeville, handkerchiefs, canes, and top hats became part of the dance, as did other kinds of objects in various stage routines. Some European folk dance also included special objects, such as the sticks and handkerchiefs used in the Cotswold Morris dance in England.

10. Competition. Competing through dance is a widespread custom in West and Central Africa. In America in the 1700s and early 1800s, whites gained understanding of the custom, in part because some Europeans came from backgrounds in which competition was also common, such as Irish jig dancing. Sometimes whites leaped into the black dance

Willie and Winnie, "The Aristocrats of Rhythm," use chairs in their performance, probably 1950s.

arena to try their skill in the "cutting contest." The tradition survived in all sorts of challenge dances such as the one between William Henry Lane and John Diamond in New York around 1840, in come-one-come-all buck dancing contests in minstrelsy and other traveling shows, in Cakewalk contests in which dancers competed for the prize of a cake, in Break Dance rivalries in which young men asserted their machismo through acrobatic performance, in Jitterbug competitions where young couples demonstrated their speed and coordination, in step shows in which African American Greek letter societies showed off signature moves on college campuses, and many other events, including a contemporary television show *So You Think You Can Dance?*

EUROPEAN DANCE CHARACTERISTICS

In contrast to African dance, which contained both ritual and secular dance and often added elaborate pageantry and symbolism in the context of an outdoor religious festival, European court dance at the time of the founding of the North American colonies was almost entirely secular and was often practiced in the context of indoor ballrooms. This dance also employed a movement vocabulary and responded to an overall aesthetic very

In this 1888 engraving, "The Dancing Lesson of Our Grandmothers," a young woman dances with a dancing master.

different from those of African dance. Folk dance, from the Fandango to the Morris dance to the Irish jig, adhered to many of the same values, postures, and movement vocabularies. Among the key distinctive features are the following:

1. Political and Elitist Basis. Much of European dance arose from court dance, which reflected nobility's vision of society, a context in which people interacted in an extremely organized, patterned fashion so as to showcase and enhance their status. The Italian *balli* or pantomime dances are excellent examples: "any [persons] of quality could take part in the *danzi* [ordinary couple dance], but the *ballo* was reserved for the most noble personages. They acted out, through dance alone, that etiquette of courtliness—advance, retreat, encirclement—which ruled their lives."[26]

At Versailles in the court of Louis XIV in the late 1600s, dance was a complex, demanding form of courtiership, a way of currying favor with the king, asserting one's noble rank, and jockeying for power. In fact, it is said that Louis built Versailles to hold his nobles and to control them. Isolated at court, they had to leave their estates, their personal enterprises, and most opportunities for trouble making behind them. Dance was a primary occupation at court, an entertainment through which Louis demonstrated his ascendancy in the arts and shaped the nature of formal dance for many years to come.

The rest of Europe shared elitist view of dance. It was an activity demanding large amounts of leisure time, expensive education at the hands of dancing masters, costly clothing and accessories, vast and richly decorated rooms in which to give and attend balls, the hiring of ensembles of musicians who could play classical music expertly, and knowledge of the intricacies of courtly manners. Dance was an activity that separated the noble from the lowly.

Dance also was an activity through which the wealthy and highborn pursued their political goals, and the ballroom was a place where people practiced conspicuous consumption and made marital alliances.

As such, it most definitely was not a veil through which to see and meet God or a moment in which one abandoned one's sense of self to give embodiment to a supernatural power.

2. Verticality and Heavenward Orientation. Much court dance had a basis in ballet, that art form shaped by and personally danced by the French king. Eventually, this form was dominated by professionals, the virtuoso performers who represented the height of art. Its body postures were vertical, with a skyward orientation. Dancers rose up on their toes, raised their arms toward the heavens, and gave preference to light movement, as if denying the corporeality of their own being. The torso was moved as a unit. Hips and shoulders were not articulated separately.

This vision of dance was reflected around the courts of Europe. In ballrooms across the continent, dancers kept their backs straight and assumed poses designed to communicate dignity and control. With men in tight breeches and women in corsets, a freer dancing style was not possible. From the Irish jig to the Highland Fling to the German Allemand to the Quadrille, Cotillion, and Minuet, dance posture across Europe echoed ballet and its vertical, skyward postures.

3. Couple Dance. Seventeenth and eighteenth century European dance was based on the couple as the essential unit of society. At a time when marriages were financial and political alliances, men and women faced each other in dance lines and then paired, unpaired, and stepped into and out of each other's space in repetitive patterns.

Like African dance, the action was highly stylized, not personal. Dancing was not openly sexual, and touching was heavily restricted. The Waltz, with its closed-couple format and intimate embrace, was still a century away. Even when it appeared, the waltz was regarded as scandalous for a long moment before it became acceptable. European dance movement, though stylized and only symbolically sexual, was nevertheless based on coupling and still reflected the importance of pairing off.

4. Geometric Patterning. The popular and long-enduring Minuet, the Cotillion, and the Quadrille in all its manifestations were danced in geometric formations. The British Morris, a folk dance dating back to the 1400s and 1500s, was performed in geometric arrangements of six or eight dancers. Figures of such dances could be and were represented as lines, circles, and arrows on a page, and this idealized configuration of moving bodies again reflected a mathematical, intellectualized concept of society. Many of the patterns were captured and fixed in the dance books of the period, including John Playford's seventeenth century *English Dancing Master*, first published under Oliver Cromwell's Commonwealth in 1651.

These patterns were learned by the well-to-do in a rote fashion, often from a dancing master. After the French Revolution (1789–1799), a number of ousted and impoverished French aristocrats found employment in the new United States, where they taught manners and dance well into the 1800s. They assured that the elite would come prepared to the ballroom, and any improvisation would have signaled ill breeding. As one group of writers point out, "dancing provided an excellent mark of rank. It was wholly nonutilitarian. Furthermore, the complex minuets and country dances of the eighteenth century required study. Study required leisure."[27] Dance education, that is, was for the rich. Perfect rendering of known steps was one of the behaviors that separated the wealthy from the rabble.

Highland dancers perform in the Crystal Palace in the Great Exhibition of 1851 in London.

In America, however, the lower classes—many of whom were both illiterate and untutored—danced the forms as well. In this, they were aided by the fiddler, often African American, who called out the figures so that the dancers did not have to know them in advance. The African American caller had simply transmuted the African tradition in which drum rhythms signaled certain kinds of movement.

5. Country Dances. As early as Queen Elizabeth I (1533–1603), the British court amused itself by adopting the dances of ordinary people. These lively dances, mostly

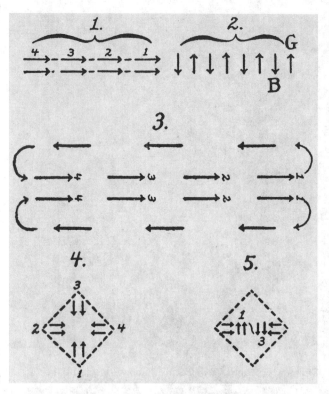

Diagram illustrating how four couples move across the dance floor in geometric patterns in a performance of the Minuet.

rounds and line forms with patterned figures, quickly became part of the repertory of the elite. Called country or *contre* dances, these were exported to France, revised, and then carried back to England. They were also popular in Germany. This family of dances later traveled to America, becoming the contra dances of New England and contributing to the development of Square Dance.

In America in the 1700s and early 1800s, wealthy and prominent families performed both court dance and country dance in the ballrooms of the great houses. In spite of the new theories of democracy, long tradition was not to be denied. Individuals with titles or rank often opened a dance, and the country dances, like the court dances, were led off by the elite.

6. Individual Dance. The most widely known example of European individual dance is the jig, an extremely old form arising from a solo country dance of the sixteenth century. One of Shakespeare's contemporaries, William Kemp, who performed in many of Shakespeare's plays in the late 1500s, often danced jigs on stage. Later, the jig was taken up by Irish immigrants and so became identified with the Irish. This vertical-posture dance with complicated footwork merged with African-based forms to create succeeding generations of precursors of tap dance. Both blacks and whites danced the jig opposite each other in pairs or larger groups, and both danced it as a competition dance.

CONCLUSION

When the two dance traditions came together on the eastern shore of the North American continent, they immediately began to have an impact on each other. White plantation owners brought slave dancers to entertain guests and used slave musicians to provide music for European-style dances. Whites observed and remembered African body postures and movements, and some adventuresome whites on occasion went to the slave quarters and danced with the blacks. Black musicians at white balls imposed African musical techniques upon European dance tunes and thus changed the music to which whites danced.

Blacks in turn began to incorporate European forms like the Cotillion into slave parties and festivals, and by the middle of the nineteenth century, this crossover of forms was common. When blacks danced European forms, however, they incorporated African-style

A late nineteenth century engraving of affluent European Americans dancing the Cotillion.

Illustration from an Italian postcard, in which Spanish dancers perform the Flamenco, a folk dance that is centuries old.

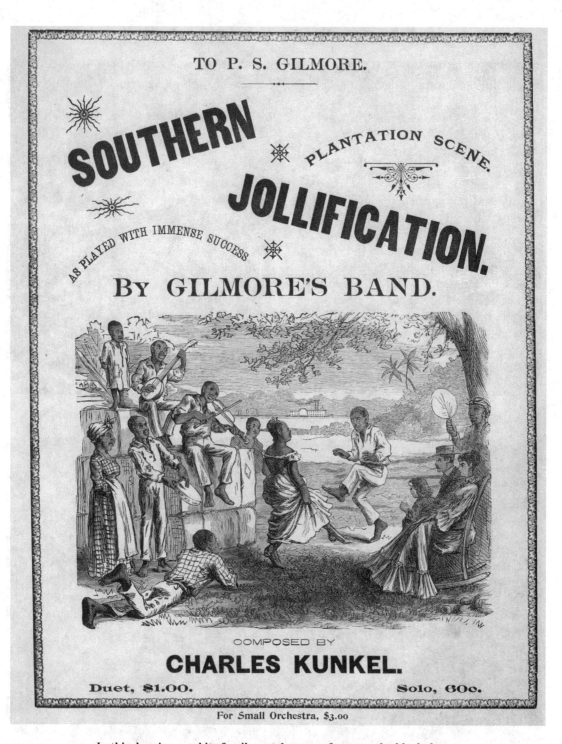

TO P. S. GILMORE.

SOUTHERN

PLANTATION SCENE.

JOLLIFICATION.

AS PLAYED WITH IMMENSE SUCCESS

By GILMORE'S BAND.

COMPOSED BY

CHARLES KUNKEL.

Duet, $1.00.   Solo, 60c.

For Small Orchestra, $3.00

In this drawing, a white family watches a performance by black dancers.

movement and musical rhythms, changing the forms significantly. Furthermore, both free and enslaved blacks on occasion adopted the formal ball as a way of distinguishing themselves from more common or lowly blacks—copying white culture, that is, indicated one's own elitism. Under the oppression of white masters, Africans hid and eventually revised their ancient ritual dances into secular forms that yet retained African dance characteristics. All the while, white painters and writers were deeply interested in black dance and spent time capturing its details and contexts, thus leaving us with a number of depictions of it.

This crossover and transformation of dance forms did nothing, however, to change the set of basic African dance characteristics that survived intact and marked most of the dance performed by African Americans.

Furthermore, the long love-hate relationship whites felt for black culture was beginning, and it focused heavily on dance. Whites were shocked by what they saw as the sexuality and undignified postures of black dancing and yet were drawn to its artistic complexity and profound beauty. Finding a way to enjoy black dance while still distancing themselves from it was a concern for white Americans for virtually the entire nineteenth century, during which time the minstrel show became the country's most popular form of entertainment and a reflection of its racism. The minstrel show, however, was but one of a long succession of methods by which white Americans condemned African-derived dance and yet tried to assure themselves of an opportunity to watch it or participate in it. The 1930s Cotton Club, where a whites-only audience watched an all-black cast of singers and dancers in a set that recalled the plantation, was a later manifestation. The Other, it seemed, called to white audiences, and they reacted by isolating it onstage. As Brenda Dixon Gottschild demonstrates in her account of the vaudeville career of Harold Norton and Margot Webb[28], African American dancers could over time secure their access to the stage, but in most cities and towns where they performed, they could not get a hotel room or go to a restaurant in white areas. Not being familiar with all the neighborhoods of the cities where they performed, black performers were often confined to their backstage dressing rooms. Despite all its contradictory and ugly realities, this disguised and denied love affair of white audiences with black dance metamorphosed throughout the twentieth century until it culminated in an open embrace of African American dance by mainstream culture in the late twentieth century.

For their part, African American dancers endured brutal repression while continuing to practice treasured cultural arts, especially dance. Through the harsh years of the minstrel show, black vaudeville, and other segregated entertainment, blacks watched their dances being stolen by white performers. Simultaneously, black entertainers immersed themselves in a long struggle for equality in the theatrical world. Enduring poor working conditions, low pay, racist violence, and inadequate credit for their work, they nevertheless transformed a nation's dance, making it so exciting and unique that it is copied around the globe. Today, Africanist dance is the dance of America and the world.

2

Black Dance in the Slavery Era: The Ring Shout and Buzzard Lope

When the English colonies in North America became the United States in 1776, slavery existed in both the North and the South. Over the decades following independence, slavery dwindled and disappeared in the North, where the states abolished it according to their separate timetables. Nothing like this happened in the South. Because of the development of cotton as a profitable crop throughout the Deep South after Eli Whitney's invention of the cotton gin in 1793, the need for black labor in the cultivation of rice in South Carolina and the Georgia Sea Islands, and a host of other economic situations, slavery did not die out in the South.

On the contrary, it thrived, creating a new cash enterprise in the slaves themselves. Raising slaves for sale and trading in them became profitable businesses in the half century prior to the Civil War. Slave coffles heading west and south in the first half of the nineteenth century to new plantation lands in Alabama or Mississippi (admitted to the Union in 1819 and 1817) were common sights, and slave traders used the slave pens or jails that began to dot the landscape as places to keep traveling slaves at night.[1] In fact, a number of slave narratives tell of the horrors of being torn from one's family, and in many cases the coffles were filled with children who later recalled the long trek to an uncertain and much feared future, where they faced both loss of all friends and family and death from overwork in a frontier situation.[2] Separation of families was only one of the many horrors of slavery. Slave songs, like the Shout songs described in this chapter, were cultural documents that remembered and gave emotive expression to the agonies blacks endured within the "peculiar institution," as well as their refuge in Christianity and their hopes for a better life beyond this one. It is important to remember that the slave coffles also carried with them African American culture, including African-based dance, and dispersed it across the South and Southwest.

Although there were shared realities that affected most enslaved Africans, the experience of slavery was not homogeneous, but was different from place to place and era to era. Slaves found themselves in widely varying circumstances from one geographic area to another, from large plantation to small farm, from rural areas to urban, and even from work on one kind of crop to work on another.[3] Despite these variations, however, most slaves had something in common: they came together on southern plantations in numbers sufficient to form communities. Drew Gilpin Faust notes:

> Only 12 percent of owners possessed more than twenty slaves, the number usually considered the minimum necessary to comprise a plantation. Only 1 percent held more than one hundred. For

Slaves being readied for sale often slept in slave jails within slave traders' pens. Courtesy Library of Congress.

owners, therefore, slavery was most often experienced on a fairly small scale. But because of the existence of some large concentrations, the majority of slaves in fact lived in plantation-size units. By 1860, the South contained more than forty-six thousand such holdings. Thus most blacks lived within groups large enough to make community and family life possible.[4]

This was especially true in South Carolina, where even by 1720 about three-fourths of all slaves lived on plantations in groups of ten or more.[5]

Such slave communities were crucial in fostering African and African American arts like dance. A late eighteenth century painting, *The Old Plantation*, for example, shows blacks dancing in a traditional African way. African dance characteristics are clearly visible. Dancers are bent at the waist toward the earth. Surrounded by other community members, they incorporate strips of cloth and a stick or staff into the dance. Musicians play a gourd banjo (the banjo or banjar is an African-derived instrument) and a drum, the latter

The Old Plantation, probably painted in South Carolina around 1795. Courtesy Abby Aldrich Rock-efeller Folk Art Museum, Colonial Williamsburg Foundation, Williamsburg, VA.

for percussion. Africans often danced as a group, and group identity was key to the continuation of African-derived dances.

As decades of enslavement turned into centuries, African-based dance continued to survive, although it was shaped by the conditions of slavery. White masters restricted the times and places of slave dancing, for example, or attempted to prohibit certain African musical instruments. Moreover, European religion affected black dance, as the following discussion of the Ring Shout will illustrate. Black and white dance forms also influenced each other, as with African and European jigs. Whites and blacks watched and participated in each other's dances, and both were changed.

THE RING SHOUT

The Ring Shout is the oldest continuously practiced African-derived dance in the United States and is still performed in the Georgia Sea Islands today.[6] Most likely an amalgamation of several African circle dances, it is also the oldest African American religious dance.

The Ring Shout flourished among blacks in the United States, surviving into the present time for a variety of reasons. First, the dance was strongly African, and through its African ritual and communal characteristics it provided a rich and nurturing experience for both enslaved and free blacks. Secondly, blacks maintained the Shout as a dynamic folk tradition, constantly adapting it to the demands and conditions of, first, slavery, and later, life in Christianized African American communities. Third, it formed a repository

"The 'Shouting' in Full Blast," from *The Illustrated American*, **September 19, 1896. This engraving shows that children as well as adults were involved in shouting.**

of cultural and religious content that remembered the past of slavery and looked forward to the spiritual joys of the afterlife, thus reminding African Americans of their proud history and future. Fourth, the Shout represented a variety of resilient African musical and dance traits that transformed themselves to reappear again and again in African American cultural arts, from the Cakewalk to jazz and rock 'n' roll to tap dance. The Ring Shout was to be profoundly influential, and this chapter will explore its most enduring traits.

RICE CULTURE AS A CONTEXT

Although the form was carried across the U.S. by migrating blacks from generation to generation, the Ring Shout found its stronghold in the Georgia Sea Islands and South Carolina low country. There were good reasons for the Shout's survival in this coastal environment. Among them were the large population of slaves brought there for the cultivation of rice; the danger of malaria in the swampy low country or island plantations, which drove whites away for much of the year; and the ongoing arrivals of smuggled African-born captives right up through the 1850s. All these circumstances protected African cultural practices from extinction. Another factor was support and encouragement from scholars scattered over the past century and a half, some of whom initially came to performances with negative predispositions and over time acknowledged the Shout's power and beauty.[7]

Thus the history of the Ring Shout begins with the history of rice culture and the unique conditions it imposed on blacks and their white masters. Some West Africans, particularly those from Senegambia and the Windward Coast, had a long tradition of cultivating rice, and many of them were imported through Charleston to bring their skills to the rice plantations that dotted the coast and the Sea Islands. The captives also understood how to process the rice, husking it in African mortars and pestles and winnowing it in African rice fanner baskets. Well into the twentieth century, these implements were still in use in the old plantation areas, and the ability to create fanner baskets continues with African American artisans. Among the blacks who worked the fields were the Mende from Sierra Leone. In Sierra Leone, ring dances had been described as early as 1721. In that year, traveler John Atkins gave an account of a local circle dance including hand clapping, drums, and "a great deal of Agility."[8]

The work of growing rice in America was unpleasant and dangerous, as Ira Berlin points out:

> ... for a large portion of the year, slaves labored knee-deep in stagnant muck, surrounded by buzzing insects, under the scorching sun. In August, even after the fields were drained and the crops laid-by, there was little respite. If the fields were drained, the insects remained, and they were joined by a host of slithering reptiles that had been displaced by the movement of water and earth.[9]

It's no wonder whites did not want to do the work. Instead, they refined the forced labor system in which skilled blacks did the heavy tasks of digging ditches, draining fields, building dikes, tending the crop, and processing the product.

By 1700, South Carolina was exporting more than three hundred tons of rice per year, and by 1708, rice was the colony's largest export.[10] Of rice production in South Carolina, William Pollitzer writes, "At its peak 150,000 acres of swamp and tidal marshes were under cultivation. In 1860, nine of the fourteen slaveholders in the country owning more than five hundred slaves were rice planters."[11] The swampy lands that favored rice bred malaria and other illnesses, and this led to absenteeism among white planters, which in turn led to the isolation and neglect of the black workers. Some of the plantations on the islands grew cotton, but the owners of these found the environment just as forbidding. In the 1830s, Fanny Kemble, the wife of a largely absentee Sea Island plantation owner, gave vivid descriptions of the deprivation and cruelty in which the slaves lived in the area. "Great intervals of many years pass," she wrote, "and no master ever visits some of these properties.... In other cases, the visits made will be of a few days in one of the winter months, the estate and its cultivators remaining for the rest of the year under the absolute control of the overseer...."[12] Owner absences, she felt, were in part responsible for the suffering of the slaves under the callous supervision of the overseer.

The intensive labor required by rice resulted in a burgeoning black population. South Carolina's population figures reflected the growth of slavery on the coastal plantations. In 1685, for example, there were approximately 1,500 whites in South Carolina and only about 500 blacks. By 1760, there were about 55,000 blacks to about 35,000 whites.[13] By 1860, more than 400,000 blacks lived in South Carolina, representing 58 percent of the population.[14] In the rice-growing areas of the state, slaves outnumbered whites in even higher proportions.

Furthermore, because of the task system under which the slaves worked on rice plantations, a system that was itself brought from Africa, there was less direct supervision than slaves had in other parts of the country. This higher degree of seclusion, in spite of the hardship that often came with it, permitted the retention of many African customs, as did

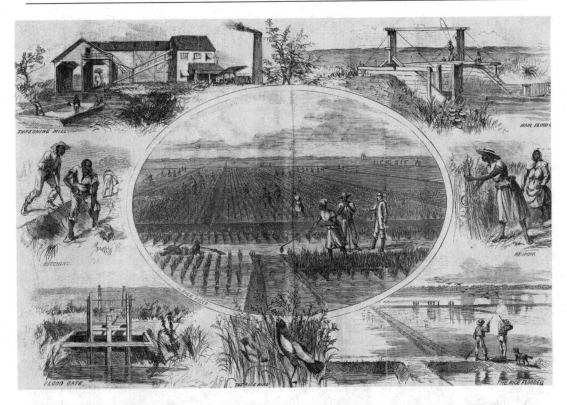

"Rice Culture on the Ogeechee, Near Savannah, Georgia," sketched by A. R. Waud. From *Harper's Weekly*, January 5, 1867. In the center illustration, blacks hoe the plants in standing water. In the surrounding vignettes, we see blacks digging the ditches and reaping rice, along with drawings of floodgates, the threshing mill, and a flooded field.

the tightly knit communities of African Americans living on plantations in the Sea Islands.[15] Among these customs was the dancing of the Ring Shout, whose preservation required a cohesive community that remained together over time.

FORM OF THE RING SHOUT

The Shout is a counterclockwise circle dance performed as religious worship. The form showed remarkable and vital flexibility. When African Americans began to convert to Christianity, the Shout was remade to fit the new religion, allowing them to continue to worship in a traditional African way, a way that was deeply communal and in which the worship lay in the interrelationship of song, dance, emotion, and belief.

As they move around the counterclockwise circle, participants sing their own improvised hymns, called Shouts, in call and response format, often pantomiming the action described by the song. In the Shout song "Adam and Eve," for example, the repeated lines "pickin' up leaves" signal participants to bend forward and pretend to pick something up off the floor. Likewise, "Rock, Daniel" leads some shouters to rock their bodies as they move their feet. Moreover, because the songs are loosely narrative, telling the stories of centuries of oppression and hardship as well as devotion to God, they form a body of historical-cultural as well as artistic and religious material. Some songs comment on Bib-

"Ring Shout in the Cabin" first appeared in Lydia Parrish's *Slave Songs of the Georgia Sea Islands*, published in 1942. The photos in the book represent people and experiences Parrish knew firsthand. In this photo, we see the traditional counterclockwise circular movement of the shout, the slightly bent posture of shouters, and the hand clapping by people who stand outside the circle. Courtesy University of Georgia Press, © 1942 by Lydia Parrish, 1969 by Maxfield Parrish, Jr.

lical figures and events, while others recall slavery. "Jubilee," for example, describes the hypocrisy of the cruel slave owner who pretended to be a Christian: "Call me Sunday Christian/ Oh, my Lord / Call me Monday devil/ Oh, Lord, Jubilee!"[16]

Contemporary descriptions help give us a sense of how the Shout was danced. Laura Towne was a northern teacher who came to the Sea Islands in April, 1862. The Union Army had captured the area in 1861, and Towne came as part of the Port Royal Experiment, the first major government effort to help former slaves. She founded a school and stayed on for thirty-eight years. She described a Ring Shout in 1862:

> Tonight I have been to a "shout," which seems to me certainly the remains of some old idol worship. The negroes sing a kind of chorus,—three standing apart to lead and clap,—and then all the others go shuffling round in a circle following one another with not much regularity, turning round occasionally and bending the knees, and stamping so that the whole floor swings. I never saw anything so savage. They call it a religious ceremony, but it seems more like a regular frolic to me.[17]

The cultural prejudice contained in Towne's account was to frame some attitudes toward the Shout for many years.

Other observers, however, were less dismissive. William Francis Allen, who later helped publish an important collection of slave songs, described a Christmas shout in 1863

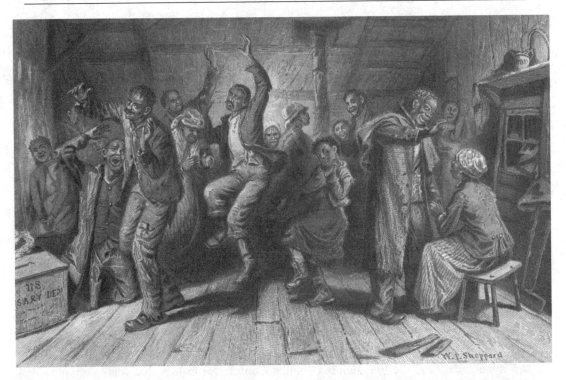

"**Prayer Meeting in a Contraband Camp—Washington, 1862,**" **by W. L. Sheppard. The engraving shows escaped slaves who have followed the Union Army and thus been declared contraband of war. The picture captures the religious enthusiasm that met with such mixed reactions from outsiders.**

in positive terms. Allen took the trouble, for example, to recognize skillful shouting, and to learn the term ("basing") for singing the choral responses:

> We went to see their regular Christmas shout in Peg's house last night. They had a praise meeting first.... At last they cleared the room and began, and a strange sight it was.... Billy sang, or rather chanted, and the others "based" him as they say, while ... [six dancers] moved round the room in a circle in a sort of shuffle. This is the shout. Some moved the feet backward and forward alternately, but the best shouters—and Jimmy, I was told to-day, "is a great shouter," keep the feet on the floor and work themselves along over the floor by moving them right and left. It seemed tremendous work for them ... and I saw the most skillful ones moved very easily and quietly.... Altogether it was one of the strangest and most interesting things I ever saw.[18]

The custom of keeping the feet on the floor, the call and response singing, the clearing of space for the dance, and the use of it to celebrate important religious holidays were all part of the Ring Shout customs.

John and Alan Lomax, folk music collectors and scholars who traveled across the United States during the middle of the twentieth century, also saw Ring Shouts. Their description expands on the two prior accounts:

> We have seen "shouts" in Louisiana, in Texas, in Georgia, and in the Bahamas; we have seen vaudou dancing in Haiti; we have read accounts of similar rites in works upon Negro life in other parts of the Western hemisphere. All share basic similarities: (1) the song is "danced" with the whole body, with hands, feet, belly, and hips; (2) the worship is, basically, a dancing-singing phenomenon; (3) the dancers always move counter-clockwise around the ring; (4) the song has the leader-chorus form, with much repetition, with a focus on rhythm rather than on melody, that is, with a form that invites and ultimately enforces cooperative group activity; (5) the song contin-

ues to be repeated sometimes more than an hour, steadily increasing in intensity and gradually accelerating, until a sort of mass hypnosis ensues.[19]

The Lomax account matches others. Even the "mass hypnosis," which many writers simply saw as emotional enthusiasm, was a key characteristic of the Shout and will be discussed in greater detail later in this chapter.

EFFECTS OF CHRISTIANITY

In 1896, a black participant told a writer for *The Illustrated American* that "Shout always bin yar."[20] Indeed, it is very old, even in its Christian form, and its African roots are of indeterminate ancientness. Shouters move around the circle in a pattern that has been described in print for nearly two centuries, and this form takes some of its characteristics from its Christian context. Sir Charles Lyell wrote about the dance in McIntosh County, Georgia, in 1845, giving us one of the earliest narratives about a Christian Shout:

> Of dancing and music the Negroes are passionately fond. On the Hopeton plantation above twenty violins have been silenced by the Methodist missionaries.... At the Methodist prayer meetings, they are permitted to move round rapidly in a ring, in which manoevre, I am told, they sometimes contrive to take enough exercise to serve as a substitute for the dance....[21]

An even earlier description may have come from John Watson, a Methodist minister who saw a black dance at the Philadelphia Annual Conference in 1819 that was "very greatly like the Indian dances." He wrote that "With every word so sung, they have a sinking of one or the other leg of the body alternately; producing an audible sound of the feet at every step.... If some, in the meantime sit, they strike the sounds alternately on each thigh."[22] Watson's account may include the circle format, as suggested by the phrase "greatly like the Indian dances," and notes other Shout features such as the rise and fall or curtsey-like motion of the body, the sound of the feet hitting the floor, and the body percussion provided by those outside the ring. He added that the practice was already affecting whites' religious worship. Later, in 1903, in *The Souls of Black Folk*, W.E.B. DuBois similarly commented, "the religion of the poor whites is a plain copy of Negro thought and methods."[23]

Shouters use a sliding, scuffing step that seems to arise out of a nexus of values, beliefs, and attitudes related to Christian worship. Here we must remember that European-style worship was not part of slave life for many years, for the slave population was not widely Christianized until well into the nineteenth century. During the 1600s and 1700s, the majority of slaves retained their African religions, and found their worship undisturbed by their so-called Christian masters. Many masters, in fact, were reluctant to allow their slaves to be converted. Some whites believed that Christian baptism would automatically confer freedom on their slaves, and others feared the assembly of slaves for worship.

Allowing slaves to come together in groups might have given them the opportunity to plan insurrections, and any hint of such a potentiality shot terror through the white community. Part of the reason for the fear was the fact that blacks outnumbered whites in many parts of the South. In the coastal areas where rice was grown, the black population was disproportionately large, and physical control over them was always tenuous. Insurrection plots came to light from time to time, suggesting the horrors that could occur if the planters' vigilance wavered. A 1730 letter from a writer in Charles Town (Charleston), for example, cites a black dance as the context for a slave plot:

The Georgia Sea Island Singers perform a Ring Shout song in 1964. Courtesy Bess Lomax Hawes.

> I shall give an Account of a bloody Tragedy which was to have been executed here last Saturday night ... by the Negroes, who had conspired to Rise and destroy us.... They soon made a great Body at the back of the Town, and had a great Dance, and expected the Country Negroes to come & join them; and had not an overruling Providence discovered their Intrigues, we had all been in blood.[24]

Slave owners wanted to avoid circumstances that would precipitate rebellions, and so allowing slaves to gather together, for entertainment or even for worship, had to be carefully evaluated.

Thus converting slaves to Christianity was not a priority for many slave owners, at least not in the first two centuries of slavery. As late as 1829, for example, the owner of a rice plantation on the Combahee River commented on his slaves' spiritual health by saying, "We don't care what they do when their tasks are over—we lose sight of them till next day. Their morals and their manners are in their own keeping. The men may have, for instance, as many wives as they please, so long as they do not quarrel about such matters."[25] Frederick Douglass' master Hugh Auld said, "If he learns to read the Bible it will forever unfit him to be a slave. He should know nothing but the will of his master, and learn to obey it."[26]

On the other hand, whites wanted to keep slaves content insofar as they could without interfering with profits. Many owners compromised by balancing limited mobility with limited leisure time for dance, which was a favorite slave activity. Before slaves adopted Christianity, their worship would have been African, and their dance African ritual dance. Furthermore, the long years in which blacks worshipped in the old ways established ritual dance as part of African American culture. Hence many blacks who had been born on this continent, some with parents and grandparents who had been born here as well, very likely grew up with African ritual dance as part of their American way of life.

"The Sunny South—A Negro Revival Meeting—A Seeker 'Getting Religion,'" by artist W. L. Sheppard. Printed in *Frank Leslie's Illustrated Newspaper*, August 9, 1873. Here we see the cataleptic
states and religious excitement witnessed at the Methodist meetings during the Great Awakening.
These may also have a kinship with the possession states in African ritual dance.

At the same time, the Great Awakening was beginning to sweep across the South. As
early as the mid 1700s, Baptist and Methodist ministers, as well as those from other denom-
inations, began to preach to blacks and whites across the South, converting many blacks
who in turn preached to black congregations wherever they found them. By the second
quarter of the nineteenth century, these evangelical preachers were effecting profound
change in African American religious allegiances. Nevertheless, such salvation experiences
for blacks could not and did not strip them of their culture. Christianity transformed black
worship in many ways, but it did not stop traditional dance. Instead, the dance became
part of the new religion, adapting itself so effectively that it was no longer even recognized as dance.

Throughout the upper South, whites and blacks mingled in emotional camp meetings
where there were mass conversions, ecstatic religious experiences such as cataleptic states
and visions, and torchlight processionals. The Ring Shout, danced by black attendees, was
commonly seen at such events, but it most emphatically was not considered dancing. Dance
was sinful, and the black shout was not. So long as the feet were not crossed or lifted from
the floor, neither the church nor secular society regarded the movement as dance.

Whatever the shout step had been like before Christianity affected it, it afterward
observed these church rules. Shouters, in the slightly bent posture of African dance, slid
one foot forward, drew the other up to it in a scuffing, hitching motion, and then slid the
first one forward again.[27] At the beginning of each new verse, or each new line sung by

This lithograph, published in 1829, shows a white camp meeting. In the grip of religious enthusiasm, women lost their bonnets and raised their arms to God. Courtesy Library of Congress.

the leader who "set" the shout, the circle of dancers would lead off with the other foot, switching feet again at the beginning of the next verse. Those who got the spirit or otherwise lost control so as to cross their feet or lift them high in a jig-like motion were pulled out of the circle to compose themselves—at least until such a degree of religious enthusiasm ensued that the rules of decorum were loosened for all present.

AFRICAN TRAITS

The Ring Shout clearly included circle formation, polyrhythms, pantomime, and community participation. Orientation to the earth was important, for the shouters bent slightly forward as they moved around the circle. Syncopation, a dominant element in much West African music, was part of the rhythm of a Shout. In 1868, Wendell Phillips Garrison, son of the famous abolitionist William Lloyd Garrison, described it: "Instead of clapping the hands in unison with the accented parts of the measure, the singers uniformly beat the time in syncopation; i.e. striking the hands together immediately after the accented notes were sung."[28] This practice added complexity and layered texture onto the instrumentation and vocalizations, reflecting a very African and highly developed musical taste.

The lead singer who set the shout told a story or unfolded a truth from line to line, feeling free to improvise in building the song, much as the lead singer improvised in a black work song or boat song. The rest of the singers or "basers" kept up a repetitive

These two photos were taken in a Nazi prisoner of war camp during World War II. They show black soldiers performing a circle dance to entertain fellow prisoners of various nationalities. One performer creates the rhythm on a drum, and several others carry pieces of cloth, perhaps handkerchiefs.

refrain, alternating with the lead singer but beginning their line of song before he had finished his own:

> Blow Gabriel
> > at the Judgment
> Blow Gabriel
> > at the Judgment Bar!
> Blow 'um easy
> > at the Judgment
> Blow 'um easy
> > at the Judgment Bar!
> My Lord call you
> > at the Judgment[29]

In the 1950s, scholar Bruno Nettl pointed out that this responsorial technique, in which the leader varies his or her part while a chorus sings a line that changes little, is typical of equatorial Africa.[30] Through the alternating lines, the leader gains the chance to take a breath while the basers sing a repeated phrase.

The multi-part singing, which reflected improvisation in timing and pitch by the singers, often bewildered and moved observers with its complication and poignancy. Participants created a song that was heartfelt, repetitive yet new, individually expressive yet profoundly cohesive, apparently untutored and yet musically sophisticated, and sung in the tones of an African scale so that it defied transcription into western musical notation.

Whites present at Ring Shouts sometimes tried to describe the effect in words such as "wild," "most interesting," and "strangely beautiful." Those who wrote down the words and tried to capture the music sometimes admitted that it was impossible to convey it with the customary notes and symbols.

In a Ring Shout, worshippers move into and out of the circle as exhaustion claims them or rest permits them. Those on the outside of the circle sing, clap, pat, and beat time with a stick. Even today, the "sticker" is a person of key importance in a Shout, providing the percussion much as the drummer provides it in a West African dance event. The sticker sits to one side, beating time with a broomstick or other stick on a wooden floor, in effect making the floor a drum and creating a resonant beat. When Bess Lomax Hawes filmed a Ring Shout performed by the Georgia Sea Island Singers in 1964, one of the participants was John Davis. Davis often wielded the stick. He was, as Hawes noted, "always very particular about the correct resonance of this instrument and would refuse to 'beat stick' on an asphalt tile or linoleum floor."[31] This concern for a resonant floor was reflected in black dance tradition throughout the nineteenth century. Individual dancers often carried a portable platform or "shingle" a few feet square, and slaves frequently erected a large platform for plantation dances.

Blacks may have begun the practice of beating time with a stick because of the ban against drums, one result of the Stono River Rebellion. At the Stono River in South Carolina in 1739, between fifty and one hundred slaves gathered together under the leadership of an Angolan slave named Jemmy. Armed with stolen weapons, they marched toward Florida, where they knew the Spanish government would give them freedom, killing the whites they met along the way. In the battle with colonial militia that followed, about twenty whites died.[32] About forty to sixty blacks were killed then and later as they were

This photo of an outdoor circle dance was probably shot in the American South around 1920. To the left, a man shows some steps to a young child. Near the center of the ring, another man plays a drum. In the foreground, two men sit in chairs. The picture appears to have been taken through a window, for a shutter is visible to the left.

captured. Slave communication through drums was implicated in the revolt, and as a result drums were widely banned.

But enslaved Africans found other forms of percussion, including not only the stick used in the shout but also body percussion such as clapping and patting. Foot percussion became important, as well. By the 1920s, it had become tap dance, in which a dancer's feet, with the help of metal taps on the soles of shoes, beat out the rhythm of the performance. The stage, like the older and simpler wooden platform, also became a drum. The Ring Shout may have been one of the sources of tap, because many Ring Shouts incorporated foot percussion. In the 1930s, Lydia Parrish noticed the complicated rhythm tapped out by shouters. She wrote, "The shouting proceeds with a curious shuffling but controlled step which taps out with the heel a resonant syncopation fascinating in its intricacy and precision."[33] In fact, Parrish saw shouts in which the heel tapping substituted for the stick percussion.

Thus the dance forms that came together in the Ring Shout may have been entirely African in nature prior to 1808, but by the late slavery period they had combined to embody Christian worship and include songs partly made up of fragments from English hymns. The Ring Shout always had an African core or base that was constantly refreshed by new importations of Africans right up to the eve of the Civil War. African elements included circular formation, percussion, pantomime, polyrhythms, orientation to the earth, improvisation, and centrality of the community—seven of the African dance characteristics listed in Chapter 1, as well as call and response. Further examination shows that the other three—African body movement, with hip and shoulder shaking, as well as competition and even the use of special objects such as handkerchiefs—were also part of the Ring Shout.

Hip shaking, for example, was relatively common. Parrish wrote that local resident

BLOW FOR BLOW.

Entd accg to act of Congs in the year 1863, by William A. Stephens in the Clerks Office of the Dist. Court of the US for the E. Dist of Pa

Whites in the antebellum South knew that, given the chance, many slaves would resort to violence to gain their freedom. The print is "Blow for Blow," a lithograph first published in 1863, showing a slave turning the tables on an overseer, who still has a whip in his hand. Courtesy Library of Congress.

Margaret "wiggled her hips shamelessly" while shouting[34] and Robert Gordon noted in 1931 that "the body sways at the hips, and dips and the knees bend."[35]

Gordon also described competition as part of the shout. "Not infrequently," he wrote, "two singers would shout facing one another in a sort of competition of skill or endurance." On occasion, the competition blended with unchurchly body movement. "Sometimes this was done with great dignity and grace," Gordon continued, "but not infrequently one of the singers, in an attempt to outdo the other, would introduce body motions that seemed to have very little to do with religion."[36]

Use of handkerchiefs appears in both description and old sheet music. Lawrence McKiver, a member of the McIntosh County Shouters who was in his nineties when he spoke to a researcher, remembers women using handkerchiefs in the shout. Referring to a song about a slave who betrayed others in the community to the master ("he would tell the old slave master every thing that the slaves do"), McKiver said that when the women did this shout in the past, they waved handkerchiefs: "They be throwing up their hands, they have a handkerchief, 'drive 'im from the window, drive 'im from the do.'"[37] Old sheet music bears out the use of handkerchiefs. "I'm Flying High," an 1886 minstrel song that attempted to express the slave's sense of joy in religion, pictured a Ring Shout on its cover, with women and children waving handkerchiefs.[38]

NEGATIVE REACTIONS TO THE RING SHOUT

The Ring Shout, because of its obvious links to Africa, has often drawn negative reactions from whites and middle class blacks. Many felt that it was idolatrous or barbaric, and that the religious enthusiasm that it engendered was irrational and demonstrated loss of self-control.

In the nineteenth century, funeral rites were strongly associated with the Ring Shout. Historian Sterling Stuckey, who argues that slaves were still essentially African in culture at the time of Emancipation, considers the Shout to be part of an African reciprocity between the living and the dead, part of communication with ancestors.[39] This link to death rites is supported in an historical account by Letitia Burwell. Burwell, daughter of a Virginia plantation owner, was writing about her girlhood prior to the Civil War. She remembered the death of Aunt Fanny, the family cook who was a staunch Christian. Yet as her death approached Aunt Fanny either called for or permitted an African ring dance around her bed:

> Several days before her death.... Her room was crowded with Negroes who had come to perform their religious rites around the death-bed. Joining hands, they performed a savage dance, shouting wildly around her bed. This was horrible to hear and see, especially as in this family every effort had been made to instruct their negro dependents in the truths of religion.... But although an intelligent woman, [Aunt Fanny] seemed to cling to the superstitions of her race.

Horrified, the narrator suggested gently to Aunt Fanny that this dancing might make her worse, but the dying woman held firm. She said, "Honey dat kind o' 'ligion suit us black folks better 'en yo' kind. What suits Mars' Charles' mind karn't suit mine."[40] While slaves might humor masters by acting out adherence to white styles of worship, many actually found much more comfort in African ways of communicating with the divine.

Shouting withstood efforts to eradicate it. Like Burwell, other whites viewed it as a remnant of old, idolatrous rituals. Some slave owners tried to repress it. During the

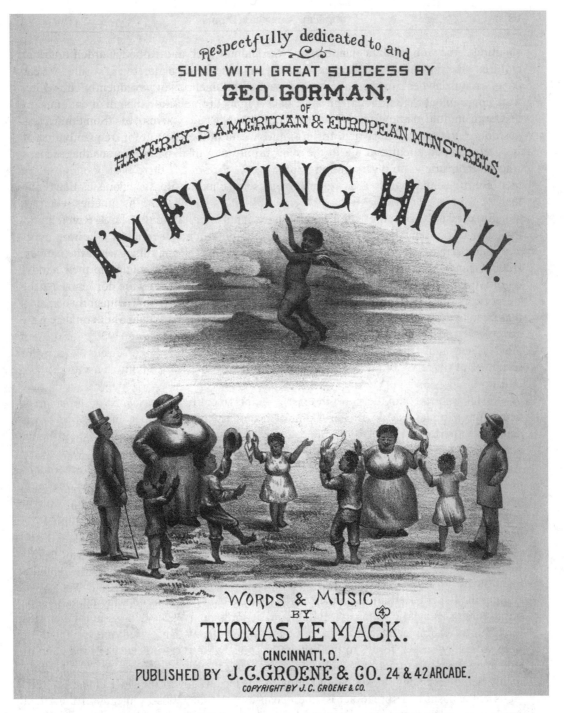

"I'm Flying High," by Thomas Le Mack, published by J. C. Groene & Company in Cincinnati, 1886. Courtesy Brown University.

slavery era, many blacks resorted to clandestine, outdoor shouting, sometimes at night and usually outside regular church services. Some blacks believed that an overturned iron pot would catch the sound and prevent whites, especially slave patrollers, from hearing the singing.

After the end of slavery and well into the twentieth century, the greatest danger to shouting came from middle class blacks, who did not wish to be associated with African culture. Many of them had adopted mainstream American perspectives, seeing African dance as a throwback to the barbaric behavior of an unchristian world. In effect, whites were continuing to repress African-style dance by making blacks ashamed of it. Thus, by and large, middle class African Americans wanted to distance themselves from the African past, not reinvigorate it. Parrish, for example, wrote in the 1942, "Genuine Negro music is confronted by a real menace in the scornful attitude of those Negro school teachers, who do their utmost to discredit and uproot every trace of it." Instead of being proud of their contribution to world music, some of these teachers treated it "like a family skeleton."[41]

Sheet music like "A Warmin' Up in Dixie" (1899) or "Africana" (1904), which portrayed blacks as dancing wildly in a circle formation around a fire, may have been especially embarrassing. To many in the black middle class, it may have seemed that just when African Americans were gaining opportunities in education and presenting a more dignified image to the world, less educated community members were perpetuating the stereotypes of minstrelsy. These stereotypes were part of a stream of negative images that stretched far into the twentieth century. As Hollywood established itself, these negative depictions of non-white native peoples were seen in *King Kong* (1933), the Tarzan movies, and many films with safari scenarios. Prejudicial images of circle dance were so powerful that they blinded mainstream America to the Ring Shout as a vibrant folk tradition.

Black ministers did their part in these attempts to eradicate Africanist religious practices. For example, A.M.E. Bishop Daniel Alexander Payne, who became the first president of Wilberforce University in 1865, opposed shouting. When he saw a shout being performed by a number of people at a camp meeting, he said, "I then went, and taking their leader by the arm requested him to desist and sit down and sing in a rational manner. I told him it was a heathenish way to worship and disgraceful to themselves, the race, and the Christian name." The leader responded, "The Spirit of God works upon people in different ways. At camp-meeting there must be a ring here, a ring there, a ring over yonder, or sinners will not get converted."[42]

Indeed, the camp meeting, especially during the nineteenth century, was a hotbed of Ring Shout activity and other kinds of religious enthusiasm. There, blacks often came under the influence of Methodist preachers who represented a tradition of ecstatic experiences. Among the British Methodists in their early years, these were common, including unconsciousness or cataleptic states, trembling, and visions. John Wesley, in his journal entries for 1739, for example, described several church participants who cried out, trembled, or were struck by unseen forces to the ground.[43] Those who were so seized felt the hand of God upon them and sometimes spoke of seeing themselves held over the pit of hell before finally being saved and "raised up" filled with "peace and joy in the Holy Ghost."[44] Religious enthusiasm had spread across the ocean by the mid 1700s by means of the Great Awakening, setting America afire for Christ. By the early 1800s, the camp meeting was spreading across the United States, and by the late 1800s, it was a phenomenon many Americans had experienced personally.

The shout's rhythmic beat also led to trancelike experiences, and these were akin to the possession sought in African dance. Descriptions of such experiences are legion. Parrish wrote of shout participants: "They began to move quietly, as if in a trance, and it was soon evident, from a peculiar heart-clutching quality in the rhythm, that they were 'possessed' by it."[45] She added, "I saw a 'lone shouter' fall into a trance that lasted half an

"A Warmin' Up in Dixie," by E.T. Paull, 1899.

"A Negro Camp-Meeting in the South," published in *Harper's Weekly*, August 10, 1872. **Courtesy Library of Congress.**

hour. She was covered with a coat and left where she fell until she returned to consciousness."[46]

Jon Michael Spencer attributes the altered states of consciousness, lesser forms of which may be called "getting happy" or "getting the spirit," to the repetitive rhythms of the shout, which produced emotional catharsis.[47] Many black Christians, on the other hand, saw this as a salvation experience or a time of spiritual beauty in closeness to God. Whites could be horrified or frightened by the frenzy that shouts seemed to produce. Frances Butler Leigh, daughter of Fanny Kemble Butler, returned after the Civil War with her father to his Sea Island plantation. The black people there presented a shout to honor her birthday. Here is her description, first published in 1883:

> … in the evening about fifty of them, of all sizes and ages and of both sexes, headed by old Uncle John, the preacher, collected in front of the house to "shout." First they lit two huge fires of blazing pine logs, around which they began to move with a slow shuffling step, singing a hymn beginning "I wants to climb up Jacob's ladder." Getting warmed up by degrees, they went faster and faster, shouting louder and louder, until they looked like a parcel of mad fiends. The children, finding themselves kicked over in the general *mêlée*, formed a circle on their own account, and went round like small Catherine wheels.

Eventually, Leigh could watch no longer. She wrote, "When, after nearly an hour's performance, I went down to thank them, and to stop them—for it was getting dreadful, and I thought some of them would have fits—I found it no easy matter to do so, they were so excited."[48]

Stuckey points out that some of the characteristics of the shout that made Leigh so uneasy, the increased speed and communal unity in particular, were African:

Wherever in Africa the counterclockwise dance ceremony was performed—it is called the ring shout in North America—the dancing and singing were directed to the ancestors and gods, the tempo and revolution of the circle quickening during the course of movement. The ring in which Africans danced and sang is the key to understanding the means by which they achieved oneness in America.[49]

The Ring Shout was part of Christian worship, but under the veneer of Christianity was African worship, with its core values of spiritual unity and ecstatic experience—experience in which individual consciousness was abandoned for a personal yet communal merging of the self with the deity.

A shout could and often did continue all night until dawn. It was usually danced only on special occasions, such as Christmas or the Watch Night of New Year's Eve, and the long hours in which to dance were seen as a spiritual blessing by many Christians. These long hours also provided enough time for individuals to fall into ecstatic states.

Typically, a shout was held after, not during, a church service because of the disapproval of the pastor and some church members. African American poet and song writer James Weldon Johnson (1871–1938), writing in 1925, remembered the phenomenon from his youth in Florida:

The very monotony of sound and motion produces an ecstatic state. Women, screaming, fall to the ground prone and quivering. Men, exhausted, drop out of the shout. But the ring closes up and moves around and around. I remember, too, that even then the "ring shout" was looked upon as a very questionable form of worship. It was distinctly frowned upon by a great many colored people. Indeed, I do not recall ever seeing a "ring shout" except *after* the regular services. Almost whispered invitations would go around, "Stay after church; there's going to be a 'ring shout.'" The more educated minister and members, as fast as they were able to brave the primitive element in the churches, placed a ban on the "ring shout."[50]

Despite this disapproval, the shout persisted because of the spiritual blessings it conferred. When Bess Lomax Hawes filmed a shout in 1964, she found that even on a sound stage in Los Angeles with cameras running, a participant named Mrs. Jones became "filled with the spirit" during a performance of "Yonder Comes Day." Mrs. Jones ignored the end of the filming and continued to sing while the camera crew packed the equipment.[51]

During the Civil War, blacks were permitted to enlist in the Union Army beginning in 1862. The shout's spiritual gifts brought comfort to these African American soldiers, who faced much greater danger than white northern soldiers. Outraged that the North would arm blacks, the South said it would execute any black soldiers taken in battle. Southerners' anger derived from their historical fear of armed blacks and slave insurrection. The Confederacy did execute some black prisoners. Other blacks were treated as lost property and sent into slavery. Southern resentment of black Union soldiers could also fuel fury in battle. At Fort Pillow, for example, where about half the Union soldiers were black, their casualties were disproportionately high. The blacks were massacred, while most of the white northerners were taken alive.

With these bleak prospects before them, many black soldiers took refuge in the Ring Shout. Col. Thomas Wentworth Higginson, a white officer who served with black troops in the Civil War, saw a Ring Shout in camp, "not rarely & occasionally, but night after night." Higginson said the shouts took place in "a little booth, made neatly of palm leaves and covered in at top, a regular native African hut," and that the hut usually contained a fire. Crowding into the structure, black men sang "one of their quaint, monotonous, endless, negro-Methodist chants, with obscure syllables recurring constantly." For percussion,

Nathan Bedford Forrest was the Confederate commanding officer at the Fort Pillow massacre in Henning, Tennessee, where the fort overlooked the Mississippi River. After the war, he became one of the early leaders of the Ku Klux Klan.

there was "regular drumming of the feet and clapping of the hands, like castanets."[52] The experience included gifts of the spirit: "Then the excitement spreads: inside and outside the enclosure men begin to quiver and dance, others join, a circle forms, winding monotonously round some one in the centre; some 'heel and toe' tumultuously, others merely tremble and stagger on, others stoop and rise, others whirl, others caper sideways, all keep steadily circling like dervishes...."[53] In the darkest times, a shout, with its rhythms, fellowship, and spiritual rewards, appeared to give solace, even to men who might face death in the coming hours.

In the dark years of American slavery and post-bellum economic oppression, the shout offered nurturing and spiritual fulfillment to a people whose lives were otherwise shadowed by pain and deprivation. Lawrence McKiver captured some of this feeling when he said, "If they set that song right, and I get my blood sort of warm, I can shout. It make you feel good, you get something out of it."[54] The survival of the shout was no accident, but happened because of the personal and spiritual value of the experience.

After the Civil War, when African American churches were able to get buildings with benches and pews, the furniture obstructed shouting. Often, dancers would simply move the benches aside, but other accommodations developed as well. The rocking and stepping of the Ring Shout survived in individual form as worshippers stayed in place but danced when they were caught up in the spirit during religious service.

VARIATIONS, RELIGIOUS AND SECULAR

There were also variations on the traditional form of the shout. One of these is "Down to De Mire." In this form, a sinner was called to the center of the circle and through his posture symbolically demonstrated the nadir of sin. In the version described by Parrish, the person in the center is on his knees, with his head touching the floor. He rotates his body as the circle revolves around him. Individual shouters reach into the center and press his head "down to de mire." The accompanying words use the center person's name and emphasize the necessity of bowing low:

This glass slide is captioned "The Contraband Camp at City Point: An Evening Prayer Meeting." With a lighted candle on the counter before him, a man preaches to fellow escaped slaves, who sit on wooden boxes or overturned baskets.

> Sister Emma, Oh, you mus' come down to de mire.
> Sister Emma, Oh, you mus' come down to de mire.
>> Jesus been down
>>> to de mire
>> Jesus been down
>>> to de mire
>> Jesus been down
>>> to de mire
>> You must bow low
>>> to de mire
>> Honor Jesus
>>> to de mire
>> Honor Jesus
>>> to de mire
>> Lowrah lowrah
>>> to de mire
>> Lowrah lowrah
>>> to de mire
>> Lowrah lowrah
>>> to de mire
>> Jesus been down
>>> to de mire

Sister Josie, you must come down to de mire
Sister Josie, you must come down to de mire[55]

When Alan Lomax asked shouter Peter Davis what it meant to go down in the mire, Davis answered, "Now that means humble your heart, humble yourself to the Lord. That's the muck of sin which your heart and mind are all—you know—contaminated in. And then when God pull you out of there, you can be free and shout round."[56] Thus the form reenacts the conversion experience, in which the sinner must acknowledge that he is in "the muck of sin" and admit his condition to God. Then and only then can he participate in the shout, a praise dance that brings him closer to God.

There were secular variations of the shout, as well. African American composer James P. Johnson remembered such performances in his childhood home: "They danced around in a shuffle and then they would shove a man or woman out into the center and clap hands." Szwed and Marks conclude that the shout's "use as a secular form as well as a sacred one is not well documented, but fits patterns of multiple functions seen in the West Indies."[57] One ex-slave quoted by Epstein mentions another play-party circle dance: "Saturday night we played and danced, sometimes in the cabins and sometimes in the yards.... We would get in a ring and when the music started we would begin working our foots while we sung, 'You steal my true love, and I'll steal your'en.'"[58] These secular forms may have developed from the sacred shout, or may have been offshoots of other African circle dances.

INFLUENCES

Looking backward to African ritual dance, the Ring Shout also looked forward to later African American dance, which drew liberally on the older form's repertoire of movement vocabulary and cultural content. Shouts, through their narrative that signaled pantomime, cued dance steps and gestures, a practice that may have had sources in the signals African drummers give dancers and that may have later contributed to the calling of the American Square Dance. The strong polyrhythmic beat and layered texture look forward to jazz and rock music. The pantomime is part of the same dance aesthetic later seen in the Swim, Hitchhike, Stroll, and other mimetic social dances, and the sliding, scuffing steps augmented with staccato heel tapping contributed to tap dance. The Ring Shout was most likely the source for the Walk Around of the minstrel show and may later have evolved into the Cakewalk. As the oldest African American dance form, the Shout represented an even older African musical tradition that had enormous influence on the dances that followed it.

THE BUZZARD LOPE

The Buzzard Lope, like the Ring Shout, is very old and also bears marks of African origins. The dance pantomimes the action of a buzzard finding and eating carrion. Photos in Lydia Parrish's 1942 *Slave Songs of the Georgia Sea Islands* show a performance of the Buzzard Lope. One person lies in the pose of death on a wide veranda, while another person dances in a "stylized pattern of the bird's awkward steps, without any attempt at realism." The stylized motion is consistent with the abstract nature of African dance; one African example is the Mandinka Lenjengo dance, which pantomimes the flight of the egret

Bess Lomax Hawes filmed this circular singing game in a Los Angeles schoolyard in 1967. The game was played entirely by girls, and involved their dancing in a circle while clapping and chanting. The format is call and response, with players moving in response to each line and improvising variations on standard moves. Courtesy Bess Lomax Hawes.

and can be seen in contemporary film footage.[59] Commenting on the Buzzard Lope dancer she observed, Parrish noted, "His is indeed a high form of rhythmic approximation, and those who have seen it at the Cabin are fortunate."[60]

A third participant stood aside, providing the percussion and keeping time through patting, while a fourth called out cues such as "March aroun'," "Get the eye," and "Look aroun' for mo' meat!"[61] These cues demonstrate the ability of folk creators to get into character, seeing and thinking as a buzzard would—or from the African point of view, in some sense to become the buzzard.

Anthropologist Melville Herskovits reported that a similar dance could be found among the Ashanti-Fanti peoples of the Gold Coast, who venerated the vulture as a sacred messenger connected with the gods. In the early 1930s in Surinam, Herskovits saw a performance of a vulture dance by descendants of enslaved Africans. They called it *Opete*, the Twi word for vulture. In a state of possession, dancers would go forth to find dead animals for food. Herskovits wrote, "Those who danced for the buzzard ... went about in a circle, moving with bodies bent forward from their waists and with arms thrown back in imitation of the bird from which their spirit took its name."[62]

Hawes filmed a version of the Buzzard Lope by the Sea Island Singers, who interpreted it as a Christian commentary on slavery. Instead of a human who lies on the floor, impersonating a dead animal, a white handkerchief is placed in the center of dance area, representing the body of a dead slave who has been denied burial. This theme is an impor-

This postcard is postmarked 1915.

tant one, reflecting the value placed on burial rites in African and African American cultures as well as the cold cruelty of the slave master. In describing the dance, Hawes writes, "The Buzzard tiptoes around the body, advancing and retreating to make sure it is truly dead, and finally fulfills the ancient African role of messenger by carrying the sacrifice back to the Lord."[63]

To give words to this African allegory in which the Buzzard carries the body of the dead to God, the singers chose a Christian Shout song:

> Throw me anywhere, Lord.
> > in that old field
> Throw me anywhere, Lord
> > in that old field
> Don't care where you throw me
> > in that old field
> Since King Jesus own me,
> > in that old field
> Don't care how you do me
> > in that old field
> Since King Jesus choose me
> > in that old field
> You may beat and bang me
> > in that old field
> Since King Jesus saved me
> > in that old field

This sequence of photos shows the Buzzard Lope in performance. From Lydia Parrish, *Slave Songs of the Georgia Sea Islands.* **Courtesy University of Georgia Press, © 1942 by Lydia Parrish and 1969 by Maxfield Parrish, Jr.**

> Don't care how you treat me
> > in that old field
> Since King Jesus meet me
> > in that old field
> Throw me anywhere, Lord
> > in that old field
> Throw me anywhere, Lord
> > in that old field.[64]

Through the song, singers transcend the brutality of slavery, triumphing in God's love and salvation. They are able to dismiss the experience of being treated like carrion by juxtaposing it with the joy of being chosen by King Jesus.

This is not to say realism was unimportant. The dancer in this case was John Davis, who expressed concern about making the "wings flap better." He added that in his younger days he had picked the handkerchief up with his teeth and whirled around with it before carrying it off in the character of the buzzard. The quality of the pantomime documented the authenticity of the natural world, which was nevertheless infused with spirits and represented an overarching spiritual framework that was moral and that gave meaning to human life.

John Davis portrays the buzzard in a performance of the Buzzard Lope in 1964. Courtesy Bess Lomax Hawes.

The Buzzard Lope shows its African origins not only through the dance characteristics of communal performance, orientation to the earth, and pantomime, but also through its ritual quality. It survived into the twentieth century to be documented and described by Parrish and Hawes, but is performed no longer. As Hawes lamented, "now that he [John Davis] is gone, we may never see it again." Sadly, she was probably correct.

3

Early Black Festivals and Congo Square

The formation of the new American nation in 1776 seemed to initiate a time of hope for African Americans. Through its Declaration of Independence, the U.S. had declared that all men were created equal and that God endowed them with certain rights, including the right to liberty. Moreover, the Constitution had forbidden further importation of slaves as of 1808. During the first years of the nation's existence, some of the states seemed to be headed toward granting freedom to slaves. In 1780, Pennsylvania passed a law that emancipated slaves gradually. In 1783, Virginia granted freedom to blacks who had fought for the patriot side in the Revolution. In the same year, Massachusetts declared slavery illegal within its boundaries. In 1783, New Hampshire freed its slaves, and in 1784, Rhode Island and Connecticut passed gradual emancipation acts. Other northern states individually freed slaves on varying timetables. In this time of hope, many African Americans practiced their cultural arts, especially dance, openly in an atmosphere of sympathy from, or at least acceptance by, many whites.

During this period and in some cases up through the end of the nineteenth century, a variety of black festivals and gatherings helped preserve and showcase African-based dance. In both the North and the South, they gave an oppressed people the opportunity to come together to dance in ways that nurtured them and helped keep alive the memories of who they were and where they had come from. Among these special occasions were Pinkster in New York and New Jersey; John Canoe in North Carolina; Negro Election Day in Massachusetts, Connecticut, New Hampshire, and Rhode Island; General Training Day in New England; the corn shucking across the South; and dancing in Congo Square in New Orleans. The first five events were held annually, while the fifth was a weekly assembly of blacks on Sunday afternoons in a public square in the first half of the nineteenth century.

The celebrations were countenanced by civil authorities, allowing blacks to break free of white domination for a few hours, a few days, or even a week to express treasured African customs and traditions, in some cases to speak the languages of their ancestors, and to socialize with family and friends. In the North, where blacks lived as farm workers, house servants, or artisans, sometimes in a master's attic or cellar, isolation from one's family and peers could be much more severe than in the South. Furthermore, where blacks lived in closer proximity to whites, they were often subject to tighter control and harsher treatment. Hence, it was no surprise that slaves needed an occasional release from control. Many African Americans above the Mason-Dixon line eagerly persuaded masters and employers to permit them to travel across the countryside to attend the annual celebration of Pinkster, and others worked extra hours or sold goods to finance their involvement.

This 1856 engraving shows the election of a leader among the Yoruba. From *Harper's New Monthly Magazine*, July 1856.

The festivals demonstrated a range of African American values and behaviors that, although usually not tolerated, were temporarily accepted by local authorities. One of these was a degree of social and political autonomy. Blacks often had the freedom to choose their own leaders for the duration of the celebration and to negotiate some of the terms of the event with whites on a basis of temporary equality if not superiority. Whites may have considered this behavior as a social safety valve, a brief time of release that made it possible for blacks to endure heavy burdens and tight controls, which snapped back into place after the gathering was over. At the southern corn shucking, for example, blacks who contributed their services to neighbors were often accorded courtesy, feasting, and space for dancing that they otherwise would not have received.

In selecting their own leaders, blacks showed a preference for noble and African birth, impressive physical size and strength, and oratorical or musical ability. They also often divided into tribal groups for the duration of the festivities, mapping out a cultural comfort zone that largely vanished when the event ended. Within this comfort zone, moreover, they sometimes felt secure enough to comment satirically on white society in general and on individuals in particular. Whites generally tolerated the derision as part of an unspoken contract in which liberties were granted for only a limited time.

In all these festivals, dance was a major focus. For the black community, celebration *was* dance, and it went on for hours if not days. Furthermore, it was African-based dance, dance in which polyrhythms dominated, people joyfully moved in African ways, and hand-clapping supplemented drumming. Dancers might move in and out of a circle or line as

Albany is advantageously located on the Hudson River. The city was declared the state capital in 1797. In 1806, the cornerstone was laid for a state capitol building on Pinkster Hill. The building stood on the north side of State Street in Capitol Park, east of the current capitol building.

exhaustion claimed them and rest reinvigorated them. There was the delight of improvisation and competition, and the fulfillment of communality. Even in situations where participants danced conventional European forms, African movement vocabulary and musical styles pervaded the experience.

The pleasure arising from this Africanist dance was perhaps difficult for whites to comprehend. Sterling Stuckey captured some of the feeling when he wrote of Pinkster, "The vigor of the dancers and their faces—which often conveyed a certain joy—not uncommonly meant that dance to them was a form of spiritual recreation, which compounded the problem of understanding for those outside slave culture, inclining them to underestimate ... the gravity of much of slave dance."[1] Dance embodied spiritual meaning, communal sharing, and personal nurturing.

The celebration gave participants distinction and power, albeit temporary, within the white community. Across the symbolic and physical performance space, whites and blacks surveyed each other with varying objectives and degrees of negotiating strength. Whites often came to watch, and in the case of the corn shucking, used the performance as an entertainment for invited guests. Many whites wrote down accounts of what they saw. These narratives, sometimes written long after the events, are typically overlaid with nostalgia and recall their excitement and beauty. From such commentaries, we can gain some sense of context, as well as see how satisfying the dance was to both the dancers and appreciative spectators. A few writers, however, interpreting the experience through their own cultural lens, criticized the dance as lascivious or as lacking artistry. The range of perspectives once again reflected the love-hate relationship European Americans had with black culture.

Some of the festivals were discontinued early in American history—Pinkster reached its zenith in New York state between 1790 and 1810, and its entertainments were forbidden in Albany in 1811. Other festivals lasted much longer—the corn husking was still common in the early twentieth century. Some are re-enacted today, including Pinkster by Historic Hudson Valley and Jonkonnu by Somerset Plantation and Tryon Palace in North Carolina.

PINKSTER

Pinkster was originally a religious celebration of the Dutch in old New York. The name came from the Dutch word for Pentecost, first used in a 1667 Dutch book of sermons[2] and commemorating the descent of the Holy Spirit on the Apostles after the Ascension of Christ. Celebrated seven weeks after Passover, the holiday usually fell in May or even early June.[3] It was a time for rejoicing in the renewal of spring and the sprouting of young crops, and it marked the first lull in farm work after planting. "The Pinkster Ode," written in 1803 by an educated person possibly using a pseudonym (Absalom Aimwell), says it was the time of year "When leaves the fig tree putteth out,/When calves and lambs for mothers cry...."[4] The event was associated with the bright pink azalea, "Pinkster Blummachee."

By the late eighteenth century, the Dutch religious festival had become a predominantly African American celebration that took place in Albany, New York City, and Long Island, as well as in other New York towns and in eastern New Jersey.[5] For as long as a week, blacks could gather on open land or in a market area, set up booths and stalls to sell food and other goods, and dance together. One of the largest of the Pinkster celebrations occurred regularly at Albany.

Albany in 1790 was a sizable town with a significant black community, in a large county. The census for the year tells us that the total population of Albany County, which covered a vast territory, was 75,980 people, of which 3,929 were slaves and 170 were free. Albany County was by far the largest in the state, and parts of it would later split off into separate counties. The area was dotted with large towns, including Albany, which had about 3,500 inhabitants, and was by no means the largest. Albany, however, would triple and quadruple in size in the next three decades. New York City and County in 1790 had a substantial population of 33,111, of which 2,369 were slaves and 1,101 were free blacks.[6] Moreover, between 1701 and 1774, 43% of all Africans sold into slavery in the North came directly from Africa[7], assuring a strong infusion of African culture among northern blacks.

Albany had a long history stretching back to its Dutch roots in the 1640s, and before the end of the Revolutionary War the city had more than six hundred buildings, some of which were substantial brick structures. After the war, it became something of a boomtown, with people from New England as well as new European immigrants flooding into the area to seek land and economic opportunity.[8] In this period, Albany had an international flavor, was filled with the sounds and sights of buildings being erected, and by the standards of the times, was liberal toward its blacks. Alice Morse Earle reflects some of this smugness a century later when she writes of Pinkster, "Nowhere was it a more glorious festival than at Albany, among the sheltered, the cherished slave population in that town and its vicinity."[9]

In Albany, the festival was held on Pinkster Hill, later the site of the state capitol building. On the grass there, blacks set up an arbor for King Charley, whom they chose to reign over the proceedings. Charley, a native Angolan, was said to be of royal birth

Modern day dancers reenact Pinkster festivities at Philipsburg Manor. Courtesy Philipsburg Manor Upper Mills in Sleepy Hollow, New York, a property of Historic Hudson Valley.

Costumed musicians play their instruments through town streets as they march to the Pinkster festival site at Philipsburg Manor. Courtesy Philipsburg Manor Upper Mills in Sleepy Hollow, New York, a property of Historic Hudson Valley.

("for a scepter he was born, /Tho' from his father's kingdom torn, /And doom'd to be a slave"[10]) and of imposing physical stature, standing over six feet tall and demonstrating vitality and agility despite being more than seventy years of age. He was dressed as befitted his status in a richly decorated British brigadier's coat with buckskin breeches.[11] The "Pinkster Ode," published in 1803, describes him as a figure of leadership, honor, and authority:

> You'll know him by his princely air,
>   And his politeness to the fair;
>   And when you know him, then you'll see
>   A slave whose soul was always free.
>   Look till the visual nerves do pain,
>   You'll "never see his like again."[12]

This is part of the appealing picture "Pinkster Ode" gives of the celebration, in contrast to other less appreciative descriptions.

Brush arbors, small booths made of interwoven branches, housed food and liquor vendors and were arranged in an amphitheatre facing the royal arbor. On the second day of the Albany festival, King Charley paraded through the streets on a cream-colored horse, followed by a large procession.[13] At the festival site, he demanded payment of one shilling each from blacks putting up tents and two shillings from whites. Those who failed to comply saw their tents instantly demolished.[14] During the festival, he served variously as master drummer setting the dance rhythms and as lead dancer. At the end of the festival, he descended from the hill in another procession, this time calling at local residences "demand-

Costumed musicians reconstruct Pinkster music at Philipsburg Manor. Courtesy Philipsburg Manor Upper Mills in Sleepy Hollow, New York, a property of Historic Hudson Valley.

ing tribute," which seems to have been paid by both cheerful and hostile householders.[15] The levying of tribute, the power to demolish whites' tents, and the bold parade through the streets all underline the real, if temporary, power possessed by the chosen Pinkster king.

Although Pinkster in its later years also featured sideshows with rope dancers, circus riding, and wild animals,[16] the real attraction was the dancing, and the audiences were large. One contemporary source says a "motley group of thousands" awaited the arrival of the king on the hill in Albany, and James Fenimore Cooper left a fictional description that counts thousands in attendance at the celebration on the commons in New York City in the 1750s.[17] "The Pinkster Ode" mentioned "Men of every grade," including native born Americans and people of a variety of nationalities.[18] The practice of importing slaves directly from Africa suggests strong West African influence on the dance. Cooper writes that American-born blacks regarded native Africans as "ambassadors from the land of their ancestors."[19]

There are only scanty descriptions of the music and dance, but despite the failure of white writers to convey them clearly, the accounts point to African characteristics. Percussive drumming, singing, and handclapping, for example, accompanied the performances:

The principal instrument selected to furnish this important portion of the ceremony was a symmetrically formed wooden article usually denominated an *eel-pot*, with a cleanly dressed sheep skin drawn tightly over its wide and open extremity.... Astride this rude utensil sat Jackey Quackenboss, then in his prime of life and well known energy, beating lustily with his naked hands upon its loud sounding head, successively repeating the ever wild, though euphonic cry of *Hi-a- bomba, bomba, bomba*, in full harmony with the thumping sounds. These vocal sounds were readily taken up and as oft repeated by the female portion of the spectators not otherwise engaged in the exercises of the scene, accompanied by the beating of time with their ungloved hands, in strict accordance with the eel-pot melody.[20]

At least some of the dance was circle dance, and people moved in and out of the circle as dictated by their "utmost energy" or "extreme fatigue."[21] One writer described "the most disgusting attitudes" and the "most lewd and indecent gesticulation, at the crisis of which the parties meet and embrace in a kind of amorous Indian hug, terminating in a sort of masquerade capture, which must cover even a harlot with blushes to describe."[22] Despite its negative tone, the account conveys pantomime and may also mean that the dance incorporated torso or hip movement. Furthermore, two drummers wore feathers and cow tails, and these speak of West African symbolism and masquerade.

In Cooper's narrative, a Negress "jabbered away explaining the meaning of different ceremonies to a cluster of very interested visitors,"[23] indicating that the events contained foreign or arcane cultural content that locals or Europeans could not be expected to understand without help. Contemporary description also emphasizes the pleasure the experience gave to enslaved Africans: "The blacks were collected in thousands in those fields, beating banjoes, singing African songs, drinking and worst of all laughing in a way that seemed to set their very heart rattling within their ribs."[24]

We are not told that participants divided into cultural groups to celebrate, but we know such things happened elsewhere in the North in the same period. John Fanning Watson, who wrote in the early nineteenth century, described a still-remembered Philadelphia practice of allowing the last days of local fairs for blacks to create their own celebrations. As many as a thousand people would be present, "divided into numerous little squads, dancing and singing, 'each in their own tongue,' after the customs of their several nations in Africa."[25]

The descriptions of Pinkster give us a rare glimpse of a celebration created largely by and for slaves and free blacks and tell us something about both blacks and whites of the period in the North. Whites, although permissive or fearful enough to grant liberties to their slaves and desirous of attending their performances, also found some of the content offensive. The dance, in particular, aroused both love and hate—people wanted to see it, but its West African body movement was unacceptable to European morality. Whites probably found the authority of an African king endurable only for a brief period of time. Moreover, as abolitionism gained ground and slavery was thrown into moral question, northerners became more and more defensive about their "servants." Racist views came more to the fore, and some of the liberties of the black population were canceled.

When New York's gradual manumission began to take effect, slave owners faced the loss of both usual comforts and personal investments. Some sold their slaves in the South before they could claim freedom.[26] Growing resentment of blacks and the push for emancipation manifested itself in a variety of ways across the North. Black parishioners were expelled from churches, abolitionist presses were destroyed, and showers of racist literature and prints were produced. Still, blacks continued to become free citizens of the North, to compete for jobs, and to demand equal rights. The liberties granted to blacks by a paternalist society whose "generosity" was based on concepts of superiority and control of its slaves were in many cases gradually withdrawn. Pinkster dancing and entertainments were banned by the Albany Common Council in 1811.[27]

Costumed actors at Philipsburg Manor reconstruct dance as it might have been at the Pinkster festival. Courtesy Philipsburg Manor Upper Mills in Sleepy Hollow, New York, a property of Historic Hudson Valley.

JOHN CANOE

John Canoe, John Kooner, or John Kuner was a dance-masquerade custom practiced by blacks in North Carolina and some parts of Virginia at Christmas time during the eighteenth and nineteenth centuries. The custom had roots in Africa, by way of the Caribbean, and its performance characteristics are in many ways similar to those of other early African American celebrations.

In Hillsboro, Edenton, Wilmington, and other places in North Carolina, and on plantations such as Somerset, slaves celebrated Christmas by dressing in costumes of rags, feathers, and animal skins. To the accompaniment of drumming and chanting, they danced as a group to the master's house. There, they boldly demanded a contribution of money

Jonkonnu celebration in Belize, ca. 1910. Some of the participants are dressed as brides, while others wear long streamers of cloth similar to those of the Ragman in other Jonkonnu traditions. All wear the wire mesh "flour sifter" masks common to the period, and we can see knee rattles on most of the performers. Courtesy Midwest Jesuit Archives.

from the master and from other white residents of the plantation.[28] In one account in December, 1823, a white overseer said that on Christmas Eve, "the slaves were preparing to go in a serenade with the exhibition of John Canno a sport common in this part of the state with Slaves on Holy-Days."[29] Harriet Jacobs, a former slave who had escaped to the North in 1842, remembered of the slave holiday that, "Every child rises early on Christmas morning to see the Johnkankus ... companies of a hundred each, turn out early in the morning and are allowed to go around until twelve o'clock."[30]

The custom continued long after slavery ended. In 1926, Dougald Mac Millan, after consulting the memories of friends, wrote that in Wilmington the Kuners had once paraded around town in a group, drawing both children and adults out of their houses. The Kuners sang a song that went "Hah! Low! Here we go!/ Hah! Low! Here we go! /Hah! Low! Here we go! / Kuners come from Denby!" and "this chant, shouted in regular cadence, could be heard for blocks; and the accompaniment of the rattle of bones, the blowing of the cows' horns, and the tinkle of the triangles added the air of gruesome mirth...."[31] The participating blacks were dressed in "tatters," especially "strips of cloth of gay colors sewn to their usual garments," topped with grotesque masks. The masqueraders were all men, but some were dressed as women. After singing, the men danced "chicken in the bread tray" or "cutting the pigeon wing." Then their leader collected money from spectators, and the group moved on to the next house or street.[32] Numerous other accounts, both before and after the Civil War, echo these characteristics, including the holiday setting, the all-male procession, masking (including dressing as women), dance, percussive music, and collection of money.[33]

The singing was based on African American verse structure. Some of the stanzas asked for a donation:

> On poor Koners
> For me, for me my Lady
> Give the poor Koners one more cent
> For me, for me my Lady.

Or the song might simply assert the slaves' right to a gift on Christmas:

> Christmas comes but once a year
> Ho rang du rango
> Everyone should have a share
> Ho rang du rango.[34]

Other songs were satiric, especially when the requested contribution was refused:

> Poor Massa so de say
> Down in the heel
> So de say
> God Almighty bress you
> So de say.[35]

Another version that commented on stinginess was:

> Run Jinnie run!
> I'm gwine away
> Gwine away to come no mo.'
> Dis am de po' house.[36]

Some of the lines exhibit classic African American improvisational content with call and response structure—a pattern of refrains repeated by the "basers" while the lead singer composed loosely narrative or comedic lines, sometimes with the use of words we can no longer interpret (perhaps these are words we no longer understand the meaning of, or words from an African language) to fill out the metrical structure of a line. The rhythm for the song and the dance was created on a gumba box or gombey drum, which was probably brought to this country around 1770 via Afro-Caribbean traditions.[37]

In the late nineteenth century, Winslow Homer visited the South and painted *Dressing for the Carnival* (1877), which shows a family preparing for a John Canoe procession. The central figure, in bright colors, contrasts with the two female figures in dull colors working on his costume. His patchwork may be a later development from the Afro-Caribbean Jonkonnu figure Pitchy-Patchy, discussed below.

Like other black holiday traditions, John Canoe was a time for social inversions, when slaves could cast aside the subservience otherwise forced upon them and with some audacity go to white homes and demand rewards. Contemporary historian Simon Spaulding noted that it "provided a sort of safety valve for a system that no one would deny created some terrible, intolerable pressures on the people who were part of the system."[38]

The John Canoe tradition probably came with slaves to mainland North America from the Caribbean, where large numbers of black captives were taken for a time of "seasoning" before being sold northward. In Jamaica, where the custom has been in continuous practice for three centuries, its name is Jonkonnu, and observers described it very early. Edward Long's account, published in 1774, emphasizes the animal disguise of the all-male dancers:

> In the towns, during the Christmas holidays, they have several tall or robust fellows, dressed up in grotesque habits, and a pair of ox horns on their heads, sprouting from the top of a horrid sort of visor, or mask, which about the mouth is rendered very terrific with large boar tusks.[39]

This passage is very similar to Dr. Edward Warren's description of slaves on Somerset Plantation in North Carolina. He said that in the custom of "John Kooner," the slaves went in a procession to the master's house, with the lead dancer wearing a mask of "two great ox horns, attached to the skin of a raccoon." In the Cape Fear area, Rebecca Cameron said the "John Coonahs" wore "the most fantastic garb, representing birds and beasts and men."[40] Another, earlier description of a Jamaican event (1688) by Hans Sloane may also refer to Jonkonnu. Sloane saw dancers with rattles on their legs and waists and "Cowtails to their Rumps," who "add such other things to their bodies in several places, as gives them a very extraordinary appearance."[41]

The name John Canoe or Jonkonnu originates either on the Caribbean islands from which the festival probably came to the mainland colonies, or from West Africa. It may be the name of a real person called John Conny or King Conny, a powerful tribal leader on the Guinea Coast who participated in the slave trade in the early 1700s. If so, this may explain one of the Jonkonnu disguises from two centuries ago, a figure with a multi-level houseboat structure on his head. Within the boat were tiny figures, including soldiers, sailors, and slaves. The boat might have represented the slave ships that carried off black captives, and the dance might initially have re-enacted slave-taking or propitiated spirits who could protect against it, or satirized the white enslavers.

Throughout the Caribbean, in Jamaica, the Bahamas, Virgin Islands, Belize, Bermuda, St. Kitts-Nevis, the Dominican Republic, and other island areas, the festival usually occurred on the scanty holidays permitted slaves at the turn of the year—Christmas Day, Boxing Day (December 26), or New Year's Day. Maskers were usually male, although sometimes the men were followed or accompanied by Set Girls, groups of women who danced in the parade while attempting to out-dress and out-perform rival bands.

There are other possible sources for the name Jonkonnu: it might derive from *gens inconnus*, French for "unknown people," meaning the people behind the masks. Then there is *jeunes canneurs*, a French name for young cutters of cane on sugar plantations, and the Ewe term *dzonko nu* meaning "sorcerer man." There is also the Bambara word *kono* for masquerade, and even the phrase "junk anew" to signify the found materials from which costumes have traditionally been made.[42] Some writers also point to the German word *könig* meaning "king" and recalling the Prussian participation in the slave trade.[43] Any of these are potential sources for the name Jonkonnu.

In the Caribbean, the characters that were portrayed in the festivities appear to descend from both West African masquerades and British mumming or masquerading traditions,

This candlelight procession of Jonkonnu figures took place as part of the 2005 Christmas celebration created by Tryon Palace in New Bern, North Carolina. Courtesy Tryon Palace Historic Sites & Gardens.

which came together on the islands. The mixture is now so ancient that the origins of the individual characters are a matter of mystery. In Jamaica, stock characters include:

- Cow Head and Horse Head, probably from West Africa. The costumes include real cow's horns and a real mule skull in combination with clothing and fabric covering the dancer's entire body. The roles may have come from Igbo, Papaw, or other West African traditions.
- Belly Woman, whose large stomach is very reminiscent of the Gelede masquerade among the Yoruba. Belly Woman wears a mask and is portrayed by a man, just as she is in Nigeria. Traditionally, among the Yoruba, the pregnant figure dances in a ceremony about fertility and dresses in cloths borrowed from the women of the village. Belly Woman's light skin and staring eyes also recall Gelede masks.
- Pitchy-Patchy, a figure whose head-to-toe costume is made up of strips of cloth that fly into the air as he dances.[44] He may derive from a British ragman figure, or the British Jack-in-the-Green, who was encased in leaves and vegetation. On the other hand, Pitchy-Patchy may descend from the Yoruba Egungun ceremony, a performance of awesome spiritual power evoking ancestors and probing the mysteries of death itself. The Egungun figure may also appear covered with bright strips of cloth, narrow or wide, and may in early times have had vegetation instead of cloth as a costume.[45]
- House Head, the houseboat character described above.
- Actor-Boy, an elegantly dressed masker who quoted Shakespeare monologues.
- A mélange of many other roles, from Wild Indian, Devil, Policeman, and Bride to Frosty the Snowman and Santa Claus. This flexibility to incorporate new characters and social roles itself reflects African masquerade traditions.
- Parades of women, the Set Girls, who competed with each other for the best costumes and performances. In the first half of the nineteenth century, Set Girl groups could include a Queen as well as a King.

Five Jonkonnu musicians and dancers celebrate on the grounds of Tryon Palace in New Bern, North Carolina. The drummers hold handmade drums similar to those used in the early nineteenth century. Courtesy Tryon Palace Historic Sites & Gardens.

• Stilt dancers, described as early as 1791 by William Young, figures that were and are found in many West African cultures and also in Europe.[46]

The characters often carry special objects—the Devil's trident, the policeman's baton, a wooden sword, a shield, a cane, or other item. In many parts of the Caribbean, wire mesh masks imported from Germany or made from flour-sifter parts came into use around 1900. All the costumes and dance are marked by improvisation on an established theme. Music comes not only from the gombey drum, but also from other drums, the fife, tambourine, triangle, and other instruments,[47] similar to the variety seen in North Carolina. In the Bahamas, contemporary instruments also include drums, tom-toms (a manufactured snare drum with one head removed), cowbells, and bicycle and foghorns.[48]

Often, dancers covered themselves entirely to assure anonymity during various gestures of audacity, demand, or protest. Cow Head and Horse Head, for example, may leave their dance groups to engage in aggressive behavior, such as chasing members of the audience.[49] But historically, dancers went much further, as Robert Dirks explains:

Slaves of all sorts—domestics, craftsmen, and field hands—enjoyed incredible license. Indeed, their behavior constituted such an antithesis to ordinary life that the slaves' Christmas stands as more than a historical curiosity. The event could be called a rite of reversal, a term anthropologists use to describe a ritual event in which everyday patterns are turned topsy-turvy.[50]

Caribbean dancers have a long history of asking for donations, and of singing derogatory songs about those who deny them. In Jamaica, blacks also ignored the rules against night

In this artwork by Isaac Mendes Belisario, we see the Set Girls who followed the early Jonkonnu figure in his parade through the streets of Jamaican towns. The women dance dressed in fine gowns, to music provided by drummers. Jonkonnu images appeared in Belisario's *Sketches of Character of the Negro Population on the Island of Jamaica* in 1837.

assemblies to conduct rites over the graves of their dead. On many plantations, slaves invaded the manor house and enjoyed the planter's food and drink. They played music and danced in the master's home, "joining in satirical songs aimed at their hosts or boldly offering free advice concerning plantation affairs."[51] When evening came, the reversal was over, and slaves returned to their quarters.

Whites feared the outbreaks of misrule and complained about the loud music and the liberties slaves took, which even in their most innocent form left the affluent without servants for a day in the middle of a holiday season. Few tried to suppress the celebration, though, for fear of reprisal. Samuel Martin of Antigua, after forbidding his slaves' Christmas holiday, was chopped to death by them in 1701. As Dirks notes, "whites looked forward to Christmas with a good deal of dread and apprehension—and with good reason."[52] Slaves at Christmas had not only come through a long year of grueling work, but also had endured horrors of starvation resulting from the limited provisions available to them in late autumn. The starvation time was scarcely over when the Christmas season began, and memories of severe malnutrition with pellagra, beriberi, and bloody flux were still vivid. It's little wonder the workers demanded liberties.

In the Bahamas, rural traditions of masking and dancing at holiday time seemed to differ from urban customs. Louis Diston Powles, who observed rural blacks around 1886, said that blacks divided themselves into tribal groups for the holidays. In August, the Yorubas, Egbas, Ebos, and Congos elected a queen to rule them on certain matters. At Christmas, he wrote, "They march about with lanterns and bands of music." Many of the groups he saw did not parade in Nassau, suggesting that there was a distinctive rural Bahamian tradition.[53] DeCosmo

These two Jonkonnu musicians wear Ragman-style costumes with headdresses made from animal skins and horns. Courtesy Tryon Palace Historic Sites & Gardens.

adds, "In the descriptions of Junkanoo in the 1860s and 70s, observers wrote that Junkanoo-ers were divided into groups characterized by African ethnicity."[54]

Junkanoo performers masked to help ensure safe political protest in Nassau in the early twentieth century.[55] An elderly man interviewed by Bettelheim in 1976 had been a Junkanooer since 1910. He said, "In those days coming out meant ... nobody knows you

Winslow Homer visited Virginia in 1876, and it is likely that he saw his subjects for this 1877 painting during his trip, as they prepared for a Jonkonnu celebration. If so, the image shows us how costuming had changed during the nineteenth century. Instead of masks of animal skins and horns, worn with ragged clothing, we see a multi-colored fabric patchwork shirt and trousers, worn with a hat. *Dressing for the Carnival,* Oil on canvas. Reproduced by permission of the Metropolitan Museum of Art, New York, NY.

and that was the beauty of it."[56] By the 1930s, though, the festivities were drawing tourists. One *New York Times* article about Bermuda, for example, said, "Groups of Negroes, garishly dressed in multi-colored trousers and jackets and wearing peacock-feather headdresses, twist and twirl their way through the streets of Hamilton and vicinity all day long to the throb of drums and the shrilling of a fife or tin whistle."[57]

Today, many of the troupes, in a new climate of governmental support and public appreciation of their art, no longer need to hide their faces. John Canoe is becoming more and more a major arts event that draws audiences from across the hemisphere and beyond. Since the 1950s, crews have competed for publicly offered prizes, and their art has been a matter of national pride in Caribbean countries.

John Canoe dance exhibits basic Africanist characteristics—polyrhythms, body parts moving to separate rhythms, and orientation to the earth:

Jonkonnu dancing involves the knees, pelvis, and shoulders moving separately, even as they move in unison. Furthermore, distinct aspects of each motion are accentuated. This genre of movement—distinct body parts moving simultaneously, or multi-metric movement—is basic to African and Afro-Caribbean dance. In many respects, Jonkonnu dancing is a version of African dance. The body parts act as separate and distinct units capable of moving independently of one another.... Observers often comment on the "get down" quality of Jonkonnu dancing. Jonkonnu dancers are not afraid to touch the earth. Many steps are executed in a low, deep knee bend position, similar to steps in African dance.[58]

In this ad for an Alcoa cruise, we see the classic Jonkonnu houseboat figure, surrounded by Wild Indian, Devil, and Horse Head, with musicians in the background. From *Holiday* magazine, ca. 1950s.

The main or central part of Jonkonnu dance in Jamaica is a Break Out, when the procession pauses for individual dancers to do solo performances. In Belize and Guatemala, there is solo dancing in a slightly different context. Characters are not differentiated by costume, but there is a king, who signals others when to do individual dances.[59]

The Afro-Caribbean and North Carolina celebrations both arose from West African sources. In North Carolina, though, the African American population gradually abandoned the John Koner or Kooner tradition after Emancipation. To them, it was associated with slavery and oppression. This negative connotation can be seen in the slang of the period, in which the word "Koner" came to mean a clown or foolish person. Still later, at the end of the nineteenth century, the masquerade crossed racial boundaries and was taken up by groups of white teenage boys. For example, Henry Bacon McKoy wrote of his boyhood:

> The boys of my neighborhood around the turn of the century engaged in "Coonering" no other time except between Christmas Day and the New Year. A group of five to ten boys would don whatever costume or garment he was able to get. There were sashes and shawls, overcoats and long pants. There were red bandannas, shirts, and dresses. Everything had to be old and ill fitting. And then there was always the mask or "Coner" face.[60]

McCoy did not even know he and his friends had been enacting the remnants of an African American masquerade tradition.

The John Canoe custom, in its many variations, illustrates the strength of African dance and ritual traditions. Today, historic sites in North Carolina, such as Tryon Palace at New Bern and Somerset Plantation in Creswell, are re-enacting the old John Koner performance as a way of understanding and appreciating the past.

NEGRO ELECTION DAY

For about a century beginning around 1750, blacks in several New England colonies/states were able to elect their own leaders. Mostly, these leaders were called governors, but in crown colonies, they were called kings. In Connecticut, the practice began with the election of London, a slave of Thomas Seymour, in 1755. Perhaps slaves, who accompanied their owners to Hartford for the election of the colony's governor, decided to choose their own leader while there and thus began a longstanding custom.[61] On Election Day, as Aimes notes, the black community "took a holiday and gathered in the towns to vote."[62] The annual event represented both an important political activity and a time for enjoying African American cultural arts, especially dance.

Black governors had limited power, but their office gave them status and power to mediate between white authorities and the local black populace. In practice, the governor could uphold the law and mete out punishments to black offenders, allowing white authorities to avoid direct intervention into blacks' affairs. Some of the governors had assistants and sheriffs to enforce their judgments.[63] In effect, Negro Election Day created a shadow government composed of African Americans. The custom, moreover, may have been a continuation of an established tradition on the Gold Coast in West Africa, where leaders were selected through election.[64]

The office was actually local rather than statewide, and blacks were elected in a variety of towns in Connecticut[65], Rhode Island, Massachusetts, and New Hampshire.[66] The elections were held at different times from state to state, but usually in May or June.[67] Voters, many of whom were not literate, cast their ballot by voice or simply stood in line behind

"First Annual Ball of the Skidmore Guard, A Colored Military Organization, at the Seventh Avenue Germania Assembly Rooms." In this 1872 engraving, we see a formal African American ball in a large assembly room. Participants appear to be dancing European-style couple dances. Courtesy Library of Congress.

a candidate. Winners were usually respected figures within the African American community, and sometimes were the servants or slaves of prominent whites.[68] In addition, the black governor often was African born, was physically impressive, and/or was a powerful speaker. Webster Brooks writes:

> The Black Governors were the embodiment and expression of Black pride.... Many of the early 18th Century Black Governors like "Quaw" of Hartford (served in 1760) and "London" of Wethersfield (served in 1755) were born in Africa. King Nero of Portsmouth, New Hampshire, was the son of an African tribal chief as were several black governors in Connecticut. Some Black Governors were educated, others were illiterate; some were businessmen, others were overseers of large farms owned by whites; some fought in the Revolutionary War in Connecticut's 4th Regiment, and still others were elected because they were the strongest and most physically imposing figures among their peers.[69]

Black governors tackled major issues. In Rhode Island, for example, they met and wrote a petition to the state legislature demanding an end to slavery. Thus, through their elective franchise, African Americans made their voices heard.

Negro Election Day usually ended with an inaugural parade through which African Americans publicly called attention to their right to elect a governor. This was followed by a dinner and dance. Stuart writes of the newly elected governor:

A troop of blacks, sometimes an hundred in number, marching sometimes two and two on foot, sometimes mounted in true military style and dress on horseback, escorted him through the streets. After marching to their content, they would retire to some large room which they would engage for the purpose, for refreshments and deliberation. This was all done with the greatest regard for ceremony.[70]

The ceremony was an important element, harking back to Africa, and the festivities at the post-election party included dinner and dancing until dawn or later. One writer described the event as a family occasion:

Families went entire, a babe in arms being no drawback, as the tavern-keeper set apart a room and provided a caretaker for them. Sometimes more than a dozen little woolly-heads would be under surveillance, while the light-hearted mothers shuffled and tripped to the sound of the fiddle … they danced and feasted … spinning out the night and often far into the next day.[71]

Information about the celebrations is sketchy, but we know that dance was a central event, and we can make informed guesses about it. The party likely began with European dances, often favored by middle class blacks, followed by African-based forms such as jigs and circle dances. This format was common at black dances both North and South. Like other African American festivals and holidays, Negro Election Day was a time for dance.

GENERAL TRAINING DAY

General Training Day, a military holiday across New England[72] in the seventeenth, eighteenth, and early nineteenth century, arose out of the settlers' need to be ready for Indian attack. Eventually, the day became a sort of family outing day that had less and less to do with military service. It also became a black holiday in which blacks socialized and danced.

The history of the day lay in the years of Indian warfare. Telfer Mook comments, "After 1675, especially, frequent Indian wars made it necessary that the people should have some knowledge of military procedure and know what to do when attacked."[73] New England towns set aside land for the drilling of the militia. The general court of Massachusetts, for example, beginning in 1631 required every township in the colony to allocate space for a weekly militia drill.[74] Later, many such spaces became town commons where public buildings such as schools and courthouses were erected. With few exceptions, all adult males, from teenagers to the elderly, were required to serve in the militia and, moreover, were required to own and possess arms in serviceable condition. The training day often provided for inspection of these weapons to make sure they would fire and that men kept cartridge boxes with adequate ammunition.[75] The sacredness of the militia concept, as it simultaneously protected the nation from a standing army and provided for its defense, became rooted in the Constitution.

When the settlements became safer, though, the drilling became less necessary. Since they took men away from the fields and placed a burden on town treasuries (the town often paid for the militia's lunch when it drilled), the number of training days were steadily reduced. Mook notes, "About 1750, each person liable to duty attended annually two 'little training days' and one 'great training day.'"[76]

In time, General Training Day became a local holiday in small towns across New England. It often took place in early summer, like Pinkster, during the first break in farm work after planting.[77] Mook writes, "Everybody went to muster: the soldier to perform his duty and drink eggnog, his wife to admire him, and his children to eat gingerbread and

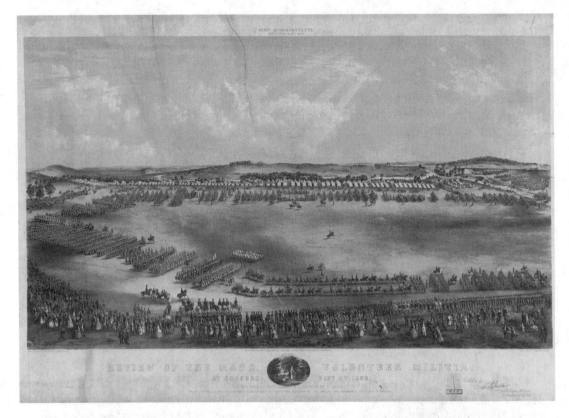

"Review of the Mass. volunteer militia, at Concord, Sept. 9, 1859, by his Excellency (Commander in Chief) Nathaniel P. Banks." The engraving shows the vast spaces used in militia training, as well as the many onlookers on the edge of the scene. Courtesy Library of Congress.

sweets."[78] Training gradually grew into a carnival, with peddlers and sideshows thronging the edges of the commons, flags flying and drums rolling, men drinking too much, and women and children taking in the sights of the town. Remembering his childhood in New York, Franklin Butler Van Valkenburgh wrote about Training Day in New York between 1835 and 1847:

> On the morning of this great day we awakened to find the south end of the square pretty fully occupied with Booths and Tents and farmers wagons, which were in their turn occupied by the itinerant vendors of such commodities as the free born American citizen of that day and generation was accustomed to indulge in on festive occasions of the general training day order. Chief among these were the tents, made by stretching a sheet or two over the end of a wagon, in which Sweet Cider and Trainer's Ginger Bread were dispensed to the hungry and thirsty warriors and their friends and relatives.[79]

Training Day was a major social event across the North, a time when ordinary people could cast aside their dull daily routine and have a good time.

In the late eighteenth and early nineteenth centuries, federal law forbade blacks to serve in the militia, except as musicians and non-combatants. Blacks had served in the Revolutionary War in the troops of Rhode Island, New Jersey, New York, Maryland, and other states, in some cases receiving their freedom and cash payments for their service. Shortly after the war, though, in 1791, Congress passed a law barring blacks and Native Americans from the peacetime militia.[80]

Here a single volunteer militiaman in a re-enactment fires his weapon in a cloud of smoke. Courtesy Colonial Williamsburg Foundation.

"First Division of Massachusetts Volunteer Militia, Passing in Review, at North Abington," from *Gleason's Pictorial*, September 10, 1853.

Despite this law, blacks served in local militias and participated in training days, sometimes on separate training days designated especially for them.[81] Furthermore, blacks, like other residents of New England towns, often received General Training Day as a holiday from work. Shane White notes:

> The other important holiday for many northern slaves was variously called Negro Training or General Training and usually occurred in June. Blacks would come from miles around, ostensibly to watch the black militia drill. In New England, this occasion was sometimes held on a separate day, as in Windsor, Connecticut, where, according to the town's historian, Henry Stiles, Negro trainings were common.[82]

White adds, "General Training was particularly important in New Jersey. It was a 'great day' for the 'Bedminster colored people' that was 'always celebrated by Dick and Nance,' slaves in the 1790s...."[83]

In his painting *Militia Training*, first exhibited in 1841, James Goodwyn Clonney (1812–1867) depicts a General Training Day in a small town. In the background, the troops are practicing, but the painter's focus is on the foreground, far from the military practice. Here, people engage in various leisure activities. Women chat and look onto the distant field. Vendors offer wares for sale, men get into a fistfight, and some people are clearly inebriated. In the center of the painting are two black dancers doing what seems to be a jig in fast time, perhaps in competition with each other. A fiddler supplies the music, and hand clapping provides more percussion. When Clonney's work was exhibited, one reviewer commented, "The Negroes are painted with great truth."[84]

This painting focuses on the holiday festivities surrounding militia training in the first half of the nineteenth century. The central figures are two black dancers and a white fiddler, while the troops are rendered in tiny size in the distance. Notice also the quintessentially American patchwork quilt being used as a canopy over the vendor's booth to the left, the American flag flying, and the black fiddler at rest in right center. *Militia Training,* **Oil on canvas, 1841, by James Goodwyn Clonney. Reproduced by permission of Pennsylvania Academy of Fine Arts.**

The painting gives us a glimpse of the characteristics of the black jig at mid century. One dancer crosses his right foot over his left in a fast, virtuoso move, while the other strikes his heel against the ground, perhaps as part of a heel-and-toe routine. Both are slightly bent at the waist, and the dancer to the right waves his hat in time with the rhythm. If the dancers had had a shingle or a wooden floor on which to perform, the beat they created with their feet would have provided audible percussion to augment the fiddle sound. Beating time with one's feet was often part of the jig, and agility and perfect timing were key elements of a good performance.

During this time period, dance competition was common, although we cannot know for sure if the two dancers in the painting were engaged in it. In a challenge dance, two people set against each other showed off their improvised routines, lightning moves, and precise meter. In formal competitions, dance judges watched the dancers and listened to the sounds made by their feet before awarding prizes. Black dancers were hungry to show their talent and win prizes, and new Irish immigrants, who brought the tradition of the Irish jig with them from their homeland, were eager to compete as well. People gathered to watch, and some public competitions drew crowds and were reported in newspapers.

The big competitions and the growth of the jig into something that later became tap dance would occur, though, more in the cities than the country. Northern blacks who obtained their freedom moved to urban areas in large numbers, helping to assure that that was where the next major development of black dance would take place. Negro training day was one of the northern festivities in which African Americans could socialize and show off their dance in such competitions.

THE CORN SHUCKING

The corn shucking was a harvest festival in the South, both during the slavery period and long afterward, well into the twentieth century. Blacks from a neighborhood gathered together on a plantation to shuck, or husk, its entire harvest of corn. In return, the master or owner of the plantation provided a generous supper for the workers, and the evening typically ended with a dance lasting far into the night. The celebration developed its own customs and order of events, and these conventions were similar to those of other early black celebrations, with a central focus on dance, unusual power or autonomy granted to blacks, election of black leaders or generals, and expression of African-based musical traditions. In addition, there were white observers whose accounts were permeated with nostalgia.

The corn shucking, incorporating excitement, competition, singing, feasting, and dancing, was an important part of the harvest in the South, one much enjoyed and often written about. Many hosts invited white guests to view the performance, usually serving them a separate supper after the entertainment. The narrator in Fred Mather's fictional account, who appeared in Chapter 6 in *The Louisiana Lowlands*, was a guest of a southern plantation owner[85], and John Cabell Chenault's *Old Cane Springs: A Story of the War Between the States in Madison County, Kentucky*, notes that after the shucking, "A splendid supper was prepared for the white guests."[86] Family members, too, looked forward to the husking and watched it with pleasure. Marion Harland recalls that she and her sister as children sat "in our outlook at the window of our room that gave directly upon the lively scene. We had sat in the same place for seven successive corn-shuckings...."[87] The corn shucking was a festive event not to be missed, and autobiographical or fictionalized accounts recalled it with a tone of both delight and loss.

Narratives reprinted by Roger Abrahams show that guests, sitting to one side in the shadows, sometimes wagered on the outcome or were the subject of public singing by the huskers. James Battle Avirett writes:

> While the corn shucking is going on and these men are warming up fully to their work, let us look into those wagons over there. The young people from a number of the adjoining estates have come over to enjoy the fun ... they begin to wager, here a pair of kid gloves, there a handsome driving whip or a silver dog whistle, or this and that and the other, on the corn shucking.[88]

But a front seat at the scene could be a double-edged sword. Some of these young plantation elite became the subject of the songs being improvised on the spot by the lead black singer on the corn-shucking team.

> Dere's Mr. Travers lub Miss Jinny;
> He thinks she is us good us any.
> He comes from church wid her er
> Un don't go back ter town till Monday.
> Hooray, hooray, ho!

Thus, for the evening, slaves became celebrities of a sort, received special courtesies from white proprietors of estates, and lampooned them in their songs.

For the huskers, the corn shucking evening began with the walk to the plantation host-ing the event. Often, the slaves came from their home plantations in groups, singing as they walked. At the end of the evening, they returned in the same fashion, singing songs whose beauty was long remembered by witnesses. Letitia Burwell, in her *A Girl's Life in Virginia Before the War*, wrote:

> Although the most perfect timists, their music, with its wild, melancholy cadence, half savage, half civilized, cannot be imitated or described. Many a midnight were we wakened by their wild choruses, singing as they returned from a frolic or "corn-shucking," sounding at first like some hideous, savage yell, but dying away on the air, echoing a cadence melancholy and indescrib-able....[89]

Great companies of blacks came to the husking as darkness fell. Mather wrote, "Parties streamed in with torch and song until there were at least 300 negroes, 100 women, and a lot of pickaninnies...."[90]

The darkness and firelight gave the event a strangeness and vividness that empha-sized the reversals it enfolded. Burwell comments, for example, that "the glare of the torches on the black faces, with the wild music and impromptu words, made a scene curi-ous even to us who were so accustomed to it."[91] Mather adds, "The fire-light, the pictur-esque costumes, which were heightened by that light, and the quaint songs and chorus in the rich voices, were beyond description."[92] The specialness of the scene set it apart from everyday reality, and signaled behaviors different from those of ordinary life.

As the workers arrived, the master who would be their host often personally welcomed them, and they responded as well-mannered equals. In Chenault's memoir, for example, the host says to the huskers, "Men you have done me the kindness to come here tonight to shuck my corn.... I thank each of you now for this volunteer service tonight, for I know that you are not here by order of your masters." The men reply, "No, suh; no suh. We come 'cause we wanted to he'p you all."[93] The dignity of this response suggested some of the role reversal that came into play. The event also displayed and idealized both sides of the white-black relationship, bringing them to the fore in a highly visible arena where both were intent upon showing themselves in the best possible light. The master appears gen-erous and respectful to the workers, and they in turn are creatively and physically in com-mand of much of the experience.

A mountain of corn in the husk typically awaited the workers, sometimes thirty feet high and more than a hundred yards long. Francis Fredric remembered one that was 180 yards long.[94] The corn was divided in half by various methods, the most common being the simple placing of a pole atop the pile at the center of its length, determined by eye or by use of a tape measure. The workers then commonly chose their captain or general them-selves. Burwell writes, "Selecting one of their number—usually the most original and amusing, and possessed of the loudest voice—they called him 'captain.'"[95] Harland calls him "the biggest man present and the best singer."[96] Abrahams quotes Mary Banks on the subject, who says "an important conference" was held by slaves on her father's plantation to choose the leaders of the shucking. "After some confabulation, one slave, Talbot, is cho-sen, 'whose duties it will be to make a speech and conduct the ceremonies generally, though leading the singing is considered the most important feature of the occasion.'"[97]

Next, the captains chose their teams from the dozens or hundreds of workers pres-ent. Barrow says, "Two 'gin'r'ls' are chosen from among the most famous corn-shuckers on the ground, and these proceed to divide the shuckers into two parties, late comers

An 1861 drawing shows black workers husking a pile of corn, atop of which sits a fiddler playing music for the event. From "American Home Scenes," in *Harper's Weekly*, April 13, 1861.

reporting alternately to one side or the other, so as to keep the forces equally divided."[98] The general was important in motivating his team and maintaining the rhythm of the work through the call and response songs he orchestrated. Barrow said, "The corn-song is almost always a song with a chorus, or, to use the language of corn-shuckers, the 'gin'r'ls give out,' and the shuckers 'drone.'"[99] That is, the leader follows the classic practice of singing improvised lines that carry the story of the song, while the other singers respond with repetitious lines that overlap with the leader's lines.

Corn songs might seem to have little serious content to the casual listener, like this one quoted by Mather:

> De cawn's in de shuck, but we gwine to get him out.
> O, roun' up, roun' up de cawn.

**This antebellum corn shucking was illustrated in David Barrow's "A Georgia Corn-Shucking,"
printed in *Century* magazine in October, 1882. The two generals sit and stand atop the pile of corn
in the husk, with the dividing stick visible between them. The huskers, including women, work
below them. The workers are singing the corn songs, and the air is full of flying cobs. To the left,
arms folded, is the plantation owner, who is neither husking nor singing.**

> An' de possum's in de gum tree, but we gwine to get him out,
> > O, roun' up, roun' up de cawn.
>
> W'en de cawn's in the tossel, and de punkin's in de bloom,
> > O, roun' up, roun' up de cawn.
> Den de darky take a res' an' he watch de harvest moon,
> > O, keep on a-roundin' up the cawn.

Furthermore, as Mather comments, these songs seem endless: "There were yards, rods,
and furlongs of this verse, and Jake seemed competent to spin it out forever."[100] The song,
though, actually reflected the black perspective on the event, in which the huskers were in
control, taking charge of a task, completing it successfully, and accepting a well-earned
reward. Other songs may have used animal characters as metaphors for the slave himself:

> Rabbit in the gyordin
> Rabbit hi oh.
> Dog can't ketch um.
> Rabbit hi oh.
>
> Gun can't shoot um.
> Rabbit hi oh.

Mon can't skin um.
Rabbit hi oh.

Cook can't cook um,
Rabbit hi oh.
Folks can't eat um.
Rabbit hi oh.[101]

Here the rabbit may represent the slave, whose uncanny power for survival cannot be defeated by the repressive regime of slavery. No matter what the injustice, the rabbit, like Brer Rabbit, is able to defeat the odds, and his story is sung in the presence of whites, who do not understand the metaphor, or realize the artistic undermining of white power.

Yet another type of song satirizes whites for their unfair, cruel, or foolish behavior. Sometimes the derision was even aimed at people present at the event. One song told of a minister who made his slaves work on Sunday; in response, the slaves exposed his behavior in their corn songs, which were publicly sung and had seemingly endless verses about his hypocrisy:

The parson says his prayers in church.
It rain, boys, it rain.
Then deliver a fine sermon.
It rain, boys, it rain.

He cut the matter short, my friends,
It rain, boys, it rain.
He say the blessed Lord send it.
It rain, boys, it rain.

Now's the time for planting bacco.
It rain, boys, it rain.
Come my negroes, get you home.
It rain, boys, it rain.
Jim, Jack, Joe, and Tom.
It rain, boys, it rain.
Go draw you plants and set them out.
It rain, boys, it rain.

Don't you stop a moment, boys.
It rain, boys, it rain.
'Twas on a blessed Sabbath Day.
It rain, boys, it rain.
Here's a pretty preacher for you.
It rain, boys, it rain.[102]

In this way, slaves countered the power of oppressor with their own power as composers, singers, and satirists. Amidst the horrors of slavery, black behavior and creative practices showed that slaves were not passive victims. Instead, they formed a dynamic, reciprocal relationship with whites, one in which they asserted their own views and needs.

The shucking itself was chaotic and went at lightning speed. The quick huskers used handmade hardwood pins that, when hooked over a finger and placed on the inside of the palm, efficiently ripped open the shucks. Workers tossed the shucks onto a pile, and the ears of corn into a pen or crib. Cobs and shucks filled the air until the job was done.

At the finish, one of the teams took the prize for being fastest. Some accounts say the prize was a suit of clothing for the winning captain. Next, blacks returned their host's respect by finding him and lifting him to their shoulders:

> The first thing in order is to express thanks for the entertainment, which is done by taking the host, putting him on the shoulders of two strong men, and then marching around, while all hands split their throats to a tune, the chorus of which is "Walk away, walk away!" This honor, though of questionable comfort, or rather most unquestionable discomfort, must be undergone, for a refusal is considered most churlish, and a retreat gives too much license to the guests.[103]

The carrying of the master is part of the liberties taken by the workers in a context where for a few hours they and the master maintain the appearance of interacting with each other as equals.

Many of these characteristics continued well into the twentieth century. Reporting on early twentieth century corn shuckings, Celia Benton quotes an informant named Mrs. Jones who says, "They would take our daddy and would tote him around by the feet and head, and sing the corn shucking songs."[104] Commenting on the period, Benton adds, "At corn shuckings in general, whites and blacks shared alike in the work, though this equality would not be carried over into the social sphere."[105]

Next came a feast prepared by the host's household. Often the providers were slave women, but sometimes the host's wife was personally involved.[106] Either way, women associated with the big house served food in huge abundance and of good quality. The dinners figure largely in remembrances of both blacks and whites. Furthermore, the whole experience repeated itself throughout late autumn. One ex-slave recounted, "we 'ud go to ten or twelve corn shuckins's in one year."[107]

Finally, there was the dance, the most intensely enjoyed part of the evening. The musicians were usually a fiddler and a straw-beater. The fiddler was an important figure at the dance, and he knew his tunes from memory. The straw-beater provided a second rhythm, this one percussive, by striking pieces of broom sedge on the fiddle at the same time the fiddler was playing:

> These straws are used after the manner of drumsticks, that portion of the fiddle-strings between the fiddler's bow and his left hand serving as a drum. One of the first sounds which you hear on approaching the dancing party is the *tum tee tum* of the straws, and after the dance begins, when the shuffling of the feet destroys the other sounds of the fiddle, this noise can still be heard.[108]

Among the songs were "Money Musk," "Arkansas Traveler," "Forky Deer," and others of the period.

By the mid to late nineteenth century, slaves were dancing not only African-based forms such as ring dances, the jig, buck dance, and the pigeon-wing at corn shuckings, but also European dances such as the Reel and the Cotillion. In many of the Africanist dances, the dancer beats out rhythms with his feet, and thus needs a platform, shingle, or even wagon bed to provide amplification for the percussion. In Mather's narrative, the Reels and Cotillions were danced on the "smooth, hard-beaten ground," but a platform "had been put up about 3 ft. high for the jig and the buck dancers."[109]

In the same depiction, the narrator was asked to be a judge of the jig dancing, which entailed competition. People from far and wide would come not only to compete for prizes but also to gain names for themselves as champion dancers. One participant in the Mather

A corn shucking in Granville County, North Carolina, in 1939. The event is smaller than those in pre-emancipation times, but the essentials are the same—a huge pile of corn in the husk, and African American huskers in charge of the work. Courtesy Library of Congress.

story said, "Dey's a buck dancah fum Vernon Parish come heah to-night to dance ouah Sam. Dey is a prize o' five dollahs…."

The narrator had to evaluate the dance by sound as well as sight. The advice to him by a fellow guest also contains some description of the dances:

> Your ear for rhythm and knowledge of the intricacy of the straight jig will make you a competent judge. Of course, the straight jig is the ideal dance, the neatest, cleanest expression of music by the human foot. It makes no claim to "poetry of motion," but it is a dance to be heard as well as seen. The buck dance is of the same order, but coarser, and the dancer moves all over the stage.[110]

Both the jig and the buck were solo dances, although a performer often danced opposite a competitor or another solo dancer. Both forms, with their emphasis on sound, on crisp and perfect timing, on individual virtuosity, and on carefully defined individual steps, strongly influenced the later development of tap. The loose, elastic stance of the black dancer, who was not in the perfectly erect posture of the Irish jig but rather bent slightly forward, would also come to dominate the style of tap.

Cotillions and Reels, European forms based on geometric configurations of dancers, were also danced at many corn shuckings and other festivities on plantations, although black music and movement vocabulary changed them significantly. African American fiddlers commonly called out directions for dancers who could not read and had not had dancing lessons. Barrow, for example, says:

> With the cotillion a new and very important office, that of "caller-out," has become a necessity. The "caller-out," though of less importance than the fiddler, is second to no other. He not only calls out the figures, but also explains them at length to the ignorant, sometimes accompanying them through the performance. He is never at a loss, "Gemmen to de right!" being a sufficient

Two huskers carry the master of the plantation on their shoulders. In some cases, the master was seated in a chair, and the men lifted the chair with him in it. From David Barrow's "A Georgia Corn-Husking," *Century* magazine, October, 1882.

After the corn shucking, the workers enjoyed various dances. In this picture, a man in the center dances solo, while the couple in right center dance together, albeit without touching. A man on the far right claps out a rhythm, while the fiddler plays in the far upper left.

    refuge in case of embarrassment, since this always calls forth a full display of the dancers' agility, and gives much time.[111]

Through this improvisational technique, black musicians helped develop the American practice of calling the Square Dance. The custom of calling cues for dancers continued with later black dances, including the Big Apple. Many twentieth century black songs extended the tradition by providing directions in their lyrics for dances such as Ballin' the Jack, Black Bottom, and others.

    The corn shucking was a formalized activity in which familiar ways of interacting were temporarily put aside. Host and huskers instead often treated each other with courtesy and generosity, behaving as equals for a single evening. The workers showcased their singing, husking, and dancing, while exercising political autonomy in choosing and following their own leaders. The host and hostess were gracious to their guests, and the carrying of the master at the end reaffirmed his traditional domination, albeit with the orchestration of the black workers. Conventions of the celebration temporarily idealized the relationships and division of labor inherent to slavery, but this ideal vision was all too brief. The kind host might soon be met in his role as a patroller, arresting and beating slaves who had recently been welcomed onto his plantation.

CONGO SQUARE

    Congo Square was part of an open field on the edge of the French Quarter in early New Orleans. Circuses set up there; cockfights and dogfights were held there; and Native

Americans used it for a ball game called raquette. The grounds were variously called Circus Public Square, *Place des Negres*, and Congo Plains. In part of the field, slaves gathered to dance. Over the years the city grew, and as Cable notes, Congo Square became part of the poorer section of town, contrasting with the fashionable area at the other end of Orleans Street:

> The Place Congo, at the opposite end of the street, was at the opposite end of everything. One was on the highest ground; the other on the lowest. The one was the rendezvous of the rich man, the master, the military officer—of all that went to make up the ruling class; the other of the butcher and baker, the raftsman, the sailor, the quadroon, the painted girl, and the Negro slave.[112]

The dancing began early in the nineteenth century and, though it significantly declined before the Civil War, continued sporadically until the 1880s.[113]

The background of the dance in Congo Square lies partly in the Haitian revolution of 1791–1803, which transformed the French Caribbean colony Saint Domingue into an independent nation run by former slaves. Previously a slave colony with a harshly oppressed black population, the island society had experienced what American slave owners lived in terror of—violence that reversed the class structure. During the fighting, many slave owners fled the country, taking their slaves with them. Large numbers of them went to New Orleans, for it was one of the nearest French cultures in which they could resume their lives as plantation owners, growing cotton or sugar. With the new immigrants came Afro-Caribbean culture, including dance as well as voodoo—a set of West African (Fon, Mahi, and Yoruba[114]) religious practices overlaid to some degree with European Catholic religion.

We will not discuss voodoo here, for its practices were secret, and precisely because of that secrecy, it is unlikely its rites were publicly conducted to any extent in Congo Square.

What *was* to be seen in Congo Square was African-based and Afro-Caribbean dance. Since the late seventeenth century, the area had been an informal marketplace, as well as a place for socializing and occasional dancing.[115] But Congo Square as the site for weekly dances was officially legislated in 1817 by the New Orleans City Council. By then, the U.S. had control of the city by means of the Louisiana Purchase, and the American fear of slave assemblies made itself felt. The new legislation limited gatherings of slaves, especially for dancing, and forced them into a public place, where they could be monitored. In Congo Square, blacks could dance on Sunday afternoon until sundown. Blacks dancing there at any other time could be harshly punished.

Once called Circus Square, as well as Place Publique, the space now took on the name of the people and the dance associated with it on Sundays: Congo Square or Congo Plain. As Johnson notes, "Those names gained in popularity, especially as the square's African dances, including one called the Congo, became occasions for outings by local residents as well as tourists, and by 1850 occasionally also began to appear in official records...."[116]

Thus Congo Square became so well known for African American dance that it drew spectators of all types and became a major tourist attraction. For the dancers, it provided a large, communal space in which to practice African cultural arts. At least one account indicates that blacks gathered there in huge numbers, as many as 500–600 people at once in the early 1800s.[117]

Christian Schultz, who observed dance in New Orleans in 1807, left an account of what he saw:

> In the afternoon, a walk in the rear of the town will still more astonish ... with the sight of twenty different dancing groups of the wretched Africans, collected together to perform their worship

This contemporary photo shows a portion of Congo Square as it looked before Hurricane Katrina. A sign in the background commemorates its history. Photographer Justin Marcinkus. Courtesy Justin Marcinkus.

after the manner of their country.... The principal dancers or leaders are dressed in a variety of wild and savage fashions, always ornamented with a number of tails of the smaller wild beasts, and those who appeared the most horrible always attracted the largest circle of company.[118]

These words indicate that the dancers performed Africanist masquerade dance, divided into tribal or cultural groups, and perpetuated ritual forms. This could suggest that a number of the dancers were native-born Africans who felt most comfortable associating with other members of their own cultural groups, and that the experience was religious. These descriptions are consistent with those of other dances in early black festivals such as Pinkster and Jonkonnu, where participants wore animal horns or masks. Furthermore, the instruments described by a variety of observers at Congo Square were typically African-derived—African drums, banza (a slave-made instrument that later developed into the banjo), quills, gourd rattle, triangle, and bones.[119]

Cable and Emery tell us that among the dances one could see in the square were the Calenda and the Chica, both brought by slaves from the West Indies. From period descriptions, we can add ring dances as well as solo footwork dances of great speed, such as this one described by Henry Didimus:

The feet scarce tread wider space than their own length; but rise and fall, turn in and out, touch first the heel and then the toe, rapidly and more rapidly, till they twinkle to the eye, which finds its sight too slow a follower of their movements.[120]

"The Love Song, Drawn from Life in Congo Square, New Orleans." Appeared in *Century* magazine in 1886. The two dancers convey profound grace and dignity.

The depiction is strongly reminiscent of later ones capturing the dance of William Henry Lane, a black dancer who performed both in the U.S. and abroad. The "Negro jig" involved extraordinary speed, precision, and improvisation, and was part of the long West African tradition of competition.

Another Congo Square dance was the Calenda, which may have first come from the Guinea coast to the West Indies. Emery remarks, "The Calenda was undoubtedly danced in Congo Square, since it was a favorite dance of all the West Indies."[121] Père Labat had described it in the early eighteenth century:

> The dancers are arranged in two lines, facing each other, the men on one side and the women on the other. Those who are tired of dancing form a circle with the spectators around the dancers and the drums. The ablest person sings a song which he composes on the spot.... The refrain of this song is sung by everyone and is accompanied by great handclapping. As for the dancers, they hold their arms a little like someone playing castagnettes. They jump, make swift turns, approach each other to a distance of two or three feet then draw back with the beat of the drum until the sound of the drums brings them together again to strike their thighs together, that is, the men's against the women's. To see them it would seem they were striking each other's bellies although it is only the thighs which receive the blows. At the proper time they withdraw with a pirouette, only to begin again the same movement with absolutely lascivious gestures; this, as many times as the drums give the signal, which is many times in a row.... It can readily be seen ... this dance is contrary to all modesty.[122]

The African characteristics are clear—improvisatory call and response singing, dance moves signaled by the drums, circle and line formations, the presence of the community to support and encourage the dancers, percussion provided both by the drums and by hand-clapping, and movement expressive of sexuality or fertility.

St.-Méry, however, described the dance seventy-five years later as not immodest at all, but rather as a lively performance in which a female dancer holds both ends of a hand-kerchief that she moves from side to side as she spins, while her male partner swirls and turns around her. The pair or a number of paired dancers move together inside a circle of other dancers who enter and leave the ring from time to time.[123] This version is strikingly different from Labat's version above, and the two may indicate distinct dances, albeit called by the same name.[124]

The described dance seems to incorporate elements of another Afro-Caribbean dance, the Chica, which also likely was danced in Congo Square. St.-Méry observed in it the West Indies. He emphasized that it was also a dance of male and female partners:

> For the woman, who holds the ends of a kerchief or the sides of her skirt, the art of this dance consists mainly in moving the lower parts of her loins while maintaining the upper part of her body practically immobile. Should one want to enliven the Chica, a man approaches the woman while she is dancing, and, throwing himself forward precipitously, he falls in with the rhythm, almost touching her, drawing back, lunging again, seeming to want to coax her to surrender to the passion which engulfs them.[125]

Dances like the one described above, which may have involved a courtship theme, may be the source of Kemble's drawing, "The Love Song," which illustrated another of Cable's articles about Congo Square.[126]

The descriptions of the dances, though, with their puzzling contradictions raise questions of how much the forms changed over time, how much European influence may have been involved, and whether elements of different forms may have merged into a single form in the West Indies and/or as African and Afro-Caribbean dances traveled to New Orleans and became African American. These topics need additional research, referencing black dance in the Caribbean, as well as dance elsewhere in Louisiana in the period.

Here, two dancers move toward the center of an open space in Congo Square, surrounded by an audience and community of onlookers. "The Bamboula," by E. W. Kemble, published in *Century* magazine in February, 1886.

In Congo Square, blacks could congregate together often and regularly. There they could dance Africanist forms that with the passage of time probably showed at least some European influence. Because of the numbers of people present, blacks were able in some cases to gather in tribal groups for dances from distinctive cultural heritages. Johnson says that native African forms survived in Congo Square a century longer than elsewhere in the U.S.[127] He is echoed by Dena Epstein, who said, "Only in Place Congo in New Orleans was the African tradition able to continue in the open."[128]

Like black festivals, Congo Square was crucially important because it gave people a dance space away from the capricious controls of individual masters, a space where African Americans had freedom to practice and keep alive their dances. That the site became a tourist attraction was also in some ways fortunate. Spectators wrote down their impressions, which today we can sift through, ignoring and reinterpreting the negative to attempt to piece together a picture of early black New Orleans dance we might otherwise not have had. Like the other special contexts of time and place described in this chapter, Congo Square provided a public demonstration of the survival of African dance as it transitioned into African American dance.

4

Solo Percussive Dance

Early observers of African American dance commented on a style that became known as the "Negro jig." It seemed to be a solo form, even when two dancers performed opposite each other, a competitive or display genre rooted in African tradition. A dancer or dancers showed off original or improvised steps surrounded by a circle of community members, some of whom provided music with a banjo, drum, makeshift instruments, and/or patting or clapping. When there was a shingle, wagon bed, or even specially built platform to allow the sound to resonate, dancing feet could provide their own percussion. In effect, the platform became the drum, and the feet the drumsticks. This kind of percussion became important when drums were banned in many sections of the South after the 1739 Stono River slave rebellion. Talking drums had been implicated in the planning of the rebellion, and when they were forbidden, black dancers found substitutes, among them foot percussion.

The dancer's torso, as we can see from period illustrations, was often bent forward, and the knees were raised high in kicks or powerful stamps. Scuffing and sliding moves were important, as was speed. Audience members looked to the dancer's feet for fancy steps, and affirmed his or her efforts with rhythmic patting or singing, along with shouted encouragement. Occasionally, the torso was held straight and still because a virtuoso dancer was carrying a container of water on his or her head as an additional challenge. In competitive situations, whites sometimes joined the circle to place bets on the dancers.

The basic form, which may have represented an amalgamation of steps from more than one cultural group, came from Africa. Later, the dance combined with European jigs and clogs to form or influence a number of American styles such as Juba, buck dancing, flatfooting, and Appalachian clogging. Theatrical buck dancing eventually, in the pressurized cauldron of the minstrel show and vaudeville stage where competition was intense, developed into tap dance, which itself gave birth to countless generalized and individualized forms including rhythm tap, the class act, legomania, acrobatics, and various eccentric steps. Tap is a truly American dance form deeply indebted to African dance and African American dancers, a style that is at once abstract, timeless, elegantly and brilliantly metrical, traditional, and yet powerfully molded by the unique personalities and artistic sensibilities of individual performers. In recent times, tap has found its leadership in the genius of Gregory Hines, Savion Glover, and others.

The Plantation Jig Draws White Imitators

Beginning in the 1830s, the minstrel show was the most popular form of entertainment in the United States, lasting for nearly a century, spawning racist stereotypes whose damage to race relations and harm to the African American community has been incalcu-

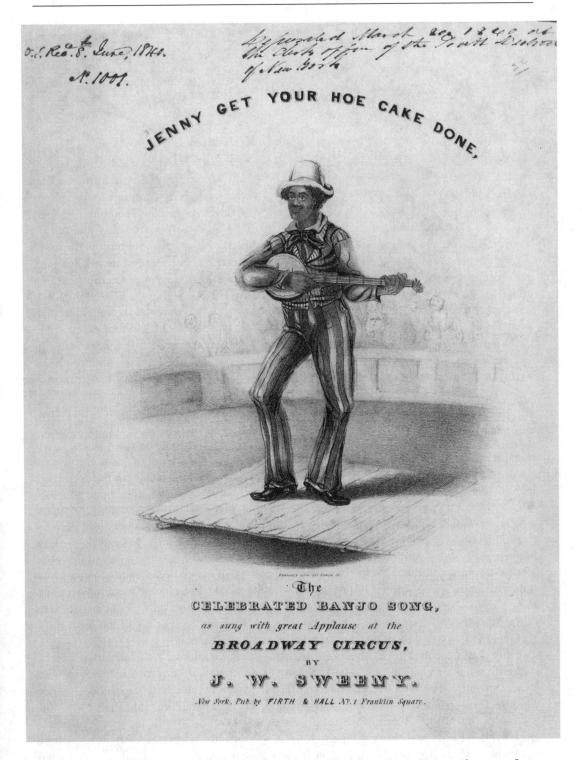

This piece of sheet music, printed in 1840, shows an early blackface minstrel attempting to perform black song and dance. The performer, J. W. Sweeny, was careful to include a shingle—often used by black dancers—in his act. When used as a portable stage, the shingle provided resonance for foot percussion. Courtesy Library of Congress.

The plantation breakdown. Two dancers perform solo next to each other, to the music of a banjo. The dance includes complex footwork as well as angular bending of the arms and legs. The wooden floor allows dancers to beat out a rhythm with their feet, and members of the community encircle the dancers to affirm and encourage them. From "American Home Scenes," *Harper's Weekly*, April 13, 1861.

lable. Minstrelsy was a curious phenomenon, in which white audiences who hungered after black culture, but had disdain for and fear of the black performers themselves, opted instead to watch white actors in blackface impersonating blacks—whites singing what they claimed were black songs and dancing what they claimed were black dances. This was a process that scholar Eric Lott called "love and theft."[1] It is a truism that, in this context of attempted cultural theft, the performances could never be authentic. Still, white minstrel dancers who wanted to present convincing black dances to white audiences did their best to observe and codify the constantly changing, improvisatory dancing of plantation workers and free blacks. The Negro jig or breakdown (an old generic term for a fast, energetic black dance) was a prime target.

It's worth mentioning at this point that the word "break" in association with black dance signifies original moves. The **breakout**, for example, is a term for the Jonkonnu main segment, which featured solo dancing. The **breakaway** is a moment in a couple dance like the Texas Tommy or Lindy Hop when the partners separate and add their own individual touches. In tap, there is a two-bar segment dubbed the **break** for solo improvisation. Even in European-style set dances done by blacks in the late nineteenth century, there were "breaks" by dancers for individually created steps, and in this the dances departed from their traditional European format.[2] And of course, Break Dance or Breakin' is all about individual acrobatic or freestyle moves to showcase agility and creativity. We can assume that a breakdown was individualistic.

Still, whites tried to standardize it. One writer, Ed James, who produced a book of dance instructions in 1873, had a special section for the "Plantation Breakdown." He admits he "gleaned" these steps from another author. One can imagine the written directions being passed from performer to performer, with readers longing to identify and memorize the elusive steps and body movements. James introduces his book by stating what every minstrel dancer knew at the time, namely that the many American jig steps were black and that whites had long imitated and were still imitating them:

> Jig Dancing is peculiarly an American institution and had its origin among the slaves of the southern plantations. No white man taught the original darkies the arts of Jig or Clog Dancing, and it is equally as indisputable that they did not pick either one of them up from reading books on the subject. It was original with them and has been copied by those who, in the early days of minstrelsy, made that a feature of their business, and by them brought down to a complete science.[3]

The last statement, "by them brought down to a complete science," was simply wishful thinking, as one can see from the book itself, which lists the steps very precisely. This sort of precise listing is by nature false, for in reality, the black dance steps were fluid like call-and-response singing: each dancer made up original moves and changed them constantly, choreographing them to be as complex and difficult as he or she could manage, for maximum artistic and competitive impact.

We can, however, read the steps James records with interest for their partial value as someone's flawed remembrance and European-based interpretation of a black dancer's steps in some time and place in America prior to 1873. Each written step is a combination of jumps, hops, taps, strikes, slides, and shuffles, and these are much the same as the units of movement for maneuvers described in James' steps for jig and clog dances, suggesting that there were critical similarities between the African American and European forms that facilitated the enormous cross-fertilization occurring between them throughout the nineteenth century. Here is James' description of the first step of the Plantation Breakdown:

> Jump on both feet crossed, then throw right foot as high as possible, at the same time hop on the left foot, (2 motions). Repeat it, leaving the right foot up in front. Then hop on left foot, bring the right down, tap it and carry it behind. Hop on left foot, (3 motions). Then make five taps quick, commencing with the right foot, which is crossed behind the left. This is the first part of the step, and is repeated on the other foot, reversed. Then done again same as first time. Then make a Cross and five taps quick, moving forward and commencing with the right foot.[4]

The big difference between James' descriptions of jigs and clogs on the one hand and the breakdown on the other is the larger number of repeated and swift crossings and uncrossings of the feet, along with high kicks or knee lifts, that were staples of the acrobatic Negro jig. These were brought to high development by its greatest performer, William Henry Lane. When Charles Dickens gave us the first written description of Lane's dance, for example, he mentioned the "cut and cross-cut" along with other elements of the profoundly impressive performance he witnessed.[5]

The dance was both Africanist and in many ways similar to foot stomping, jig-style European solo forms. The Rev. Charles Rockwell left us a description of an African dance he saw off the coast of Liberia. Written in Boston in 1842, his account notes that:

> Sometimes, when the sailors were at leisure in the evening, they would collect the Kroomen on board together upon the forecastle, and get them to show off some of their native dances. These had not a little of the kick and shuffle peculiar to the negro dances with us, though at times there were violent motions, somewhat like those of the shaking Quakers and howling Dervishes. They kept time to a loud, harsh, monotonous kind of music, somewhat resembling that used by the Spanish peasants, in connexion with the fandango and other national dances.[6]

A CABIN IN THE GOOD OLD TIME

COPYRIGHTED 1888 BY J.H. BUFFORD'S SONS

Victorian trade cards were used by businesses to call attention to their merchandise or services—their "trades." Often, both front and back of the card were printed. On one side, there was an interesting or entertaining illustration, and on the other side, advertising. People collected these colorful trade cards and sometimes kept them in scrapbooks. Here, the "Good Old Time" is a dance event in a cabin. Two people jig opposite each other, while music is provided by a banjo and hand percussion. The black jig involves a loosely held torso, often bent forward, angular legs and arms, and knees raised high.

Rockwell, then, saw similarities between the West African dance and African American dance he is familiar with, as well as with the Fandango, a stamping dance that may have contributed to American tap dance via the European jig. The Fandango is also danced by two people opposite each other who do not touch. In fact, the Fandango can be traced back to the Moors, making it African in style and origins.

Robert Schomburgh, who in 1847 described a black dance he saw in Barbados, though, echoes the comparison to European dances. First, he carefully distinguishes between the dance he witnessed and the European set dances being adopted by the elite blacks there: "This dance," he says, "is a remnant of African customs, and only practiced by the lower classes of the Negroes. The black aristocracy have long since abolished this barbarian custom, which has been replaced by quadrilles and the fashionable polka."[7] Next, he points out that the dance shares something with white forms: "The grotesque figures of the dance, in some of its motions resembled an Irish jig, in others, by the various contortions of the body, their advance or retreat, the voluptuous dances of southern Europe."[8]

It would be easy to assume that one way in which the African-based and European dances could be contrasted was body posture. But the plantation jig was not in every case performed in orientation to the earth. On the contrary, sometimes the posture had to be rigidly vertical, because dancers held a container of water on their heads and isolated all the speed and movement in their hips and legs. Ex-slave James Smith, born in Texas some-

The breakdown was almost any black solo dance with fancy and swift footwork. This glass lantern slide shows an example from around 1900.

time in the middle of the nineteenth century, recounted just such a jig with containers of water:

> Master ... had a little platform built for the jigging contests. Colored folks comes from all around, the see who could jig the best ... on our place was the jigginest fellow ever was. Everyone round tries to git somebody to best him.... He could ... make his feet go like triphammers and sound like a snaredrum. He could whirl round and such, all the movement from his hips down.... There was a big crowd and money am bet, but Master bets on Tom, of course. So they starts jigging ... they gits faster and faster, and that crowd am a-yelling. Gosh! There am 'citement. They just keep a-gwine. It look Tom done found his match, but there am one thing yet he ain't done—he ain't made a whirl. Now he does it ... the other fellow starts ... but just a spoonful of water sloughs out his cup, so Tom is the winner.[9]

Acrobatic dancers from both Sierra Leone and Tunisia perform such container dances, with isolations, and we may assume African sources for it.[10] In another slave narrative,

Volume 18, Number 11.   Copyright, 1891, by D. LOTHROP COMPANY.   *January* 10, 1891.

THE PANSY.

AN ·APPRECIATIVE AUDIENCE.

A drawing shows a black boy dancing a breakdown to a tune created on the banjo by another young boy, while a girl watches—yet another reflection of the white audience for black arts. Again, we see the slightly forward torso with bent knees and elbows. From *The Pansy*, January 10, 1891.

Published in 1882, this sheet music shows two African American children in a jig or breakdown, with a third child providing music by playing the banjo. A cotton boll at the bottom of the illustration symbolizes the plantation. The creators of such sheet music did their best to capture black music and dance for mostly northern audiences.

Allen Parker says, "Some slaves … could dance so steadily that if a glass of water were placed on their heads none of the water would be spilt. I have often seen a girl dance for ten minutes with a glass cup filled with water on her head without any of it being spilt."[11] This means that black dancers, accustomed to isolating body parts in dance, would have adjusted easily to the motions of the rigid-torso Irish jig or Lancashire Clog.

In its usual manifestations, though, the black jig utilized all parts of the body with special emphasis on the feet, which executed complex steps as well as provided the beat for the dance, rendered in perfect rhythm. Acrobatics and speed are often emphasized in period descriptions, as are makeshift musical instruments. Several of these characteristics are mentioned in William Cullen Bryant's account of a black dance at a corn shucking in South Carolina in 1843:

> When the work of the evening was over the Negroes adjourned to a spacious kitchen. One of them took his place as musician, whistling, and beating time with two sticks upon the floor. Several of the men came forward and executed various dances, capering, prancing, and drumming with the heel and toe upon the floor, with astonishing agility and perseverance, though all of them had performed their daily tasks and had worked all evening and some had walked from four to seven miles to attend the corn-shucking.[12]

The Negro jig, then, included percussion, community involvement, competition, improvisation, polyrhythms, special objects such as water jars, African movement vocabulary, and often orientation to the earth.

COMMONALITIES WITH EUROPEAN JIGS AND CLOGS

The black jig or breakdown had a number of commonalities with European solo dances. These facilitated dance exchange as well as muddying historical accounts, with both whites and blacks claiming credit for tap dance, the ultimate child of the two dance traditions. To see the profound shaping influence of the black tradition, one might begin by comparing the Irish jig or English clogging with American tap dance.[13] The differences are essentially African American characteristics. The involvement of all parts of the body, a loosely forward stance with flexed knees, posture angled toward the earth, polyrhythmic music, closeness of the feet to the ground in scuffing and sliding steps, involvement of the hips, acrobatic moves, and improvisation—all these are Africanist.

The European jig is danced in a very vertical posture, with the eyes held straight ahead. The legs and feet do all the rapid work of the dance, as the arms and hands simply dangle loosely and the hips are relatively quiet. In his 1873 pamphlet, James advises, "Hold the head well up, standing erect; do not look at the feet at all, as that has a tendency to stooping, which is a very bad and ugly habit. Let the arms, the hands being open, dangle perpendicular and without straining at the sides."[14] James' illustrations emphasize this verticality, reflecting his European values. His descriptions emphasize the jumping and hopping steps that are also part of its skyward orientation.

So strong is this preference for very straight posture, that even later white-written tap-instruction books emphasize it. "Stand erect, that is, chest held high," says Rita Ramsey in her *Home Lessons in Tap Dancing* (1932). "Hold the chin up and look straight ahead. Never watch your feet in any exercise or step. To look down, throws the entire body out of position and creates an awkward, ungainly appearance."[15] But Bill Robinson, one of the greatest tap dancers of all time, did just what Ramsey advised against. Watching his feet was part of his showmanship—he drew audience's attention to the magic of his feet. And

ON THE O HIGH O!

HENRY KEYES & COMPANY,
MEN'S CLOTHING BOYS'
HATS, CAPS, AND FURNISHING GOODS,
424 Main Street, - - - - Springfield, Mass.

A trade card presents its advertisement directly below the image of black dance on board a river raft on the Ohio River.

the illustrations in the front of Ramsey's book and in other contemporary instruction booklets show tap dancers in a quintessentially African stance, with the body bent forward, knees flexed, and arms thrown forward or outward. While this position may have been used simply to finish a routine or add a flourish to one, it nevertheless reflects a shift from traditional European body posture, in a time when African American stage dancers used a wide variety of postures and moves to distinguish their routines from others, all the while exerting tremendous influence on their white contemporaries. By the early 1930s, the traditional rigidity of the European torso had already been discarded in American tap dance, and the basic contrast between white and black styles was being quickly forgotten by white tap dancers as the black style dominated.

Despite differences, though, there are strong similarities between African American and Irish styles. Solo Irish dancers took pride in their complex footwork, and they competed with each other publicly, albeit mainly to see who had the most endurance. Dancers were also known to take doors off their hinges to provide a small dance floor, and this practice is strongly reminiscent of the African American shingle. Moreover, dancers sometimes held objects as they danced, a handkerchief or a stick called a shillelagh, which could be twirled in the dance. Some Irish dancers put glasses of beer on their heads as they danced, too, to show off their balance and their ability to isolate movement below the hips. In the eighteenth century, there were Irish dance masters who traveled from village to village giving instruction, and this suggests fairly fixed forms. But when Irish immigrants began competing with black Americans and other Europeans in urban areas in the nineteenth century, most dancers improvised.

English clogging derived from older step forms. It takes its name from shoes called clogs, which had wooden soles and heels. In the eighteenth and nineteenth centuries, English mill workers developed percussive styles based on striking these soles onto hard

To the left is the jig dancer from James' 1873 booklet, and to the right (and next page) are modern tap dancers from a 1940s how-to booklet.

surfaces. They "developed a form of challenge dance in which they pounded out elaborate rhythms on floors and cobblestone streets…. When this exciting percussive noise was added to the complex footwork already existing in such step dances as the jig, hornpipe, and reel, and in Morris dances, a new dance form … was created."[16] Like Irish step dance, clogging keeps the torso relatively uninvolved and the posture vertical. In the Lancashire clog, though, improvisation is prized, and this gives it a commonality with African American dance.

Appalachian clogging is a more recent derivative of older stepping and clogging styles, and shows the influence of African American dance. In this form, the body motion is down (in contrast to that of step dancing, where it is up), and the feet engage in a flat-footed

shuffle. That's why it's called flatfooting in many Appalachian areas. "Hold your feet on the floor the best you can," said flatfooter Hoy Haden in an interview. "That's really the old-time flatfoot."[17] American clogging is not done with wooden shoes or soles, however, but with leather soles enhanced with metal taps.

When Irish, British, and African Americans met in mainland North America, they brought with them a collection of solo footwork dances such as the Jig, Clog, Hornpipe, Highland dances, and African competitive/display styles. But some plantation blacks may already have had contact with Irish before they set foot on this shore. Oliver Cromwell deported many thousands of Irish to the new English islands in the Caribbean in the middle of the seventeenth century. There, the Irish became indentured servants who worked side by side with African slaves for a century, sharing their cultures, having mixed-race children together, learning each other's music, and dancing together. By the time some of these "seasoned" slaves and servants came to the mainland of North America, they had already influenced each other.[18] The form of solo dance we call the Irish jig, however, had probably not developed into a recognizable form at the time of this earliest Caribbean cultural exchange[19], but characteristics of earlier Irish dancing were there for the sharing. Notwithstanding this limited cultural exchange, observers and commentators on the black jig during the slavery period did not see it as a form of Irish or European dance.

Later, in the United States, in the first decades of the nineteenth century, Irish immigrants arrived in significant numbers, bringing the fully developed Irish jig with them. Here, they lived in many cases in the same crowded, poor neighborhoods as blacks. In New York City, where the largest of these mixed neighborhoods could be found, slaves had been emancipated as recently as 1827, and importation of slaves from Africa had only stopped as of 1808. African American culture lived closely with Irish culture and, to a lesser degree,

Lawrence, Publisher, Dublin.

THE OULD IRISH JIG.

"Then a fig for the new fashioned waltzes
Imported from Spain and from France,
And a fig for the thing called to polka,
Our own Irish jig we will dance."

The Irish jig, like the Negro jig, often involved two people dancing opposite each other, whether in competition or not. There were significant differences, though, including body posture and focus on the feet. In the Irish jig, the legs and feet move swiftly through a complex series of steps, while the arms are either raised skyward or simply held quiet. Torsos are kept vertical, and eyes look straight ahead. In this depiction, the man carries a stick or shillelagh in one hand, and a third performer provides music. The card was published in Dublin and mailed in 1904.

242. Roustabouts ot Play.   A. SELIGE SOUVENIR POST CARD CO., ST. LOUIS.

Top: In this stereo view from around 1900, a young boy shows his friends his steps. This may have been a challenge situation in which the boys took turns trying to top each other's performances. *Bottom:* A postcard, titled "Roustabouts at Play" and probably produced around 1900, captures two men showing off some steps for co-workers' entertainment.

with English and other cultures. The groups struggled for the same jobs and turned similar resentments toward each other. They also intermarried, competed on the dance floor, and influenced each other's art and customs. One result was a dance form called the Juba, a dance that fused elements from the dance traditions of the time and yet remained Africanist.

Five Points was a New York slum, populated in part by Irish immigrants and free blacks. It was here that Charles Dickens saw William Henry Lane in a dancing cellar.

JUBA

In 1842, Charles Dickens visited America. When he landed in New York, the city threw a party for him, and many prominent people attended to welcome him. What he really wanted to see, however, was the poorer neighborhoods of the city. So, attended by two policemen, he went to Five Points, a notoriously impoverished and vice-ridden part of town. Blacks and Irish—both of whom were at the bottom of economic ladder at the time—made up the larger portions of the population of the neighborhood. Foreign-born Irish residents, in fact, formed 66% of the adult population there in 1855. Blacks were only 4% of the local ward in that year, but there is some suspicion they were undercounted, as they were 14% of the population in 1825.[20] In the area's squalid tenements, blacks and Irish lived side by side, and despite the violence they occasionally perpetrated against each other, shared their cultures, especially dance.

Dickens is responsible, in his *American Notes*, for giving us one of the contemporary descriptions of Five Points. He went to Almack's, which was a dancing cellar, to see the local amusements. Dancing cellars were places where local people drank, danced, and socialized. In the period, dance was a way to distinguish oneself, a medium in which one could sharpen personal skills and show them off. Dance competitions, both formalized and informal, were common. The "sporting" or "flash" press publicized them in a context that gives evidence of the large number of young white men who came to the city in the 1820s and 1930s in search of work and who spent their money in interracial spaces like Five Points to purchase entertainment and sex, and to gamble. They, like Dickens, were slumming.[21] They watched and bet on the dance contests just as they did prize fights and other competitions.

When Dickens entered Almack's, however, he saw an appealing space very different from the other sights of the evening. It was a room with a low ceiling and brightly white-washed walls, presided over by a woman with sparkling eyes and a dainty handkerchief, along with the well-dressed black owner of the place, Pete Williams. There was a black fiddler, and several couples were on the floor doing a "breakdown." These dancers did not impress Dickens. But suddenly a new figure entered, a young man who was probably 16 or 17 years of age. From Dickens' account, we gather the fiddler recognized him and knew he would provide a powerful and delightful performance:

> Instantly the fiddler grins, and goes at it tooth and nail; there is new energy in the tambourine; new laughter in the dancers; new smiles in the landlady; new confidence in the landlord; new brightness in the very candles. Single shuffle, double shuffle, cut and cross-cut; snapping his fingers, rolling his eyes, turning in his knees, presenting the backs of his legs in front, spinning about on his toes and heels like nothing but the man's fingers on the tambourine. Dancing with two left legs, two right legs, two wooden legs, two wire legs, two spring legs—all sorts of legs and no legs—what is this to him? And in what walk of life, or dance of life does man ever get such stimulating applause as thunders about him, when, having danced his partner off her feet, and himself, too, he finishes by leaping gloriously on the bar-counter, and calling for something to drink, with the chuckle of a million of counterfeit Jim Crows, in one inimitable sound![22]

It is assumed by most scholars that this dancer was William Henry Lane, a free black man probably born in Rhode Island around 1825. The connection between Lane and the anonymous dancer seen by Dickens became clear when Lane went to England on tour in 1848 with Pell's Ethiopians, a minstrel troupe, where he received top billing as "Boz's Juba" (Boz was a common nickname for Dickens). Dickens, never inclined to be silent when his name was misused, said nothing, perhaps giving us a sort of backhanded endorsement of the advertisement. With that, along with the significant publicity surrounding Lane's tour, we can conclude that he was the indeed the dancer of *American Notes*.

The star of the dancing cellar in Five Points was known as a Juba dancer, and Juba is consistent with the dance Dickens described. The form has been defined by Katharine Dunham:

> In its original African form, the Juba or Jumba or Majumba, as it is called in the West Indies, is primarily a competitive dance of skill. One person steps forward in the circle of dancers and begins exhibiting his skill, whereupon he is joined by a member of the opposite sex…. The people in the circle … all the while clapping rhythmically and encouraging the competitors with song and verse.[23]

Gerstin adds that challenge dances could include "virtuoso solo display as well as challenge per se."[24] Patting Juba meant clapping and patting to keep time and to provide accompaniment during the dance. "Master Juba" was a stage name sometimes taken by Juba dancers. William Henry Lane was called Master Juba, as was his African American contemporary, Lewis Davis.[25]

As a competition dance, the Juba was a favorite of dancers in variety shows, traveling and otherwise. For example, an ad for an "attraction at Frank's Museum" in the *Public Ledger* of Cincinnati on February 20, 1841, calls readers' attention to "Master Kent, only 13 years old, the best Juba dancer living, and who challenges any man or boy living to dance for from 50 to 500 dollars, will dance at the above establishment this evening." A museum was not the storehouse of cultural or artistic artifacts we are familiar with today, but rather was a place of curiosities and entertainment. Museum performers' offers to take on all comers, especially when serious prize money was offered, gathered crowds and generated publicity.

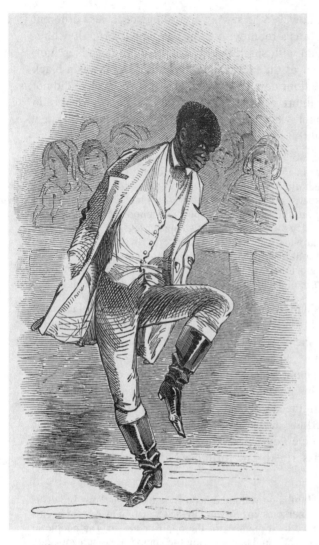

A British newspaper, *The London Illustrated News*, printed this sketch of Master Juba dancing onstage for a packed house in 1848. The sketch was part of a review of Juba's performance, which the reviewer called "the only national dance" he knew. His point seemed to be that, as an authentic folk dance of America, it was unique. The article noted that Juba would be held over for another week.

Lane himself was apparently seriously involved in dance competition in New York City. A young dancer named Juba, at any rate, was put forward by P. T. Barnum for "trials of skill" in 1840.[26] Lane then engaged in at least three high-dollar dance contests with Irish dance champion John Diamond. The *Herald* publicized one of these as follows:

GREAT PUBLIC CONTEST Between the two most renowned Dancers in the world, the Original JOHN DIAMOND, and the Colored Boy JUBA, for a Wager of $300 ... at the BOWERY AMPHITHEATER, which building has been expressly hired from the Proprietor.... The fame of these Two Celebrated Breakdown Dancers has already spread over the Union, and the numerous friends of each claim the Championship for their favorite, and ... have seriously wished for a Public Trial between them ... [to] know which is to bear the Title of the Champion Dancer of the World.[27]

The two men were to dance three jigs, two reels, and the Camptown Hornpipe, and all of these suggest traditional European solo dancing, although they certainly could have incorporated African characteristics. Evidently, Lane was pronounced winner in either this contest or later ones, for in 1845 he was billed as the "Greatest Dancer in the World/Having danced with John Diamond at the Chatham Theatre for $500 and at the Bowery Amphitheater for the same amount, and established himself as the KING OF ALL DANCERS!!"[28] Moreover, Lane's interaction with the top blackface dancers of the nation gave him great familiarity with their styles, and he later created a routine in which he began by giving imitations of seven of them ("all the principal Ethiopian dancers of the United States"), including Dick Pelham, Frank Brower (both later of the Original Virginia Minstrels), and John Diamond. Lane ended the routine by breaking into his own dance to show its superiority to the others.[29] With this routine, Lane followed a classic challenge format. He showed he could do everything his opponent did, and then went him one better.

What this meant was that Lane as Master Juba was the foremost representative of the

In this late nineteenth century illustration, a group of shoeshine boys share a moment of dance. The white boy to the left sits on his shoeshine box and claps to keep time, while the African American boy to the right performs a footwork dance. All the boys' faces show their enjoyment. From *Harper's Weekly*, April 18, 1885.

Juba or breakdown, having not only competed with other major dancers to prove himself the best, but also having conquered and absorbed their styles, as well as the forms of European solo dances, and then put together his own choreography that was better than any of theirs. Thus, the dance was no longer purely an African-based or black plantation form. Instead, it was a fusion of styles that achieved its greatest heights as improvised routines under the intense pressure of competition showcased to large audiences, all still in an African American challenge tradition.

In 1848, Lane traveled to England with Pell's Ethiopian Serenaders. One of six performers, he had top billing. His portrait on a playbill shows a well-dressed, handsome young man. Reviewers said he was five feet two or three inches tall, thin, and extremely agile. His dance was drew so much attention and was so extraordinary that he was called to perform for Queen Victoria. No one who was anyone wanted to miss the performance that had been described as "unlike anything seen in this country."[30] Reviewers were both puzzled at the unusual acrobatics and steps and overwhelmed by Lane's virtuosity. Their impressionistic descriptions in the news sources of the time give us the best information available about what the dance was like.

First, the dance was unusual. One reviewer declared, "He is the greatest phenomenon in the dancing line that Manchester has witnessed," and yet regarding the dance itself said, "The effort baffles description." Another writer says, "His steps are unborrowed from schools, unadopted from academies. They are original, novel, peculiar, curious, wonder-

12737   WAITING FOR THE SUNDAY BOAT

"Waiting for the Sunday Boat" was probably produced around 1910, from a hand-colored photograph. Notice that the dancer has chosen a wooden platform for his solo.

ful, exciting, marvelous...." Clearly this was no Irish Jig or Lancashire Clog—British reviewers would have recognized those instantly. The uniqueness of the performance was its greatest drawing card. Still, one reviewer believed he saw a few echoes of the more familiar dances: "The highland fling, the sailor's hornpipe, and other European dances, seemed to have been laid under contribution, and intermixed with a number of steps which we may call 'Juba's own.'" This insight probably correctly identified the influence of the dozens if not hundreds of jigs, clogs, and hornpipes Lane had witnessed and performed back home.

The reviewers tell us that the dances were described on the playbill as plantation dances ("Virginny Breakdown," "Alabama Kick-up," "Louisiana Heel-and-Toe," and others). Thus the audience was led to believe northern-born Lane was a representative of slave dance. And the reviewers noted how superior Lane's dance was to that of white men performing in blackface: "It is laughable betimes to witness the abortive attempts of those collier or whitewashed personations of the Ethiopian. They are just as much in character as a pig is in a drawing-room. Juba's executions are both graceful and accomplished." The dance, that is, was both brilliant and sophisticated. Had it not been, it could not have caused the stir it did among the knowledgeable and elite.

But what were the key features of the dance? Several can be identified. First, the dance included extraordinary acrobatics and was performed with amazing rapidity and agility: "Such mobility of muscles, such flexibility of joints, such boundings, such slidings, such gyrations, such toes and such heelings, such backwardings and forwardings, such posturings, such firmness of foot, such elasticity of tendon...." Lane could "turn, and twine, and twist, and twirl, and hop, and jump, and kick, and throw his feet almost with

Here is another illustration of street dance as joyful self-expression. The newspaper headline, "Yanks Win," tells us the reason for the dance.

a velocity that makes one think they are playing hide-and-seek with a flash of lightning!" The same reviewer said, "He jumps, he capers, he crosses his legs, he stamps his heels, he dances on his knees, on his ankles, he ties his limbs into double knots, and untwists them as one might a skein of silk…." Another asked, "How could he tie his legs into such knots, and fling them about so recklessly, or make his feet twinkle until you lose sight of them altogether in his energy[?]"

This picture was taken in the 1940s at Raiford Prison in Florida.

Yet simultaneously, there was control and absolutely perfect timing: "The manner in which he beats time with his feet, and the extraordinary command he possesses over them, can only be believed by those who have been present at the exhibition." The same writer said, "To us, the most interesting part of the performance was the exact time, which, even in the most complicated and difficult steps, the dancer kept to the music." The steps, moreover, were audible. "Mr. Pell would take it as a great favour if the Audience will keep as quite [sic] as possible during Master Juba's Dances; by doing so, they will hear the exact time he keeps with his extraordinary steps."

It is clear that all parts of the body were involved, not just the legs and feet: "toes and heels, ankles and calves, knees and thighs, elbows and wrists, nay even his eyes and the lobes of his ears, and the wool on his caput all dance...." Another reviewer mentioned Lane's joyful attitude and infectious laugh: "there never was such a laugh as the laugh of

Four boys dance on the sidewalk in Florida in 1932.

Juba … clear, ringing, echoing, resonant, harmonious, full of rejoicing and mighty mirth, and fervent fun…." For Lane, and because of his profoundly communicative performance, for his audience, too, the dance was joyful, a powerful experience that made spectators laugh out loud in spite of their dignity.

We can't document the individual steps of Lane's dance, but from the descriptions above, we can get some sense of it. Was the dance no longer Africanist? Did it no longer look like the plantation Juba that African American workers had performed for centuries? Compare this description of a "Juber" dance on a plantation in 1838 with the descriptions of Lane's dance:

[the banjo player was] Tumming his banjor, grinning with ludicrous gesticulations and playing off his wild notes to the company. Before him stood two athletic blacks with open mouth, and pearl white teeth, clapping "Juber" to the notes of the banjor…. [They] rested the right foot on the heel, and its clap on the floor was in perfect unison with the notes of the banjor, and palms of the hands on the corresponding extremities; while the dancers were all jigging it away in the merriest possible gaiety of heart, having the most ludicrous twists, wry jerks, and flexible contortions of the body and limbs, that human imagination can devine.[31]

Certainly, the descriptions of this plantation dance and Lane's theatrical dance are similar, if impressionistic. However, it is not reasonable to believe that Lane interacted with Irish and other European American dancers in the hothouse of competition dance for a decade and yet took nothing from European forms, especially when he achieved such a mastery of them. Nevertheless, the dance that emerged, of which he was America's greatest representative, seems still to have African characteristics: improvisation, African movement vocabulary, polyrhythms, competition, and percussion, along with the superb African sense of timing.

Stephen Johnson reflects this African content when he writes, "In the chaotic and confused descriptions of Juba I read an effort to describe several things at once—several parts of the body moving simultaneously at different speeds and in different rhythms." He adds, "I read an effort to come to terms with sudden, unaccustomed changes of tone. In the magnificent failure of description—the flood of words, the exuberant protestations that it is indescribable—I see a reflection of the speed, surprise, and exuberance of the Africanist aesthetic."[32] Johnson's view is compelling.

Lane died young in England, probably at age 26 or 27. Despite the brevity of his life, he was a major figure in the development of a prototypical dance form that took much from Africa while probably adopting something from the precise stepping of European jig, clog, and Highland dances. He gave priceless performances that imprinted themselves vividly in the historical record. Most important of all, he performed African-derived dance so powerfully that no purely European dance could overshadow it. Instead, the flexibility of African dance absorbed something from its opponents and moved on, toward buck dance and tap.

BUCK DANCE

A great deal happened between the Juba and the Buck. The Civil War happened, and within its context, many northern soldiers saw authentic southern black culture for the first time. Slaves ran away from their masters as the Union Army passed nearby, and once they were declared to be the contraband of war, they were, after some initial difficulties, allowed to take refuge with the soldiers and to contribute their knowledge and service to the troops. By 1863, Lincoln had announced that northern blacks would be permitted to enlist, and thousands came to the front. Magazines like *Harper's Weekly* sent artists like Winslow Homer and Thomas Nast to sketch what was happening there for news-hungry people back home in the North. Among these pictures were illustrations of southern African American culture, including dance. Subscribers devoured these pictures as eagerly as they did the minstrel shows at home.

After the war, black entertainers formed their own minstrel shows to wrest the delivery of African American culture from the hands of impersonators. The black traveling shows could only survive with white management, and they always suffered from the racism of the time. Yet they formed a crucible in which the old plantation dances could be broken down, polished, reworked, and recombined into new, exciting forms. One of the dances that received enormous attention was the Juba or breakdown. Individual dancers created flashy steps, and both black and white dancers found time to watch each other dance and take from each other what they could for their own routines. Amidst all this improvisation, some steps coalesced into enduring forms, and there grew up a shared vocabulary.

One result was buck dance, in which the feet were close to the earth, doing scuffing,

Ed Young demonstrates the Buck Dance in *Buck Dancer*, filmed in 1965 by Bess Lomax Hawes. She calls the form "a southern dance of male virtuosity engaged in by both black and white frontiersmen." She sees Young's "relaxed floppy arms" and "subtle sinuous trunk movements" as African, along with his "low dragging foot moves." Courtesy Bess Lomax Hawes. Quotes are from her notes, which accompany *The Films of Bess Lomax Hawes.*

sliding movements, often with audible taps. Most of the body movement was from the hips down, although the stance was still Africanist. Lots of dancers made the dance's sound by sprinkling sand on the stage and dancing in it. The softer, scratchy sound was successful with audiences, but more precise-sounding taps were part of buck, too. Makeshift metal taps for shoes gained scattered use before the turn of the century, and manufactured ones became common by the 1920s.

The basic mix of shuffle and tap was brought to a high point by one of the greatest buck dancers of all, King Rastus Brown. The King was a legend in his time, the first two decades of the twentieth century. No one knows when he was born, but he was an old man in the 1920s when young, aspiring dancers watched him and learned from him.[33] Although the young Bob Hope wanted for a time to become a prizefighter, he eventually went into show business, and King Rastus Brown helped him learn to dance. In fact, Brown was known for helping young dancers learn. He had also toured Europe successfully and, according to dancer Eddie Rector, had medals he had won in Europe "all the way down his front."[34] Brown's style represented buck dancing in the early twentieth century. It incorporated syncopation, and a flat-footed style. "He danced flat-footed, close to the floor, moving from the hips down, and swinging," Willie Covan said.[35]

Prince Spencer, a member of the Four Step Brothers, remembered that in his youth he saw King Rastus Brown perform. Brown laid out clear, clean taps that made a rhythm:

Two black children dance the breakdown in Baton Rouge, Louisiana. Members of the invading Massachusetts 41st and New York 131st Regiments, as well as the Connecticut 25th Volunteers watch. On either side, we see black soldiers in Union uniform. By the time this illustration was published, black men were permitted to enlist as soldiers on the northern side, although they were paid only about half of what white enlistees received. *Frank Leslie's Illustrated Newspaper*, **January 31, 1863.**

One particular man come to our hometown, a black dancer named King Rastus Brown. He was an old man by this time, and he danced with a cane. King Rastus Brown just impressed me so much, because his tap was so clear and profound. I didn't have any idea that feet could make this kind of a sound. I had seen the move dancers—guys Buck dancing and Shuffling and what not. And I remember the Waltz Clog and Pat Rooney. But King Rastus Brown danced so impressively that I began to see what dancing was about.[36]

At the Hoofer's Club, a back room in Harlem, Brown stopped in from time to time to mingle with other dancers and eager youngsters. With a boy playing the "Buck Dancer's Lament" on the piano, the King would do his own version of the Time Step in the first six bars. Then he, "during the two silent bars, taps out a rhythmic miracle."[37] His originality, coupled with his perfect timing and audible taps, made him one of the most admired dancers of his time.

Later, when Prince Spencer saw and heard Bill Robinson's clean, crisp taps, he said, "That's what this fellow, King Rastus Brown, was doing years ago."[38] Spencer added, "Yeah, tap dancing was an art—to excel in dancing, your feet had to have a great sense of rhythm where you couldn't afford to lose time or lose rhythm or miss a beat, or you weren't in that category of greatness."[39] Spencer felt that Bill Robinson's greatness echoed Brown's: "that was like the master putting the touch on a story and saying, 'Yeah this is where it's supposed to be.'"[40]

Like Lane, Brown was a great competitor. Older dancers remember he won a major

Contrabands, escaped slaves who followed Union troops, sometimes provided one of the entertainments around the campfire at night, giving many young northerners their first experience of authentic black culture. This drawing by Winslow Homer includes the dancer of a jig or breakdown, along with a fiddle player to the right. "A Bivouac Fire on the Potomac," *Harper's Weekly*, December 21, 1861.

buck-dancing contest in Madison Square Garden around 1910. Brown could also imitate other sounds and styles, and then top them all with his own. As Willie Glenn remembered, "He could imitate anything ... whatever the audience called for, a train, a drunk, and different nationalities—Dutch, Irish, Jewish, Scottish. Then he'd say, 'Now I'll go for myself' and top them all."[41] In this way, he continued the ancient challenge tradition.

Brown carried on the essence of the African American tradition in the solo percussive style: competition, audible percussion, perfect timing, amazing originality, and ability to both outperform his opponents and absorb their styles simultaneously. It remained for Bill Robinson to bring tap up onto its toes, lighten its feeling, and give it a different kind of elegance. By then, it was no longer buck, but modern tap.

5

The Minstrel Show and Other Traveling Productions

The minstrel show was an extremely popular form of entertainment in the United States for more than half a century (from the 1840s through 1900), although its racially negative influences and political messages lasted much longer. Yet, despite its offensive images and the adversity it imposed, African American dancers and other performers broke into show business through minstrelsy. Furthermore, they gradually transformed its format into a showcase for their talent and a vehicle for their cultural arts—a monumental achievement.

The minstrel show grew up during a time when slavery was coming under attack, and the response to abolitionism was a backlash of oppression against blacks. The Missouri Compromise (1820) put limits on the spread of slavery, and the Compromise of 1850 enacted a strong fugitive slave law. In 1839, near the beginning of the minstrel show phenomenon, a group of fifty-four African captives on their way to slavery in the Americas seized the ship *Amistad*. Later, defended by John Quincy Adams, they would sue for their freedom before the U.S. Supreme Court and win. As these events polarized American views on slavery, escaped slaves like Sojourner Truth and Frederick Douglass told their stories in oratory and published narratives, winning over thousands to the antislavery cause. Douglass also founded the abolitionist newspaper *The North Star* to argue in favor of Emancipation. A secret network called the Underground Railroad helped many slaves to escape. As slave hunters came north to look for these fugitive slaves, they sometimes carried away blacks who had never been slaves. In response, Vermont, Connecticut, Rhode Island, Massachusetts, Michigan, Maine, Kansas, and Wisconsin passed Personal Liberty Laws to protect their black citizens. With each event, hostility between pro- and anti-slavery forces grew to new heights.

Developing in this time of bitter conflict over slavery and race, the minstrel show had a strange, reflexive history. In minstrelsy, whites donned blackface and imitated blacks onstage, offering up what the mostly northern and western audiences believed was authentic black culture. The resulting caricatures became conventions of the form, and when black minstrels got their chance to perform onstage, they had to observe these conventions, blacking up and enacting theatrical stereotypes that had been in place for decades. Thus, black entertainers were compelled to imitate whites imitating blacks. In time, African American entertainers cast aside these shackles from the past and created new images for themselves, but it took decades. During those difficult years, they faced long tours through small towns rife with racism, and physical danger, low pay, poor working conditions, and other hardships to forge a new life in post-emancipation America. This chapter is the story of the challenges they faced, their perseverance, and their success.

A color postcard, dated 1908, shows Guy's Minstrels seated in the traditional semi-circle onstage, while the audience takes advantage of the sloped amphitheatre for a good view. The photograph was taken in Oriskany, New York.

ROOTS OF THE BLACKFACE MINSTREL SHOW

It is worth asking how and why minstrelsy grew to be so popular. Its roots are entwined with those of the abolition controversy in pre–Civil War America, part and parcel of the political struggle over slavery, but also drawing material from economic hard times, the restless movement of people across the continent, the growth of urban areas, and the rough humor of the frontier. As Constance Rourke noted, blackface entertainment became popular when slavery sparked heated controversy:

> The rise of the Negro minstrel coincided with a marked change in his place within the nation. Little Jim Crow appeared at almost the precise moment when the Liberator was founded; and minstrelsy spread over the land and grew in popularity as the struggle for emancipation grew in power through the '40s and '50s.[1]

At least part of the public interest in the minstrel show was curiosity about black culture and a desire to see it. Many whites who had never seen any African Americans in person had nevertheless heard or read about them, and wanted to observe their arts in a nonthreatening way. Many northern whites had opinions about slavery, and some had sympathy for enslaved Africans. Most whites, however, did not want to have contact with real blacks. Being entertained by white men who said they presented authentic black song, dance, and speech was not only acceptable but also satisfying. Eric Lott has called this "love and theft,"[2] and others have called it further commodification of an oppressed group of people from whom enormous profits had already been taken by the nation.[3]

For many audiences, the comic caricatures onstage were more than funny; they were comforting. The minstrel show made blacks less fearsome and slavery less horrific. For a mere twenty-five cents admission fee, the mysterious dark race was drained of its threat, and the plantation became a hilarious place where blacks were well treated and had leisure time to sing and dance. In the imaginative world of the minstrel show, the plantation was not a place Christian citizens had to worry about. Slaves could remain there without suffering, and whites could enjoy black cultural arts without having direct contact with blacks themselves. In cities where Irish American immigrants felt deeply angry about competing with black freedmen in the marketplace for jobs, the message of minstrel shows really resonated. Not only could working class whites feel superior to the characters on stage, but they could also take an ideology from the show. Blacks, they thought, were inferior beings that could and should stay in the South where they belonged.

Sheet music carried these racist messages across the nation. In every middle class parlor, the piano stood as evidence of social respectability and feminine artistry. Minstrel sheet music found its way there via the huge popularity of the shows, reinforcing stereotypical perspectives on black Americans.[4] In post-Civil War minstrel shows and music, the plantation comes to seem a lost and beautiful home for the African American. "Massa's in the Cold, Cold Ground" and "Old Black Joe" were only two of the parlor songs that animated the fiction of the ex-slave's longing for a vanished past. Furthermore, so attached were whites to the myth of the romantic plantation, that they expected blacks to share it. Helene Magaret described this attitude in 1932, when she wrote in a tone of sarcasm, "The 'good' Negro was one who loved to be a slave, and who wept copious tears when the Emancipation Proclamation was signed, because he no longer 'belonged.'"[5] But when African American entertainers gained space on the minstrel stage, they pointedly omitted such nostalgia for slavery.[6]

This psychological drama was reflected in popular enthusiasm for portrayals of black characters onstage. In period accounts, we read that people so enjoyed minstrel performances that they went back to the same show over and over, night after night. E.P. Gratton, who saw an 1843 performance by the Christy Minstrels said, "so droll was the action, so admirable the singing, so clever the instrumentation, and so genuine was the fun … that I not only laughed till my sides fairly ached, but that I never left an entertainment with a more keen desire to witness it again…."[7] Clearly, deep issues were being resolved, and the laughter marked both release and relief. The fact that the stage representations of blacks were false on nearly every level didn't come up.

Beginning in the 1840s, minstrelsy swept the nation. Minstrels went to the White House in 1844 to entertain President Tyler. Presidents Polk, Fillmore, Pierce, and Lincoln also enjoyed minstrel shows.[8] Minstrel troupes established themselves in their own theatres in New York City and San Francisco and sustained long runs amounting to years. Christy's Minstrels were at Mechanics' Hall in New York for seven years (1847–1854).[9] Tom Rice gave more than 50 performances of his quirky character Jim Crow in New York City as early as 1833, and overflow crowds came night after night to view his antics, even spilling onto the stage to laugh, drink, and dance.[10] Later, laws and ordinances that enforced racial discrimination took their name from this character. Places like Cincinnati, Pittsburgh, and Columbus welcomed less well-known companies such as the Empire Minstrels for twenty or even fifty performances.[11]

Blackface shows traveled around the world, embraced with as much enthusiasm in England, Europe, and Australia as they were in America.[12] Tom Rice left New York to perform in London in 1836[13] and a Mr. Ferguson portrayed Jim Crow in Australia in 1838.[14]

VILSACK'S FAMOUS MINSTRELS AT HOTEL BARTLETT, CAMBRIDGE SPRINGS, PA. NO. X44.

This downtown minstrel parade took place in Cambridge Springs, Pennsylvania, around 1900.

At Epsom, Henley, Hammersmith, and Margate, British vacationers and amusement seekers found blackface minstrels that had either traveled from America or were homegrown. Much sought by crowds, they were illustrated in the press and popular literature. Many had only learned a smattering of black dialect third or fourth hand from visiting American minstrels, but still the imitators of imitators enthralled audiences.[15]

An American commentator writing in the *Saturday Review* in 1884 had nothing but contempt for what he called "blacked-up and hopelessly *h*-less Cockneys ... attempting an exact imitation of the sayings and doings of the American plantation negro, studied by them at second-hand from some Irish-American performer who had probably never in his life seen a cotton field or a sugar-house."[16] Still, the reality was that the minstrels drew crowds. We may wonder why people overseas would be so interested. The answer may lie in colonialism. For countries busy founding empires, blackface entertainments were reassuring. Seeing subjugated people of color portrayed as happy, childlike, and of lesser intelligence made the empire more acceptable. As it did for Americans, the minstrel show may have dispelled doubt and guilt for Europeans.

Some critics maintained that minstrelsy was the first truly American stage show. *Putnam's Monthly* called the blackface theatres "The only places of Amusement where the entertainments are indigenous ... [and] vocalists, with blackened faces, sing national songs, and utter none but native witticisms."[17] It was true that ordinary people in American cities didn't flock to European-based drama. In fact, in 1849, when the British Shakespearean actor Charles Macready played Macbeth in New York, going toe to toe in competing theatres with the American actor Edwin Forrest, also playing Macbeth, some of the rowdier elements of the city rioted against Macready's theatre.[18] As Robert Toll has pointed out, working class men wanted "a 'common man's culture' that glorified American democracy

BRYANTS'

PROGRAMME.—Part First.

Instrumental Overture ...new, by Hobbs....**Bryants' Minstrels**
Opening Chorus, Operatic.................................**Company**
Old Black Oak...**J. W. Hilton**
Babylon is Fallen....................................**Dave Reed**
I am lonely to-night.................................**W. P. Grier**
Finnigan's Wake...........new................**Dan Bryant**
Mother kiss'd in my Dreams..................**Frank Leslie**
Finale—Sleigh Polka..........................**Full Chorus**

PART SECOND.—VARIETIES

GRAND TIN-PAN-O-NI-ON.

Conductor....................................**Sig. Dani Bryanto**

SALLY COME UP

Eccentric Song and Dance, Dave Reed.

The Pillywillywinck Band

Emmett, Hilton, Gettings, Mullins, Seymour and Mac.

CHALLENGE DANCE,

Dave Reed and Dan Bryant.

The Magic Echo.................................**J. Garatagui**

THE TAKE-IT-AND-LEAVE MAN

Bob Ridley..**Dan Bryant**
The Tiger............Nelse Seymour | Old Gibson..............**D. Reed**
Essence of Old Virginny.......................**Little Mac**

Influence of Mr. Rogers' Fiddle,

Morrison, Reed, Hilton, Mullen, Gettings, Mac & Seymour

Bryant's Minstrels performed from 1857 through 1866 in an incredibly long run at a single venue, Mechanics' Hall in New York City. Various members of the troupe, including Dan Emmett, who wrote "Dixie," came and went during that time. In the Civil War years, the company incorporated a number of patriotic songs into their repertoire. Notice that the program includes a challenge dance and the Essence of Old Virginny.

and the average white man in contrast to European aristocracy and effete 'gentlemen.'"[19] Again, we can see how the minstrel show identified and satisfied a need.

And in an oddly contradictory way, the minstrel show simultaneously allowed audiences to empathize with black characters, who often made jokes at the expense of their masters or offered up off-color material.[20] Identifying with the underdog, disliking elitist or well-to-do characters, and enjoying a belly laugh were also part of the reaction to the minstrel show. Working class people had endured financial panics and unemployment in the struggling new nation, had suffered the breaking of family ties to go to the new cities and find jobs, had walked long distances across the continent to find a new stake further west, had fought Indians and drought, and had survived. These audiences liked characters

Blacking up to entertain people at the seaside was once common in Britain. Children flocked to the blackface performers, who imitated American minstrels in every detail.

who were tough, who could endure oppression and laugh at hardship. They liked the malapropisms of the "negro" characters, and they howled at the hilarious, blacked-up white men who appeared in women's clothes to sing "Lucy Long" and in later years to dance the Cakewalk in drag. In its early years, the minstrel show was a frontier entertainment, a common man's amusement. As time went by, the minstrels became more refined, cleaned

BOSTON THEATRE

1881

TOMPKINS & HILL...................Proprietors

EUGENE TOMPKINS ....Manager

LEAVITT'S GIGANTEAN MINSTRELS.

M. B. LEAVITT.....................Sole Proprietor
KIT CLARKE ....Manager

"A good hearty Laugh is worth a thousand groans in any market." —LAMB.

FIRST GRAND DIVISION.

Chairman ....J. W. LAMONT

BONES.	TAMBOS.
H. J. ARMSTRONG.	LEW BENEDICT.
DAVE REED.	ARCHIE HUGHES.
JAS. SANFORD.	CHARLES WILSON.
ED. GIRARD.	TOM E. SOMERS.
SAM WESTON.	SAM BEASLEY.
WM. WOOD.	M. WESTON.
WM. WEST.	CHAS. V. SEAMON.
WM. GIRARD.	SAM SANFORD.
ED. BRYANT.	BEN. WOOD.

THE PROGRAMME.

Overture—"Racquet"....................Leavitt's Minstrels
"Star upon Star"......................Mr. R. T. Tyrrell
"Baby's Tooth".......................Mr. H. J. Armstrong
"Give Back My Heart".................Mr. Ernest Sinclair
"Paddy McFadden......................Mr. Archie Hughes
"The Blue Alsatian Mountains".........Mr. A. Cook
"Hail, Jerusalem, Hail"...............Mr. Lew Benedict
"Only to Love".......................Mr. Geo. Hammond

A GRAND INNOVATION!

INTERMEDIATE DOUBLE FIRST PART SCENE.

Herein are presented the Great Original Founders of Minstrelsy: The VIRGINIA SERENA-DERS, exhibiting as first presented upon any stage — the first attempt at an art which has become a household word in all lands, and at once demonstrating the great advance made in Modern Minstrelsy.

DAN EMMETT..........................Violin
SAM SANFORD.........................Tambo
ARCHIE HUGHES.......................Bones
DAVE REED...........................Jawbone
SAM WESTON..........................Banjo

THE VIRGINIA SERENADERS.

"Massa's in de Cold, Cold Ground"......Company
"Dandy Jim".........................Sam Sanford
"My Old Dad ".......................Dave Reed
"Boatsman's Chorus".................Dan Emmett

TIME — 10 MINUTES, GRAND FINALE.

Introducing the Laughable Interlude — "DIMPEY'S LAST STORY."

up the ribald and sexual material, and became family entertainment. But the appeal of the underdog endured, and the contradictory elements of the show continued to work.

Despite the reality that many audiences found the shows satisfying, we must never lose sight of their basic falsity. Although embraced by white society, they contained little that was authentic, either in characterization or artistic content. Nevertheless, some white performers claimed to have carefully observed African American song, dance, and speech, and others lauded the truth of the stage performances. Carl Wittke, who was an ex-minstrel himself, said, for example:

> Rice's impersonation of "Jim Crow," moreover, depended for its dramatic success entirely upon the performer's ability as an imitator of the voice, appearance and action of a genuine Negro character. Rice's mimicry was superb and absolutely true to life.[21]

In reality, a good many of the minstrels had not studied blacks first hand, and numerous 1830s minstrel tunes came from European sources: "Zip Coon" could be connected to two Irish songs, "Sich a Getting Up Stairs" was similar to an English Morris tune, "My Long Tail Blue" could be connected to a Scottish folk song, "Jim Crow" was very like an Irish folk tune, and "Gumbo Chaff" was virtually identical to an English piece called "Bow Wow Wow."[22]

Still, there were a number of early banjo tunes, commonly called jigs, which included a musical device called syncopation. Syncopation is the practice of accenting a beat that traditional European music would consider weak, that is, accenting offbeats, and it derives from African tradition. In describing these elements, Nathan says minstrel "banjo music proceeded to an idiom infinitely more complex in rhythm than could have originated within a predominately white cultural milieu and its nineteenth-century concepts."[23] The borrowings, that is, not only were technically sophisticated, but also came from African American music of the period. Their fragmentary appearance, however, reflects the extent to which whites were able to lift and market black material. The true fruition of this Africanist musical practice in America did not come until later when black minstrels presented their own music on the musical stage, giving us ragtime and its later development, jazz.

Dance was a major element of the minstrel show, and early white minstrels claimed to present the solo percussive dance steps performed by African Americans across the South. An article in the New York *Clipper* in 1878, for example, said that Billy Whitlock, an original member of the Virginia Minstrels, observed black dancers in the South: "Every night during his journey south, when he was not playing, he would quietly steal off to some negro hut to hear the darkeys sing and see them dance, taking with him a jug of whiskey to make them all the merrier...."[24] For most white performers, though, such study with an eye to theft was more likely to take place in northern urban areas, which were hotbeds of dance improvisation and competition, as occurred between William Henry Lane and John Diamond. Here traditional European and black forms influenced each other and then were carried into performance venues as hornpipes, clogs, and the Negro jig. The early minstrel show, however, often focused on comedy at the expense of virtuosity, and many observers said the imitations of black dance were poor. Fanny Kemble, a world-traveled actress who married a plantation owner, said of the minstrel dance that "all the contortions, and springs, and flings, and kicks, and capers you have been beguiled into accept-

Opposite page: **An 1881 program shows how many people in the show played either the tambourine or the bones, and the piece also emphasizes the kind of sentimental ballads sung by the performers. Management calls the audience's attention to the fact that the company includes one of the first and most famous of all minstrel companies, the Virginia Serenaders, founded in 1843.**

Sheet music sometimes gives us an idea of what a minstrel show looked like on stage. Although it was published in 1911, this cover still displays the semi-circular arrangement of the minstrels on the stage. It also suggests how large and extravagant the shows became over time, with literally dozens of people onstage at once.

ing ... are spurious, faint, feeble, impotent—in a word, pale Northern reproductions of that ineffable black conception."[25] It remained for black entertainers to introduce African-derived dance to broad American audiences.

AFRICAN AMERICAN MINSTRELS

African American entertainers were able to enter the minstrel show in very small numbers in the 1850s[26], but it wasn't until after emancipation that they began forming successful professional troupes. At the time, show business was one of the few professions open to blacks, along with ministering to a black church or teaching in a black school. Tom Fletcher wrote, "It was a big break when show business started, because singing and dancing was the way in which they had amused themselves for years." He also pointed out additional reasons for show business' appeal: "The objectives were, first, to make money to help educate our younger ones, and second, to try to break down the ill feeling that existed toward the colored people." Black entertainers who traveled across the South felt that ill will every day, but Fletcher, almost casually reflecting on their courage, said, "All of us who were recruited into show business went into it with our eyes wide open."[27]

Desire for respect and dignity were powerful attractions. For youngsters, seeing a professional black performer who was well dressed, confident, and able to show off his talent on stage was a compelling experience. Many children and teens yearned to be part of that glamorous world. Tom Fletcher, for example, recalled his boyhood experiences in his *100 Years of the Negro in Show Business*. In its early pages, he remembered that visiting companies allowed local boys to help with the parade, which occurred soon after the show hit town:

> Minstrel shows were my chief delight. They would put you in a red coat, give you a banner to carry or put you in front of the bass drum. Whenever a minstrel show came to town I always found an excuse to leave school in time to make the parade.... I made so many minstrel show parades that pretty soon they didn't have to show me how to turn corners and I was always put in charge of all the other boys, giving out coats, passes and everything.[28]

By the time Fletcher was fifteen, he was a member of Howard's Novelty Colored Minstrels. White minstrels in blackface had already taken the names "Negro Minstrels" and "Ethiopian Minstrels." African American minstrels were called "colored."

Among the first all-black companies to gain prominence was the Georgia Minstrels, which described itself as "The Only Pure Negro Troupe in the World."[29] It toured successfully in the Northeast in 1865–1866 and gained a reputation for talent and professionalism. Its performers were so respected that for the remainder of the nineteenth century, other black troupes chose names that incorporated the words "Georgia Minstrels." But Charles Hicks, the original manager of the Georgia Minstrels, and other founders of black companies quickly learned that racism was not easily overcome; most white theatre managers would not talk with them, much less negotiate bookings.[30] By the early 1870s, the majority of black minstrel troupes had white owner-managers and advance agents, a necessary arrangement for playing white-owned venues. Toll tells us, "Negroes had to struggle to retain ownership of any companies at all."[31] Still, it was a step up from total exclusion.

There were several other early black minstrel companies. Charles Hicks formed another black troupe and began touring it. Sam Hague, an Englishman and former minstrel dancer, took a group of ten black minstrels to Britain under the name Hague's Slave

Authentic black minstrels began to gain attention after the Civil War. Here, four black minstrels perform at Smith's Club House on Harlem Lane near New York City. Notice that they play the traditional minstrel instruments: bones, fiddle, banjo, and tambourine. From *Harper's Weekly*, April 6, 1872.

Troupe. The African American Hyer Sisters (May and Madah) toured a production that was not a minstrel show, but rather a drama called *The Princess of Orelia*. The sisters called their troupe The Hyers' Sisters Musical Company, starring Sam Lucas. Lucas soon became one of the stars of black minstrelsy. In fact, he was Tom Fletcher's father's favorite actor, and the elder Mr. Fletcher held him up as a model to young Tom.[32]

Hague had named his company with an eye to its appeal in England. Black minstrels emphasized their color—calling themselves "genuine" or "natural"—as well as their connection to the plantation, to compete effectively with white minstrels, whose imitation blackness and distance from slave culture suddenly became a liability. The Georgia Minstrels, now under new ownership with the name Brooker and Clayton Georgia Minstrels, advertised that they had been "SLAVES IN MACON, GEORGIA, who having spent their former life in Bondage" would "introduce to their patrons PLANTATION LIFE in all its phases."[33] Race at last worked in African Americans' favor, becoming an important drawing card and attracting curious audiences who had never seen blacks on stage.

A number of the early black minstrels did not use burnt cork to darken their faces as the white minstrels had. Perhaps some whites had actually assumed that the blackface minstrels were real blacks, or perhaps many northerners really knew virtually nothing about African Americans. Either way, observers often registered surprise at the range of skin color among the performers. One reviewer commented, for example, that black minstrels had all the "hues and complexions from light cream tint down to ... darkness."[34]

Later, though, blackface became common among black entertainers as they assumed the format developed by whites.

While the novelty of genuine black minstrels onstage filled theatres, audiences brought with them preconceptions that deprived the entertainers of credit. Among these was the assumption that African American ability to sing and dance was an inherent racial trait, not a talent or a practiced skill. "Being genuine Negroes," one reviewer wrote, "they indulge in reality."[35] African Americans who had struggled to gain the stage and spent long hours developing their skills received no praise for their achievements. Instead, whites regarded the performances as effortless.

On the other hand, when black minstrel companies began calling themselves "genuine" or "natural" and attracting audiences on that basis, the falsity of blackface became a negative. Black minstrels were thus able to give stiff competition to white troupes, which began branching out into more variety acts to avoid unfavorable comparisons. Although white shows maintained their traditional patterns until about 1870, by the mid-1870s they had moved away from imitations of plantation blacks toward lavish productions.[36] The big extravaganza increasingly became the rule for white companies, with performers numbering from the dozens to a hundred, all presented in lavish costumes and with expensive backdrops.

The switch to variety entertainment became evident in reviewers' columns. The *New York Times*, for example, commented favorably on a minstrel show in 1888: "there was plenty of fair singing,

Callender's Georgia Minstrels were a genuine African American company, and Billy Kersands performed with them through the 1870s. The program included skits, dance (the Essence and the Pedestal Clog), song, and a "plantation" sketch.

CALLENDER'S
Georgia Minstrels.

CHARLES CALLENDER ....Manager
R. G. LITTLE..............................Stage Manager

PROGRAMME.

PART FIRST.

Tambos } Moore.   McIntosh } Bones
        } Devonear.   Grace   }
Interlocutor—Wm. Morris.

Overture........................Callender's Georgia Minstrels
Early in the Morning..J. Grace
Sing Me the Old Songs Again..............................S Jones
Run Home, Levi...P. Devonear
As They Greet Me at the Door.............................W. Morris
Alex Stephens Lives..T. McIntosh
Are You Tired of Me, Darling...............................T. Chestnut
Don't You Hear de Bugle in de Morning...................N. Moore
Our Little Darling's Grave..................................R. G. Little

Concluding with the ludicrous finale entitled

The GINGER BLUES
Gen. (Black)man and his skilled recruits.

PART SECOND.

The DASHING BELLE
W. E. LYLE in Artistic Female Portraiture.

The Pedestal Clog
W. ALLEN, Champion of the World,
Danced on a surface 15 inches square, 4 feet high.

THE HAMTOWN STUDENTS
Morris, Jones, Devonear, Little.

The HEN CONVENTION
BOB MACK.

ESSENCE,   -   -   NEAL MOORE

The Entertainment to conclude with

Holiday on the Old Plantation

Uncle Ike Simpson.....................................W. Morris
Aunty Susan Simpson..................................J. Grace
Estella...............}   {...............W. Lyle
Phila Jane Della   } their daughters, {.........T. McIntosh
Rufus....   }   {............P. Devonear
Thad.....   } their sons   {............T. Chestnut
Nat......   }   {.......Young Kersands
Brother Joe Marcus}   {..........Neal Moore
Sam Lyons..........} Visitors   {............Dick Little
J. W. Marcus, Jr. }   {.............W. Allen
Peter Vandgrass Cotilion Band...........................Orchestra
Concluding with a Grand Tableau.

NOTICE.—Mr. Callender respectfully informs the public to beware of fraudulent "Georgia Minstrel" troupes, who are traveling on the name and fame which has cost Mr. Callender eight years of time and a large amount of capital to build up. He has no connection with any other party claiming the name. This is the only original company, and under his personal management.

DeVeny, "The Printer," Cleveland, O.

Like many traveling black shows, the Dixie Minstrels had to assemble its platforms and put up its tents whenever it arrived in a new place. Dancers and singers performed on the platform outside the main tent to preview the show and entice audience members to buy tickets.

good dancing, and much variety business done by jugglers, athletes, and performers on musical instruments by men with blackened faces and dressed in gaudy and gorgeous costumes."[37] One news item about a minstrel show even mentioned "a combination of three Japanese troupes of jugglers, balancers, and tumblers."[38] Another change was that blackface minstrels now often aimed their humor at non-black segments of society—government, women seeking the vote, various ethnic groups, and others.

Many people found the new productions to be less exciting and interesting, though, than earlier ones. Some remembered the old "negro" characters longingly, saw them as giving a center to the show, and felt that the variety format was not as satisfying. Writing in 1891, Conde Hamlin said of the new format, "The result has been a frivolous hodgepodge of specialties entertaining to the senses, but without motive enough to connect them into a symmetrical and consistent whole." He noted, "Skirt dances, Spanish dances, eccentrique dances, kangaroo dances, nautch dances, have been added to the more staple clog, jig, and wing dances." The result, Hamlin felt, was a poor quality entertainment.[39] Another writer remembered the old minstrel show songs with regret: "These songs retained the flavor of slave life, with all its pathos, its yearning, its hopelessness, its mournfulness."[40] Wittke adds, "This change in the technique of minstrel shows, together with the competition of new forms of amusement, slowly but relentlessly sapped the vitality of minstrelsy as a professional form of theatricals."[41] By this time, consumers had become so fond of the false images of minstrelsy that they had internalized them as real.[42]

Cost was another issue. The big sets, satin costumes, twenty-piece bands, and specialty performers were astronomically expensive. To pay for them, managers raised admis-

The size of the double company, eventually numbering more than 100, suggests the staggering expenses that helped destroy the minstrel show. Courtesy Library of Congress.

sion prices beyond what the market would bear, and still often faced bankruptcy. Audiences dwindled, and the newspapers of the time began to report on companies stranded on the road for lack of money to get home.[43] It was a far cry from the fortunes made on twenty-five cent admissions in the early days.

Some minstrel shows competed by hiring black performers. Primrose and West's Big Minstrels included both blacks and whites, advertising "our colossal double company" on its posters. Such troupes, however, were rarely actually integrated. White minstrels refused to share lodgings with black colleagues, and many hotels would not accept blacks, no matter their professional connections. Still, audiences wanted to see them, and in the early 1880s, they made the highest wages they would see in the nineteenth century. At last, black talent was driving a wedge into the market and making a place for itself.

Amateur Minstrels

By and large, though, the big white-dominated minstrel show was fading. Gradually, amateur minstrels doing benefits for various clubs and charitable organizations took over its patterns, its jokes, and its costuming. Newspapers carried countless small articles with titles like "A Minstrel Show at Cornell,"[44] "Minstrels in Aid of the New York Athletic Club,"[45] and "Society Women as Minstrels ... 'Black Up' and Give a Performance in

Brooklyn."[46] In the pages of the *New York Times* alone, we read of minstrel benefits for the Seventh Regiment, the Manhattan Athletic Club, the Essex County Toboggan Club, the Staten Island Athletic Club, Bowdoin College, the American Canoe Association, and dozens of others.[47] Publishers printed booklets of minstrel gags and skits for the use of amateur groups, and would-be actors and actresses could purchase minstrel makeup and wigs by mail.

Amateur minstrel shows were performed in places and circumstances that surprise us even today. For example, the crew of a British polar expedition with its ship *Discovery* frozen in at McMurdo Sound in Antarctica in 1902 amused itself with putting on a minstrel show. The show took place in the hut the crew had erected a short distance from the ship. Mike Pearson, who made a study of the event, writes:

> It was hard enough getting to the rehearsal, the guide ropes having become hidden in the snow. But even inside the hut it was "awfully cold" and Royds almost got his hands frostbitten while playing the piano. He later found that the tops of four fingers and thumb on his right hand had "gone." Yet the minstrels—"Bones," "Skins," "Sambo," *et al.*—only six days from their premiere, were in good voice, even as a blizzard began to rage and the walls shook.[48]

In February, 1867, an article in the *Illustrated London News* called attention to the amateur blackface minstrel show put on by a group of Lombard Street bank clerks at the Bethnal Green workhouse.[49] The audience was the destitute inhabitants of the place, and we can only wonder how they reacted to the "treat," replete with its class smugness and contempt for the Other. Unfortunately, the appeal of putting on blackface and enacting stereotypes did not die out until well past the middle of the twentieth century.

SUCCESSFUL BLACK COMPANIES

By the late nineteenth century, several large black companies were touring the United States. One of these was the Georgia Minstrels, which had been purchased by Jack Haverly, who renamed it "Haverly's European Minstrels," enlarged it, and took it overseas, where there were eager audiences for black minstrels. Among the company's top-notch talent were Sam Lucas, the beloved Billy Kersands, and the multi-talented James Bland.[50] In 1881 and 1882, Gustave Frohman organized the Callender's Consolidated Spectacular Colored Minstrels, by purchasing Callender's Consolidated Colored Minstrels in partnership with his brother and then purchasing Haverly's black company as well—and combining the two. Eventually, the Frohmans had to split the large troupe into smaller ones to save costs. By 1893, only three large black troupes were touring the country; they were the Hicks and Sawyer Minstrels, the Richards and Pringle Minstrels, and the McCabe and Young Minstrels. All had white managers.[51]

The big troupes facilitated the making of black stars. One of the biggest was Billy Kersands, who at $100 per week in the 1870s and 1880s was the highest paid of the genuine black minstrels.[52] Kersands was a widely known comedian as well as a brilliant dancer. His comedy routine took advantage of his large mouth, especially when he put a cup and saucer entirely inside it, or did a monologue with his mouth full of billiard balls. His act apparently made Queen Victoria laugh heartily during his performance before her.[53] Kersands was known to quip that if God had made his mouth any bigger, He would have had to move his ears.[54]

As a dancer, Kersands was an expert performer of the early black minstrel dance called the Essence of Old Virginia, or simply The Essence. The Essence was one of the

The bank clerks who in 1867 put on a show at Bethnal Green Workhouse in England called themselves the Delaware Minstrels. Even from the distant perspective of the drawing, it's clear they made sure they had the same instruments as American minstrels—the banjo, tambourine, bones, and fiddle.

earliest African American dances to be taken up by minstrels and performed on stage. Composed of sliding and scuffing steps that were neither fast nor flashy, but graceful, it eventually became known as "song and dance" or the "soft shoe," because it was danced in soft or leather shoes without taps. Ragtime composer Arthur Marshall described it by saying, "If a guy could really do it, he sometimes looked as if he was being towed around on ice skates … the performer moves forward without appearing to move his feet at all, by manipulating his toes and heels rapidly, so that his body is propelled without changing the position of his legs."[55] The modern soft shoe is a development of the Essence, and became a commonplace on the stage performed by both black and white dance stars.

James Bland, a singer and comedian, was also one of the greatest composers of the late nineteenth century. He wrote "Carry Me Back to Old Virginny," "Dem Golden Slippers," "In the Evening by the Moonlight," and perhaps as many as seven hundred other songs.[56] Starstruck after seeing a performance by white dancer George Primrose in 1874, he formed and managed the Original Black Diamonds in Boston in 1875. Over time, he became part of the Bohee Brothers minstrels, Sprague's Georgia Minstrels, and the Haverly Colored Minstrels. The latter troupe went to England, where Bland remained behind to become a star in British music halls, earning as much as $10,000 per year, a fabulous sum for the time. Many black minstrels followed this pattern, staying in foreign countries where there was less racism than in the U.S. Bland eventually returned to the U.S., where he died in 1911.[57]

PERSONAL. BILL BOY. BANNER. PRESS. LITHO. BAGGAGE. LOT. BILL BOARD. R. R. BAGGAGE

JULY
AUG.
SEP.
OCT.
NOV.
DEC.

J. W. JOHNSON'S
VIRGINIA MINSTRELS
The Show That is Different
SPECIAL COURTESY
WORLD'S BEST COLORED SHOW
Issued by _____

JAN.
FEB.
MAR.
APR.
MAY
JUNE

1 2 3 4 5 6 7 8 9 10 11 12 13 14 15 16 17
18 19 20 21 22 23 24 25 26 27 28 29 30 31

RESERVED SEAT
COUPON
ADMIT ONE

This ticket to an African American minstrel show bills the troupe as the World's Best Colored Show.

Sam Lucas began his career as a minstrel in 1869 at the age of 19. He was a singer, composer, and actor in a wide variety of roles. He played serious roles in two dramas produced by the Hyer Sisters, *Out of Bondage* and *The Underground Railroad*, both of which dramatized important stories in African American history. He also acted in the early, groundbreaking black musicals and was the first black man to star in a film of *Uncle Tom's Cabin*. James Weldon Johnson called him "The Grand Old Man of the Negro Stage."[58]

In addition to the big minstrel shows with well-known performers, there were dozens of smaller troupes traveling the South,[59] playing chiefly to a mainstay of black audiences. On occasion, companies also played to predominantly white audiences, for "colored minstrels were considered an amusing night entertainment in towns where there was no colored population" or only a very small population.[60] In touring the South, these companies endured discomforts, hardships, and dangers that today we can hardly imagine. To begin with, most of the minstrels found it necessary to wear blackface and retain the old format of the early white minstrel show. White minstrels shows abandoned much of the old structure and content when black companies gained prominence, but blacks continued using them. Toll explains:

> In the mid-1870s, as the white minstrels shifted their emphasis from portrayals of Negroes to lavish productions and general social commentary, black minstrels took an almost opposite direction, leading to a nearly total concentration on Afro-Americans and the plantation. By that time, black minstrels had clearly distinguished themselves from blackfaced whites and had established their primacy as plantation delineators.[61]

Thus blacks stepped into an established framework that limited and dictated many of their performance decisions.

Blackface makeup was commonplace among black minstrels. Fletcher writes of the Georgia Minstrels, "All the end men used burnt cork on their faces and grease paint on their lips."[62] Wittke adds, "Negro companies, it is curious to point out, almost always black up for these minstrel acts."[63] This was the custom as far back as a Civil War minstrel performance in Union-liberated Beaufort, South Carolina, given by refugees from Charleston. Despite their dark skin, "all the performers had given their faces a coating of burnt cork, in order that their resemblance to the Yankee minstrels might be in every respect complete."[64] Like these Charleston Minstrels, most later black entertainers found it necessary

The "minstrals" seem to be part of a larger traveling show, for next to their banner is another banner with another tent behind it. Several members of the company dance on a platform outside the tent to give onlookers a sense of what the show will be like, while the white barker stands at his podium with another man to entice customers to purchase tickets. The picture was probably taken around 1900. Courtesy National Afro-American Museum and Cultural Center.

to use the conventions audiences were familiar with. Brenda Dixon Gottschild sums up the irony:

> ... whites in minstrelsy used the minstrel construct as a way to have their cake and eat it, too—to have the power to be both outsider and insider in relation to Africanist life and culture. Because other performance outlets were closed to them, African Americans, on entering minstrelsy, had no choice but to step into a white-constructed mirror that distorted their reflection. Required to claim themselves as the original upon which the stereotype was modeled, they imitated the imitation. Yet they introduced genuine black presence, invention, and creativity into the genre.[65]

One of the greatest early black performers, Bert Williams, wore blackface for most of his career, even when he was appearing on Broadway. In 1921, when performing in the black hit show *Shuffle Along*, Flournoy Miller and Aubrey Lyles wore blackface.[66] The theatrical practice persisted in rural areas of the U.S. well into the 1930s and beyond.

One must ask, how did the stereotypes, especially comic skits, play to black audiences? Riis conjectures that the most repulsive skits were altered or tempered, and that images of the plantation were changed to keynote family unity and resilience.[67] Most likely, too, comedy then was the same as today. The comic lampoons himself and his audience, often without audience members taking it personally or even seeing themselves as the object of the comedy. The person satirized is never oneself, although he may be one's neighbor.

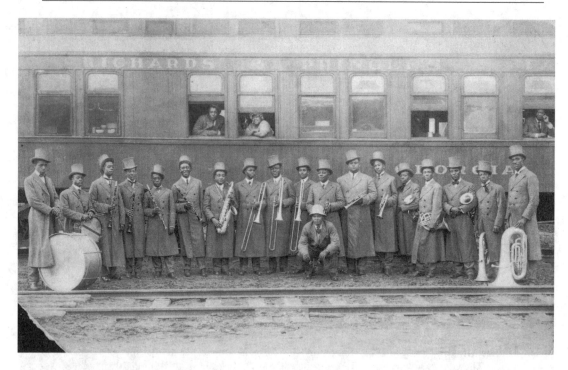

A black minstrel band poses outside its train car. A few other members of the troupe are visible in the open windows.

Ike Simond, a career minstrel, left us his reminiscences of black minstrelsy from 1865 to 1891. With it, he included some of his own comedy material, portions of which recall the old stump speeches of white minstrelsy, in which a boastful speaker, eager to impress his listeners, makes himself ridiculous by using malapropisms and made-up words. As one of Simond's stories goes, a young lady asks a plantation hand when the steamboat they're on will get to Memphis. Wanting to impress her, he says, "Well, madam, de influesence of billity am so stagnificating dat it will not stop de pommelgations of dee waters till to-morrow morning about seven o'clock."[68] Black comedy followed older formats, but softened content, still looking for laughs from the audience that was the object of its jokes.

Moreover, Simond's anecdote is much like some of the comedy of Mark Twain and other writers of the period. Consider, for example, Twain's characters the Duke and the King in *Huckleberry Finn* (1884), whose speech is just as full of ludicrous language as Ike Simond's plantation hand. During the period, there was a widespread comedic impulse at the expense of characters who were trying to make themselves appear better than their peers. The jokes poke fun at the desire to imitate classes or cultures that are perceived as more intellectual, well to do, or respected than oneself and one's neighbors.

In 1932, the *Pittsburgh Courier*, the second largest black newspaper in the country, began a campaign to remove the *Amos 'n Andy* radio show from the air. The newspaper protested the show's stereotypes, which were a throwback to the minstrel days, in a series of harsh editorials, but all to no avail. Black families continued to listen to the show, and other black newspapers ignored the *Courier*. It seemed that most African Americans wanted to support successful black entertainers, whatever their characters' voices were like. James Horton summed up the problem of black audiences by writing:

The Jubilee Minstrels show off some steps on the platform outside the tent where their show will take place. The canvas façade advertises a Cakewalk, and a few of the entertainers wear blackface. The picture probably dates to about 1910.

> There was considerable ambivalence among blacks who hungered for almost any media presentation of African-American life but were at least irresolute about this racial burlesque.... Blacks are expected to accept that which demeans them as humorous, to be a "good sport," to be "able to take a joke." Some could remain detached enough from the racial insult of "Amos 'n' Andy" to appreciate the universality of the characters.[69]

Evidently, black listeners continued to support black performances while making allowances for stereotypical material.

As they traveled across the North and South in the late 1800s and early 1900s, black troupes encountered racism that made it difficult if not impossible to get a hotel room or a meal in a white part of town. Early minstrels slept in train stations or tried to get lodgings with black families in the towns where they performed. Later companies traveled in their own train cars, and these often had hidden compartments where people could be secreted if they somehow offended a white audience member. The threat, if not the reality, of racist violence was always present.

W.C. Handy, one of the most talented American musicians and composers of the period, traveled across the South with the Mahara Minstrels for four years. His experiences tell us how brutal the life of a minstrel could be. A close friend of Handy's, trombonist Louis Wright, was lynched in Missouri. Handy's own life came close to ending just as tragically on several occasions. Cowboys in a Texas town lassoed the Mahara bandleaders during a morning parade, and Handy's refusal to play his cornet for them almost got him killed. In Orange, Texas, men sprayed the minstrels' train car with bullets just for fun as it sped by. Handy and his colleagues lay on the floor to avoid being killed. In Tennessee, he knocked a white man down to keep him from killing a fellow minstrel. Handy then hid in the train car's secret compartment until the local sheriff and his posse gave up looking for him. In Tyler, Texas, when one of the members of the company broke out in smallpox,

This traveling show still calls itself a Plantation show, despite the fact that the time is probably around 1920, long after the Civil War. Both the band members and the dancers appear ready to give pre-view performances.

the town doctor seriously suggested lynching the entire troupe as a way of controlling the disease.[70] It's no wonder many black performers left the country to live abroad.

Tom Fletcher provides a striking recollection of the atmosphere in largely white southern towns. Comparing the locals to savages, Fletcher said, "We quickly discovered that their favorite tune was 'Dixie'…. As soon as all the members of the company were on the ground we would start playing 'Dixie.'" Barely had the minstrel parade begun when the performers would hear "the old familiar cue of 'Hey, you N——-s.'" Having completed a day of parading, the company would present a concert and an evening show. "After the show that night," Fletcher continues, "all the colored people connected with the show would get together and parade down to the car. If there were no trains leaving that night we would hire an engine and get right out of town without delay."[71] The physical danger of assault and even lynching was too great for the minstrels to remain in town.

To balance these horrors, there was the welcoming applause of black or even mixed audiences. In big cities like Washington, D.C., Pittsburgh, New Orleans, and Galveston, large numbers of people came to performances.[72] The draw of Haverly's Colored Minstrels, starring Billy Kersands, in St. Louis was so great that "prejudice was half forgotten as the owners arranged for colored customers to occupy a full half the theater from the ground floor or orchestra section right up to the gallery, with whites filling the other side. In the south, a minstrel show without Billy Kersands was like a circus without elephants."[73] Blacks who became minstrels had the hope of becoming stars like Kersands and Lucas, of making good salaries, dressing well, and earning the admiration of thousands of people. In fact, when a New York promoter advertised in 1894 for forty black minstrels, two thousand people visited his office.[74] Compared to the other work available for black men

At least nine members of a minstrel company are visible on the wagon, plus a small child being rocked in the rocking chair behind the driver. The occasion seems to be a county fair where the minstrels will be one of the featured attractions.

and women, nearly all of it menial with very low pay, show business, despite its dangers, was an important opportunity.

Moreover, the black minstrel show brought authentic black cultural arts to audiences. The music offered by black minstrels was brilliantly innovative and broadly appealing, developing major genres like ragtime and jazz. Dance was another draw, including the Virginia Essence, clog, jig, and buck dance, as well as the Buck and Wing, a new hybrid dance done to a swinging rhythm, that became one of the sources of tap. The Buck and Wing combined elements from other forms—clogs, jigs, and soft shoe—along with acrobatic moves. It foreshadowed later, almost countless individualized varieties of tap, including versions of rhythm tap, flash, eccentric, and more.[75]

OTHER TRAVELING SHOWS

Black song and dance were also featured in other forms of black touring entertainment. There was more than one kind of traveling show, as Dewey "Pigment" Markham explained to interviewers Marshall and Jean Stearns:

In the old days ... show business for a colored dancer was like going through school. You started in a medicine show—that was kindergarten—where they could use a few steps if you could cut them, but almost anything would do. Then you went on up to the gilly show, which was like grade school—they wanted dancers. If you had something on the ball, you graduated to a carnival— that was high school—and you sure had to be able to dance. College level was a colored minstrel show, and as they faded out, a vaudeville circuit or even a Broadway show. Vaudeville and

MUSIC HALL
PROVIDENCE.

GRAND OPENING
BEAUTIFUL WITH DECORATIONS AND IMPROVEMENTS.
LARGE STAGE, ELEGANT NEW SCENERY

WEDNESDAY, THURSDAY, FRIDAY & SATURDAY EVENINGS,
AND SATURDAY MATINEE, OCT. 5, 6, 7, and 8, 1881.
Prices 25 and 35 Cts.   A few Reserved Seats 10 and 15 Cts. extra

C. H. SMITH'S DOUBLE MAMMOTH

UNCLE TOM'S CABIN CO.

In the Grandest Production ever given of Harriet Beecher Stowe's
immortal work, read and admired all over the world, and by
the *Clergy* and *Christian People* of *all Creeds*, who

WEEP AT THE DEATH OF EVA,
SYMPATHIZE WITH POOR UNCLE TOM,
LAUGH AT THE VAGARIES OF TOPSY,

And pay tribute to the wonderful woman who has given to the
world this great picture of Life Among the Lowly.

ATTRACTIONS WITH NO OTHER COMPANY IN THE WORLD.
FUN! LAUGHTER! TEARS!

2 FAMOUS TOPSYS. 2
2 MARKS, THE LAWYERS. 2
2 EDUCATED DONKEYS. 2
JACK AND JILL.

6 MAMMOTH TRAINED SIBERIAN BLOODHOUNDS 6
GREAT COTTON PLANTATION FESTIVAL
UNDER THE DIRECTION OF
MR. SAM LUCAS, the famous Comedian.

THE SHERWOOD SISTERS
SMITH'S COLORED TROUBADOURS,
HARPER'S FERRY JUBILEE SINGERS,
OLD TENNESSEE MINSTRELS,
THRILLING ICE SCENE, with ELIZA ESCAPING
across the Ohio River, with the savage bloodhounds in pursuit.

C. H. SMITH'S DOUBLE MAMMOTH UNCLE TOMS CABIN.

C.H. SMITH, AND HIS BLOODHOUNDS.

Opposite and above: Featuring Sam Lucas, trade card above, this production presented Mrs. Stowe's story with plenty of singing, dancing, comedy, and drama. On the reverse is a drawing of three of the six advertised Siberian bloodhounds, along with their trainer.

Broadway sometimes had the best, although a lot of great dancers never got out from under the rag, never left the tent shows.[76]

There was also the *Uncle Tom's Cabin* show, in an amazing number of variations, which presented black singing and dancing in the context of Mrs. Stowe's famous story. The *Lewiston Journal* of Lewiston, Maine, noted in 1887 that an *Uncle Tom's Cabin* show had come to town: "It consists of 18 people, comprising 14 men, 3 women, and a little girl. Its two wagons transport from place to place a tent, broad seats, and reserved chairs such as one sees in a circus. It presents that time-honored play, 'Uncle Tom's Cabin,' and little Eva's death is followed by a minstrel show...."[77] In its many forms, the "Tom" show was one of the first entertainments to place blacks on the same bill with whites, breaking a longstanding taboo against blacks and whites appearing together on the same stage.

The medicine show was a commonplace throughout nineteenth century America, passing through small towns to sell tonics, ointments, and elixirs. In his quest for profits, the medicine man needed to gather a crowd and hold it while he made his pitch, playing upon people's fears of sickness and death. Unlike more expensive professional doctors, the medicine man—who nevertheless often called himself "doctor"—often offered a product claimed to create instant cures, banish pain, and restore people from chronic illnesses, all for a small cost. Medicine show leaflets and broadsides contained testimonials, philosophy, and explanations of vague conditions like "sexual neurasthenia."[78]

In the nineteenth and early twentieth centuries, black dancers sometimes got jobs with medicine shows. The dancers' responsibility was to gather the crowd and make it comfortable while the "doctor" prepared to launch his spiel. Stars like Bert Williams,

The black band attracted an audience for the "doctor," who then made a sales pitch for his cactus juice compound.

George Walker, Ulysses "Slow Kid" Thompson, and Pigment Markham all began careers in show business by working for medicine shows.[79] Interviewed by Marshall and Jean Stearns, Thompson recalled his job with "Dr. Randolph 'Somebody.'" He said, "We hit all the dirt roads in Louisiana. We had a canvas tent in back where we dressed and a small platform out front where we danced—any step was okay—clapping our hands for accompaniment. Then the doctor went into his sales talk."[80]

Eubie Blake got a job with Dr. Frazier's Medicine Show in 1901. He played the melodeon and a small reed organ when he wasn't buck dancing on the tailgate of Frazier's wagon.[81] Pigment Markham had to take a job with a medicine show after he was stranded on the road with a carnival in Kentucky in 1921. "We just played hick towns, ol' Doc, a banjo-harmonica player, and two dancer-comedians," Markham said, "but us two dancers had a ball outshining each other."[82]

A gilly was a small traveling show that transported its few dozen people in wagons or painted trucks. Gillies, carnivals, and circuses traveled with "plantation shows" or other versions of black minstrel performances, or employed a few black dancers to do daily shows in a separate tent. There were even tiny, self-contained black shows with perhaps a dozen or fewer members who traveled on their own, finding bookings at county fairs, town halls, and churches. In virtually all of these, dancing was important. There were large vari-

The comedic entertainers in the photo collected a crowd and then shifted to a sales pitch for the "Anti-Morbific" compound, called a "cure-all." The signs explained that a woman who was thin and listless needed only to take the compound to become voluptuous and exciting.

ety shows, too, forerunners of vaudeville, as well as traveling dramatic productions that included song and dance.

One of these variety shows was Black Patti's Troubadours, led by headliner Sissieretta Jones, often called the Black Patti after the Italian opera singer Adelina Patti. Jones was a brilliant operatic singer who performed before President Harrison and at Madison Square Garden. White managers organized her company in 1895.[83] When dancer Ida Forsyne joined it in 1898, it boasted 26 performers. Their repertoire featured song and dance acts, as well as a vocal segment in which Jones herself starred with her cast behind her as a chorus. There was also a buck-dancing contest in every town, a fact stated on the poster for the show. The Troubadours was one of many black shows that continued the old tradition of allowing outsiders to show off their talent through a dance competition.

Jones had such a beautiful voice and used it so powerfully that she drew large audiences, white as well as black, wherever she went, and served as an important representative of black artists to American society. Of her, Riis writes, "The Black Patti Troubadours shows exploited the common devices of black musical theater of their day—African themes, vaudeville specialties, and ragtime songs—and were blessed with a dazzling star and several talented comedians."[84] Perhaps even more important, Black Patti's success allowed her to employ a number of black entertainers for two decades before her show disbanded in 1916. Among these were stars like Ernest Hogan, Ida Forsyne, Bob Cole, Aida Overton Walker, and the legendary buck dancer King Rastus Brown.

In Old Kentucky was a traveling dramatic production that combined white actors and actresses with black musicians and dancers. As Stearns points out, there was a "flimsy plot about horse racing and a black horse named Queen Bess, who wins the Derby."[85] The band was made up of young boys, frequently referred to as "The Famous Pickaninny Band." Tom Fletcher, who was a member of the band as a young boy, writes, "Our big scene was in the second act, down by the stable of Queen Bess, the horse that was a star in the play. This scene was where we did our band playing, singing and dancing."[86] The latter included buck dancing as well as sand dancing—a type of dance that depended in part for its effect on the sound produced by the sand the dancer spread on the floor.

Fletcher says the company always began its tour in New York City with an opening performance at the Academy of Music and then "would take to the road." He remembers, "We would play all kinds of towns and cities throughout the country and the kids, seeing and hearing us, would often get the inspiration to take up a musical career."[87]

The company's performance included a dance contest, and among the contestants were the young Bill Robinson and 16-year-old Willie Covan, who later starred in the dance team The Four Covans. In recounting his experience in the contest, Covan said, "So I came jumping out with a Wing, a Grab Off, and a Roll ... and managed to get in a lot of stuff before my time ran out." His intense performance won the prize, and the audience carried him out on their shoulders.[88] After that, Covan's name was known throughout black show business.

The young band was one of the best in the nation. "Our big hobby was," Fletcher remembers, "whenever we played the same town with a company that had a band, to get right behind their band and run them off the streets." This was fun for the boys until the tables were turned on them by the band of *Darkest America*, a traveling black show organized by Al G. Field.[89]

Sissieretta Jones became widely known as the Black Patti. Her company, Black Patti's Troubadours, was a major attraction wherever it traveled. The performances typically included Black Patti's operatic performances of superb quality. Courtesy Library of Congress.

In its early days, the minstrel show had been a man's world, but by the late nineteenth century both women and children had made places for themselves in a broad variety of traveling shows. The children, sometimes called "picks"—a shorthand for "pickaninnies," never failed to draw a positive response from audiences with their singing and dancing. So effective were they, in fact, that many white stars began to travel with picks.

Women transformed the all-male club of minstrelsy. Sam T. Jack's Creole Show, formed at the end of the nineteenth century, included women as performers and even had a woman master of ceremonies. Women made their biggest impact in the dance of the black minstrel show, especially by taking part in a dance called the Cakewalk. The Cakewalk was a plantation dance that took America by storm around the late nineteenth century. It was basically a strut, with shoulders thrown back, head held high, torso in a backward sway, and feet kicking forward. Versions of the Cakewalk had been performed during the

This show poster for *In Old Kentucky* features the famous Pickaninny Band. Courtesy Library of Congress.

slavery era as competition dances, sometimes called Walk the Chalk Line, and sometimes executed with a bucket of water on the dancer's head. The prize was traditionally a cake— hence the name Cakewalk. Shephard Edmonds and other ex-slaves later explained that the dance was a really a satiric pantomime of pretentious white manners, underlining the fact that performance satire can work in more than one direction. The water carrying, the line format, the competition, and the pantomime all marked the dance as African-derived.

When the dance became part of the minstrel show, it was first presented as comic, danced by white men in blackface whose partners were men in drag. At that point, the form was the curious product of white men imitating black men and women who had been imitating supercilious whites. In late minstrelsy, however, black dancers performed the Cakewalk in elegant dress with beautiful women as partners, stepping to ragtime music, often as a line dance. In this form, the dance became a staple of the stage. Early black musicals popularized the dance among mainstream audiences and carried it overseas to European audiences. Moreover, like many other black dances, the Cakewalk lasted a long, long time. Some African Americans remember Cakewalking at school or community events in the fifties.

CONCLUSION

Black entertainers overcame the stereotypes put in place by the exclusive world of white minstrels. Despite the searing experiences of racism encountered in small towns across the United States, African Americans remained in show business and gradually changed it to display their talents and communicate with their audiences. At the end of the nineteenth century, blacks were onstage everywhere across America—in minstrel shows, medicine shows, *Uncle Tom's Cabin* productions, other kinds of dramatic productions, carnivals and circuses, and other formats small and large. Performers brought with them their dances—jigs, buck dancing, sand dancing, Buck and Wing, and the Cakewalk. Through their improvisation and originality, they would in the next three decades introduce many more dances that would fundamentally change the way the nation moved to music.

6

Black Broadway

At the turn of the century, African Americans were suffering from discrimination, disenfranchisement, violence, and harsh poverty. Lynchings were occurring across the South as terrorist groups took away many of the rights southern blacks had been granted after Emancipation. Throughout the country, black Americans were excluded from most labor unions, professions, equal educational opportunities, and good housing. But in spite of the indignities and brutalities endured by African Americans, their arts blossomed. At the same time mainstream society retained negative stereotypes of black life, many whites embraced black arts, especially music and dance.

By 1900, black minstrelsy and variety entertainment had produced seasoned performers who would break new ground in musical theatre in New York City. Over the next three decades, leading figures such as Bert Williams, George Walker, Ernest Hogan, Bob Cole, Noble Sissle, Eubie Blake, Florence Mills, Aida Overton Walker, Flournoy Miller, Aubrey Lyles, and others would bring black-written and black-directed shows with all-black casts to large Broadway audiences. The most important of these exciting musicals and revues opened in New York, but many of them also toured the country, and some crossed the ocean to earn acclaim in England and Europe as well. Sheet music for their hit songs reached far and wide, bringing the new ragtime and jazz rhythms to parlors and bandstands in towns in every state and a number of foreign countries. People everywhere whistled the tunes and learned the dances the shows introduced.

The dances included moves that went back to the plantation and Africa. Black entertainers continuously revised and polished old material for stage routines, which was nevertheless new to mainstream audiences. The Reel, Cotillion, Waltz, Polka, and Schottische faded in popularity as the Cakewalk, Shimmy, Charleston, and Black Bottom leaped across the footlights to become all the rage among ordinary people. The dance forms not only crossed the color line to become national and international crazes, but also fundamentally changed the way Americans moved in the ballroom, in nightclubs, and at the parties and gatherings of friends. These dances also withstood a serious backlash from traditional dance instructors and conservative arbiters of taste. Jazzy dance movement was here to stay, bringing along African characteristics like syncopated rhythm, bent knees and torso, and hip and shoulder movement. Furthermore, by the 1920s, freer dance movement had influenced clothing, and shorter dresses with fringe and beading gleamed in the new electric light as couples showed off their style.

But when Africanist dance was carried into mainstream venues, some of its characteristics were changed as well. Couples now executed dances that once had been communally performed by groups. Steps that continued to be shaped and reshaped through improvisation in the black community now were snapped into a fixed format in the hands of white dance instructors and dance book writers. Energetic, swinging, hip-moving dances were "refined" for the white ballroom, toned down, and homogenized. Still, the transition

An old snapshot captures the "Fairy Shimmie Dancers" booth at an amusement park, with a roller coaster visible in the background, probably during the late teens or early twenties.

was real. America and Europe were embracing Africanist dance, and the flow of new forms based on the African aesthetic has never stopped.

Tap dance, a lighter and higher version of the old buck dance, blossomed into countless variations onstage, through the creativity of stars like Bill Robinson, Eddie Rector, Toots Davis, Johnny Nit, Charley Davis, Tommy Woods, Willie Covan, and others. Professional tap dancers developed new forms while simultaneously educating their audiences, teaching them to understand and appreciate tap. Enchanted amateurs consumed a broad range of how-to books like *Home Lessons in Tap Dancing, Tap Dancing in 12 Easy Lessons,* and *Tip Top Tapping.*[1] The diagrams and drawings in these books showed just how much American dance posture had changed. Gone was the sky-oriented vertical posture of the European jig, and here to stay was a curved, supple stance infused with both energy and control.

During these early decades of the twentieth century, African American entertainers loosened the grip of old theatrical stereotypes. Despite the lingering of predictable story elements and racist vocabulary in the shows, the relationship between black entertainers and their audiences became more direct and less mediated by white control. The white minstrels who claimed to present black culture were diminishing. Slowly, the old plantation-style stage dress vanished as well, and black entertainers appeared in elegant evening wear or costumes similar to those worn by white performers. Although some major figures such as Bert Williams, Flournoy Miller, and Aubrey Lyles continued to wear blackface, many of their colleagues discarded it. Black shows gained space in mainstream theatres and played to white or mixed audiences.

But the expectations of many reviewers remained a major challenge. These reviewers seemed to think black dance should reflect a stereotypical plantation culture and racial characteristics that existed primarily in the minds of white audiences, implanted there by

Top: The weekly Cakewalk contest at Madison Square Garden. The Cakewalk seen here in 1892 is danced entirely by African Americans, with white judges. *Bottom:* In this postcard, postmarked 1909, we see a comic Cakewalk staged by the Elks in Baltimore, Maryland. Several men play the female role in the dance, appearing in dresses and women's hats. The Master of Ceremonies holds the cake to be given as prize. The comedy, which could be off-color, harks back to earlier days of minstrelsy, when the shows drew male audiences. There are no women to be seen here.

minstrel shows, and that the reviewers could not even articulate. It would be decades before most professional critics considered the work of black dancers on its own merits.

Furthermore, other kinds of racial discrimination continued. On the road, African Americans throughout the first half of the twentieth century could not stay in most first-class hotels or eat in most downtown restaurants. Black composers and lyricists were typically paid poorly and were subject to being cheated by mainstream music publishers. Black choreographers who had powerful shaping influence on shows often received less money and public credit than white artistic directors who had small influence and yet nevertheless received substantial compensation and major billing. Finally, financing was hard to find, notwithstanding the proven success of black shows.

Despite these bitter realities, it was during this period that black musicals succeeded in gaining audiences worldwide and permanently changing the way we dance. Black entertainers and managers of the time exuded hope and excitement. Barriers were coming down, and dreams were being realized. American theatre was in the process of being incalculably enriched by black creativity, and by the treasure trove of African cultural arts it brought. Let's see how it happened.

BEGINNINGS

Bob Cole was an African American minstrel performer who had been part of *The Creole Show* (organized in 1890) before he joined Worth's Museum All-Star Stock Company and then Black Patti's Troubadours. Cole, a multi-talented writer-composer-actor, wrote sketches and skits for both the Stock Company and the Troubadours.[2] For the latter, he created one called "At Jolly Coon-ey Island." The language of his title raised few eyebrows at the time. It simply reflected the generally racist vocabulary black entertainers had to accept and work with in order to draw audiences. After Cole left the Troubadours, he and Billy Johnson expanded the skit into a full-length musical called *A Trip to Coontown*, which was first performed in South Amboy, New Jersey, in September, 1897. The show then toured successfully for three years, returning periodically to New York to play in successively better theatres, including the Casino Roof and the Grand Opera House.[3]

Coontown owed its success to its seasoned players, most of whom had learned their art in minstrel shows—Bob Cole, Billy Johnson, and Sam Lucas, and Mamie Flowers, among others. Minstrel shows had traditionally excluded women, but *A Trip to Coontown* included them. Both *The Creole Show* and Black Patti's Troubadours had put women onstage, so Cole was in a position to know how positively audiences could respond to them. One critic called the female dancing in *Coontown* "pretty and vivacious,"[4] and we can imagine its effect on audiences who once had been used to all-male minstrel performances. Cole also had engaged singer-actor Lloyd Gibbs, and later, Sam Lucas for their superb voices and stage experience, and they were instrumental in making some of the show tunes into hit songs.[5] *Coontown*, the first black-written, produced, and performed musical comedy in New York City, was a triumph.

It was quickly followed by another black musical called *Clorindy, or the Origin of the Cakewalk*. The Cakewalk had been seen on the plantation for generations and had been a comic dance in minstrelsy, performed by white men in blackface. Male couples paraded across the stage, each including a man dressed as a woman and casting sly looks at the audience, who usually roared with laughter. In contrast, the *Clorindy* cast interpreted the Cakewalk as an elegant dance, with well-dressed men and beautiful women forming graceful couples and moving to ragtime music. The music was written by Will Marion Cook, a classically trained composer and violinist who had studied in Europe and also had an understanding of black musical forms. Constance Hill notes that his music was "the product of an unprecedented borrowing and blending of melodic and harmonic complexities, which combined syncopation (derived from Africa) and melodic chromatism (derived from Europe)."[6]

Cook had planned the show around comedy dance team Bert Williams and George Walker, who were at that time performing the Cakewalk at Koster and Bial's music hall—and seeing it catch on among members of their white audiences. Eventually, however, Williams and Walker were unable to appear in *Clorindy*, and Cook got veteran performer Ernest Hogan take the lead role and to help train the dancers. Cook knew what he was doing—some old-timers of show business said that Hogan was the best dancer-comedian of all time.[7]

The ragtime music was sophisticated, syncopated, and very danceable. Morgan and Barlow explain "ragging" as a way of making traditional European music more complex so as to be more satisfying to black listeners:

> The roots of ragtime can be traced back to the practice of "ragging" European dance music, a technique developed by slave musicians in the antebellum South. Playing banjos, fiddles, and an assortment of homemade rhythm makers in small ensembles, they would overlay the basic rhythmic and/or melodic structures of European songs with alternative rhythmic schemes. This was accomplished by two or more musicians playing the competing rhythmic patterns simultaneously, or by one musician on a string instrument playing a separate pattern with each hand or with different finger and thumb combinations to achieve the desired cross rhythms. This polyrhythmic principle has always been prominently featured in the drumming patterns of West Africa, and the practice indeed may have come from there.[8]

Ragtime music, whose most famous composer was Scott Joplin, had already been brought to full blossom in southern cities like New Orleans and Memphis.

Clorindy opened in the summer of 1898, when New York theatres were hot and stuffy. In the days before air conditioning, many wealthy people left the city during the hot season for vacation homes in the Pennsylvania mountains. With fewer customers in town, there was less competition for theatrical space. Because they were open and breezy, rooftops became popular sites for productions of various sorts. The Casino Theatre Roof Garden was one of the most glamorous, and Cook was able to convince the manager and conductor there to give his show a chance. The first performance began one evening at about 11 pm. Hogan immediately discarded the libretto Cook had worked so hard to persuade the famous black poet Paul Laurence Dunbar to write. "A lot of dialogue on an uncovered roof garden after eleven p.m. would have been impossible," Cook later remembered. The decision apparently did not harm the performance, for Cook said, "When I entered the orchestra pit, there were only about fifty people on the Roof. When we finished the opening chorus, the house was packed to suffocation." He added, "My chorus sang like Russians, dancing meanwhile like Negroes, and cakewalking like angels, black angels!"[9] Hogan's song "Who Dat Say Chicken in Dis Crowd" got ten encores. The *New York Times* called the performance "sensational,"[10] and Cook exulted that the old days of minstrelsy and exclusion were over. The show continued at the Casino throughout the summer and even toured briefly with Williams and Walker in lead roles. For black performers, it was a magical moment in time.

At the time, musicals often went forward without scripts, or with scripts whose plots held the show together in only the loosest fashion. Actors took the stage and ad libbed

This drawing of a Cakewalk competition appeared in *Frank Leslie's Illustrated Newspaper* (December 31, 1870). The cakes are visible to the right of the three contestants. If the drawing is accurate, the Cakewalk changed somewhat later in the century. By 1900, dancers were performing it with shoulders in an exaggerated backward sway, a posture not seen here.

many of their lines to move the story forward to the next song or dance routine.[11] The songs and dances were the key elements, and in *Clorindy* they were memorable. "Darktown is Out Tonight" became a hit, even though the sheet music credited "Will Marion" rather than "Will Marion Cook." The way the *Clorindy* players sang and danced at the same time riveted audiences and was a first for American musical theatre.[12] The show's success was not lost on other theatre managers. The Madison Square Roof Garden and Koster and Bial's Music Hall signed up more black acts that summer and the next, including Charles Johnson and Dora Dean, a black cakewalk duo.[13]

As a result of both Williams and Walker's stage performance and Cook and Hogan's musical, the Cakewalk swept across the city and then the country, quickly crossing the color barrier into the mainstream market. Song sheets began to feature drawings of whites doing the dance. Hundreds of Cakewalk competitions became popular across the country, including one at Madison Square Garden and another at Coney Island, each with substantial cash prizes.[14] Tom Fletcher, who often entertained in the homes of the wealthy, was engaged by Mr. and Mrs. William Vanderbilt to teach them the dance.[15] Years later, Fletcher mused about the Cakewalk, "From the plantation it moved to be taught to and danced by everyone in the mansions of the Four Hundred and the palaces of the royal families."[16]

The new dance fad had its naysayers, who appeared both appalled by the dance's African origins and convinced that it led to moral decline. The *New York World*, for exam-

James Smith and the beautiful Marie Sharp appear on this sheet music. Today, we may find the language of the title offensive, but we must remember that all the words in *Clorindy*—script, lyrics, and titles—were written in collaboration by black poet Paul Laurence Dunbar and black composer Will Marion Cook, two of the most brilliant men of their time. We must assume they chose their words deliberately to be consistent with the usage of their era and, most importantly, to find a market for their work.

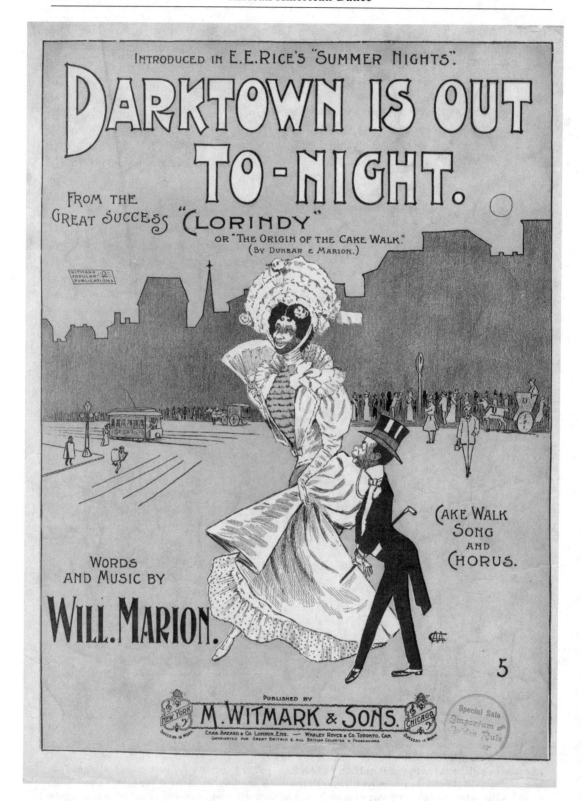

"Darktown is Out Tonight" was one of the hits of *Clorindy*.

ple, depicted the decadence of insurance heir James Hazen Hyde's 1905 costume ball in a cartoon that showed him in a high stepping Cakewalk with a drunken, scantily clad partner.[17] Some misunderstood the history of the dance. As late as 1913, Lady Middleton wrote to the *New York Times*, "We know the cakewalk, which I have seen Negroes dance, was the attempt of colored folk to represent the grand and stately menuet de la cour."[18] She apparently did not know the Cakewalk had actually begun in derision of people like herself. Furthermore, the controversy over African American dances was only getting started. For the next several decades, people who claimed to represent decency would condemn black dances and argue that they undermined morality. In the same article that quoted Lady Middleton's letter, for example, another writer who called herself Peeress commented on the new dances by calling them "the various horrors of American and South American negroid origin."

Abbie Mitchell, born in 1884, was only fourteen when she starred in Will Marion Cook's production *Clorindy, or the Origin of the Cakewalk*. A year later, she and Cook were married.

Two of the Cakewalk's primary exponents were Bert Williams and George Walker, whose 1898 run at Koster and Bial's Music Hall had lasted for forty weeks. They then produced and starred in *The Policy Players* (1899) and got it booked into Koster and Bial's after opening at the Star Theatre. This they followed with *The Sons of Ham* (1900), which toured for two seasons and garnered bookings at the Grand Opera House and Hurtig and Seamon's Music Hall.[19] Both shows were respectable efforts by the young dancer-comedians, and both provided good vehicles for their talent. Aida Overton Walker appeared with them in both, having married Walker in 1899 and transformed the Williams and Walker duo into a trio. The handsome Walkers could perform an elegant Cakewalk, while Williams provided contrast with an ungainly, comic dance that audiences loved. What the three did next was even better.

At the time this picture was published (January 5, 1899), the Cakewalk was just beginning to cross the color line to become a mainstream dance form. The main title is "Close Competition at the Cakewalk," and it describes the situation of the elegantly dressed African Americans demonstrating the dance. The sub-title is "A Popular Diversion of the Colored People, in which Many White Persons Manifest Great Interest," and it suggests that the Cakewalk is no longer always an excuse for buffoonery on the minstrel stage, but rather is now being seen as a serious dance form and being taken up throughout the country.

A DECADE OF SHOWS

In Dahomey (1902) was a major hit musical created by Williams and Walker, who starred in the show with Aida Overton Walker. Its origins lie partly in the early years of Williams and Walker's friendship. They met in San Francisco in 1893, where they decided to put together a vaudeville act, for which they earned $14 per week, billing themselves as "Two Real Coons."[20] They also worked at the Mid-Winter Exposition in Golden Gate Park, in 1894, in an exhibit of a Dahomey village, which had been created to give spectators an idea of life in Africa. George Walker reported that the Africans "were late in arriving in time for the opening of the Fair, and Afro-Americans were employed and exhibited ... Williams and Walker were among the sham Dahomians."[21]

After the real Africans arrived, the American pair visited them and were impressed with them. Walker remembered:

> We were not long in deciding that if we reached the point of having a show of our own, we would delineate and feature native African characters as far as we could, and still remain American, and make our acting interesting and entertaining to American audiences.
> Many of the themes from which some of our best lyrics have been written are purely African. We were the first to introduce the Americanized African songs: for instance, "My Zulu Babe," "My Castle on the Nile," "My Dahomian Queen." From the time we commenced to feature such songs, not only the popularity of Williams and Walker, but that of the colored performer in general has been on the increase.[22]

An example in point was their third musical, *In Dahomey*, set in Africa.[23]

In this colorful postcard, half a dozen couples perform the latest version of the Cakewalk, with shoulders thrown back and feet thrusting forward.

It got off to a good start with a road show version. By February, 1903, the show had toured for seven months and was playing at a major Broadway venue, the New York Theatre, between Forty-Fourth and Forty-Fifth on Broadway. It was the first time a black musical comedy had played an important Broadway venue to white audiences.[24] As Woll noted, "the only blacks on the main floor of the house were James Vaughn, the conductor, and the ushers."[25] The show received good reviews, partly because of Williams' irresistible comedy, in which he enacted a down-on-his-luck, sad faced character with Walker, a well-dressed dandy on and off the stage, as his straight man.[26]

In April, 1903, the cast departed for a tour of England.[27] As Jeffrey Green points out, "It was the first time British audiences would have ever seen a musical with an all-black cast."[28] There, reviewers liked the production, in spite of the fact it had no Cakewalk and its plot was so loose as to be incomprehensible to audiences. The *Daily Mail* commented, "What it is about we are unable … to understand." The *St. James Gazette* said, "Musical comedy is commonly not conspicuous for … well-proportioned plot, but the wildly inconsequential abruptness of the way in which there was suddenly no more of 'In Dahomey' about 11 p.m. on Saturday had to be seen to be believed."[29] British audiences were unfamiliar with the loose, ad-libbed way the actors set up the story, and had little experience with black comedy on stage. Notwithstanding these difficulties, the show was musically exciting and included infectious comedy. By May 23, the Cakewalk had been inserted because of "the number of letters received by the management requesting its introduction."[30] Soon the Cakewalk was a featured attraction, and some of *In Dahomey*'s publicity called attention to the dance.

Curious Brits attended the show in droves and loved its American slang along with

The British magazine *Black and White Budget* offered these pictures in its May 30, 1903 issue in a brief piece about *In Dahomey*. In the lower picture, we see George Walker and Aida Overton Walker Cakewalking with Bert Williams, who appears in blackface. Like many of his colleagues, Williams chose to wear blackface onstage, more evidence of the corrosive racism that shaped the careers of black entertainers.

In honor of the upcoming performance of the musical at the Theatre Royal, Bradford, on December 5, 1904, this advertising postcard displayed a giant cake topped with Cakewalkers from the show.

its unforgettable music and dance. The production became so popular in London that it attracted the attention of the aristocracy, and in June the company was summoned to Buckingham Palace to perform for the ninth birthday of the Prince of Wales. The Cakewalk was a favorite part of the show ("the King being one of the first to recognize its merits"[31]), and as a result the children of the royal family were seen Cakewalking on the palace lawn, all glowingly reported by the British press. Partly as a result of this incident, the Cakewalk became popular in Europe.

After he and other cast members met the King and Queen of England, George Walker said, "We were treated royally. That is the only word for it. We had champagne from the Royal cellar and strawberries and cream from the Royal garden. The Queen was perfectly lovely, and the King was as jolly as he could be...."[32] It was a heady experience for the young actor-dancers. After a seven-month run in London, the show toured other parts of England, and the cast gave performances in Scotland. When the cast returned to the U.S. in August, 1904, the show began a forty-week road trip across the U.S. and managers dispatched a second company for more travel in Britain.

Williams and Walker began work right away on an even more ambitious undertaking, *Abyssinia* (1905), again set in Africa. It could only be described as an extravaganza, with a cast of one hundred, both mock and real animals onstage, an elaborate set including a manmade waterfall, and a large number of songs. Unfortunately, none of these novelties saved it from relative failure. Although positively reviewed, it ran for only thirty performances. Four road companies were assembled to take the show to the hinterlands and help defray some of the enormous expense of putting the production together.

Bandanna Land (1908) was more successful. It also had a large cast, led by Williams and the Walkers, along with the brilliant singer Abbie Mitchell, who sang "Red, Red Rose." Williams performed his famous poker routine and sang "Nobody," a piece that was to become his trademark. Large white audiences attended during the run in New York, and a troupe of nearly one hundred took it on the road. In stereotypical fashion, a Cincinnati reviewer complimented the players for being "natural singers and comedians," adding a statement that would often be echoed by commentators on black shows: there was an exuberance and joy in the singing and dancing that white shows could not equal.[33]

Other shows during the period included Ernest Hogan's *Rufus Rastus* (1905) and *Oyster Man* (1907), as well as Cole and Johnson's *Shoo Fly Regiment* (1906), which toured in Ohio and Pennsylvania in addition to a brief run in New York, and *Red Moon* (1908), which presented a storyline about both African American and Native American characters.[34] *Red Moon* closed because of poor bookings on the road, and because Cole and Johnson could make much, much better money in Vaudeville. All these productions drew attention and appreciation to black singing, acting, and dancing.

In 1911, J. Leubrie Hill—a former member of the *Red Moon* cast—presented a skit called *My Friend from Dixie* in a Brooklyn theatre. It did not make a particularly strong showing. Two years later, Hill brought a new version of the skit, now called *My Friend from Kentucky,* to a Harlem theatre as part of a show called *Darktown Follies*. The brilliant song and dance in the show made it a major attraction in the New York theatre season. Riis says of the piece, "its dynamism was strong enough to draw white Broadway theater patrons to Harlem's Lafayette Theatre in droves, the first show to accomplish that feat."[35] Like *Red Moon* before it and *Shuffle Along* after it, *Darktown Follies* also included a serious love story about black characters, a plot element that many people had previously assumed white audiences would not accept.

Several new dances in the show were especially exciting, including two tap acts. Eddie

"MY DAHOMIAN QUEEN."
MISS MATTIE EDWARDS.

"A DAHOMIAN DAMSEL"
MISS LIZZIE AVERY.

"THE QUEEN OF THE CAKEWALK"
MISS AIDA OVERTON WALKER.

These three postcards reflect the public's admiration for the beautiful leading ladies of *In Dahomey*—
Aida Overton Walker, Mattie Edwards, and Lizzie Avery. Here and abroad, the musical ran for
more than a thousand performances.

Rector presented a "smooth military routine" in which he tapped elegantly across the stage. Toots Davis demonstrated two flashy tap steps called Over the Top and Through the Trenches.

Black Cakewalkers march around the outside of a candy tin. The dance was so popular that it was used in advertising to draw attention to a wide range of products.

Over the Top, the Stearnses tell us, "consists roughly of a figure-eight pattern in which the dancer jumps up on one leg and brings the other around and forward beneath it with an almost self-tripping effect...." Through the Trenches "is a more or less stationary running step," with the dancer "bending at the waist with arms flailing as the outer sides of the feet scrape alternately from front to back."[36]

Then there was the Texas Tommy, which was both a performance and a social dance. We can trace a sketchy history for it. A black dancer named Johnny Peters had brought it up from the South to San Francisco where it became popular at Lou Purcell's, a cabaret with black entertainment but a whites-only audience. Peters then traveled to New York, where he danced the Texas Tommy with Ethel Williams at Bustanoby's cabaret on 39th Street in 1912, the year before both joined *Darktown Follies*.[37] The Texas Tommy was a source of the Lindy Hop and, according to the Stearnses, "the earliest example we have found in the vernacular of a couple-dance incorporating, as did the Lindy fifteen or more years later, the breakaway, or the temporary and energetic separating of partners—a distinctly unwaltzlike and non-European maneuver."[38] Little or no visual documentation of the black version of the dance has survived, unless what we see in a short Edison Mutoscope recording from 1902 is an early version of the Texas Tommy.[39] In this moving film, called "A 'Tough' Dance," a couple perform a breakaway, moving swiftly from a closed couple position to an open one. Although there is no sound, there is a faintly discernible hop in the step as the partners move across the floor. The violence in the performance (one partner slaps the other) and the shabby clothes they wear seem intended to indicate lower-class origins for the dance, perhaps a racist signal that it is African American.

Another new dance in the show was Ballin' the Jack, whose name came from railroad slang. "Jack" is a black name for locomotive. "Ballin'" comes from the expression "high ballin'," the signal to start the train moving. "Ballin' the Jack" thus means powering up and moving fast. The dance is explained in the words to the song "Ballin the Jack":

> First you put your two knees close up tight,
> Then you sway 'em to the left, then you sway 'em to the right,
> Step around the floor kind of nice and light,
> Then you twis' around and twis' around with all your might,
> Stretch your lovin' arms straight out in space
> Then you do the Eagle Rock with style and grace
> Swing your foot way 'round then bring it back,
> Now that's what I call "Ballin' the Jack...."[40]

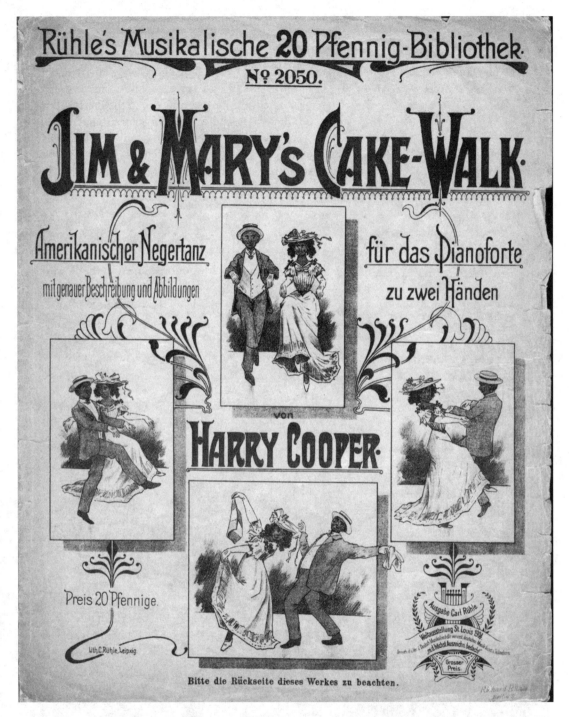

After *In Dahomey*, Cakewalk sheet music began to appear across Europe. This German version from 1904 retains an English title.

"Do the Eagle Rock" apparently meant raising and stretching out one's arms as one danced. Ethel Williams Balled the Jack at the end of Act 2, when the cast did a circle dance that the audience loved. "For the Circle Dance," the Stearnses write, "the entire company formed an endless chain, dancing across the stage and off on one end, then around behind the curtain and back on stage at the other end—circling continuously, snapping fingers

Abbie Mitchell starred in the show *Bandanna Land* along with Williams and Walker, whose pictures appear at the bottom of this sheet music.

This sheet music for the famous song from *Darktown Follies* credits J. Leubrie Hill, but features white dancers.

with a 'tango jiggle,' a 'moochee … slide,' and a 'Texas Tommy wiggle'"—all the while singing Hill's catchy tune, "At the Ball, That's All."[41]—the entire company, that is, except Ethel Williams, who did a comic version of Ballin' the Jack, much to the audience's delight.

The circle dance, with its compelling rhythms and the added zest of Williams' comedy, was the hit of the show. Ironically, however, it was *too* good. Florenz Ziegfeld went

HARRY   STELLA
WEBER AND JOHNSON
DE LUXE PEERS OF ALL
TEXAS TOMMY DANCERS
A SENSATION AT THE
Portola-Louvre Restaurant
POWELL AND MARKET STS.   SAN FRANCISCO, CAL.
HERBERT MEYERFELD, MANAGER

This 1911 postcard shows two elegantly dressed white dancers. The Texas Tommy, introduced to San Francisco in a cabaret on the Barbary Coast by a black dancer, quickly crossed the color line into white circles.

up to Harlem and purchased the song and the dance combination for his own show, the *Ziegfeld Follies*, which at the time was playing on the roof of the New York Theater. Nevertheless, New Yorkers had learned the way to Harlem and had thrilled to the demonstrations of African American dancing. In years to come, Harlem would be a beacon for many white New Yorkers interested in African American musicians and dancers.

After this decade of achievement, black Broadway—the realization of the dreams of so many performers, writers, and composers—lost momentum. One reason was the sudden death of its leading lights. George Walker, Bob Cole, and Ernest Hogan were all dead by 1911. Aida Overton Walker died in 1914. Bert Williams, devastated by the loss of his long-time friend and partner, never created another Broadway show. Instead, he chose to accept a lucrative offer from Ziegfeld Follies, in whose shows he made more money per year than the president of the United States. Black theatre found itself without its best writer-directors as well as some of its finest comedians and dancers.

Another, murkier factor was racism. Massive migration of southern blacks into major northern urban areas like New York and Chicago in the first two decades of the twentieth century had strained race relations to the breaking point. Predominantly white neighborhoods that had previously contained black families suddenly no longer welcomed black residents. Instead, blacks were isolated in their own neighborhoods, often with substandard housing for which they paid high prices. Noble Sissle, for example, grew up near the turn of the century in Indianapolis where his family had white neighbors. Kimball and Bolcom comment, "American cities were more integrated then.... It would be twenty years before the great influx of Negroes from the South would result in the huge ghettos of today."[42] In Cleveland, the isolation of the black population into separate neighborhoods played itself out between 1910 and 1920.[43] As the cities became overcrowded and people competed for jobs, there were racial tensions. When black boxer Jack Johnson won the fights in 1908 and 1910 that gave him the heavyweight championship and allowed him to keep it, there was joy among African Americans and a backlash of violence against them across the southern states. Even in the North, there was widespread resentment of Johnson's openly sexual relationships with white women. During the same period, blackface minstrelsy regained energy and African American theatrical progress stalled. It was not until after World War I that the doors of Broadway began to open again.

Jazz

The jazz age arose in the energy, optimism, and excitement of the 1920s. The Great War was over, and people turned away from bleak loss to seek amusement and self-expression. Many African Americans had left a starved, sharecropper existence in the South and migrated to the North, where they hoped to find a better life. Fueled by their creativity, the Harlem Renaissance was an outpouring of artistic expression by black artists, writers, and musicians throughout the 1920s.[44] At the center of this energy, Harlem was a beacon, not only for migrating blacks, but also for whites looking for entertainment. They found it at the Cotton Club, Connie's Inn, Small's Paradise, and other nightclubs

Shimmy Pin-Back Button

with black floorshows. Ironically, some of the clubs, especially the famous Cotton Club, were segregated, catering to an all-white clientele and excluding blacks as customers.

As the jazz composition "Take the 'A' Train"[45] pointed out, New Yorkers from white neighborhoods made nightly visits to black clubs and dance halls, "slumming" to enjoy the dance and music to be found there. Opening in 1923, the Cotton Club offered only the finest of this entertainment and gradually became a mecca for aficionados of black cultural arts. Duke Ellington's orchestra played there and broadcast its music via radio, allowing people across the country to be part of the Cotton Club audience. Through recordings and sheet music, as well as touring shows, an international audience also enjoyed the music and dance.

Jazz was the pulse of this experience. Based on African musical tradition, jazz is built on the conflict of distinct rhythms played at the same time. In European music, the basic or "ground" beat is part of the melody. In jazz, this beat is avoided in the melody and played by a separate rhythm section. Instrumental sounds are personal to individual musicians and are part of their signatures. Many notes do not begin or end on beats or even between them, but are part of improvisations, which themselves are played against complicated syncopation.[46] The rhythmic complication, the moments of individual expression and improvisation, the offbeat accents, all are African.

Brass bands were a significant force in the making of the new music. They had been common in the military for a century before the birth of jazz, in New Orleans around 1900, where it was part of a style called "playing hot." The city where so much music was played out of doors had a special fondness for brass bands. The new sound grew out of the marches and ragtime played by such bands, as well as the blues.

Another important influence was the availability of used band instruments sold off by the U.S. Army at the end of the Spanish-American War in 1898. As one of the closest American ports to Cuba, New Orleans was flooded with these, allowing local blacks an unusual chance to get affordable instruments. Many New Orleans blacks of the time lived in a poverty that contemporary Americans cannot even imagine. Operating in an African American tradition going back to slavery times, amateur and even professional black musicians of the period used makeshift instruments created from washtubs, washboards, bones, and other materials. Cheap instruments transformed these musicians' relationship to their music and facilitated the development of a new sound. The new sound went to France with black musicians in James Reese Europe's 369th Regiment "Hellfighters" band, which led the way in introducing the French to jazz.

This was the music that shaped, and was shaped by, the new American dances that came out the black experience in the first decades of the twentieth century. In their 1919 sheet music "The Wedding of the Shimmie and Jazz," Johnson and Hess wrote:

At the wedding of Minnie Shimmie and Mister Jazz

That pipe organ played the Blues,
Folks all quivered in their shoes.

Bride and Groom met their doom with a smile
The preacher with his book, simply took a look, and shook all over the aisle;

Bridesmaids waited all decorated, with "Jassamine."
Ragtime best men "walked the dog" as they came down the line;

And when the "Jazz-bo" knot was tied—the Groom "Balled the Jack" with the Bride.[47]

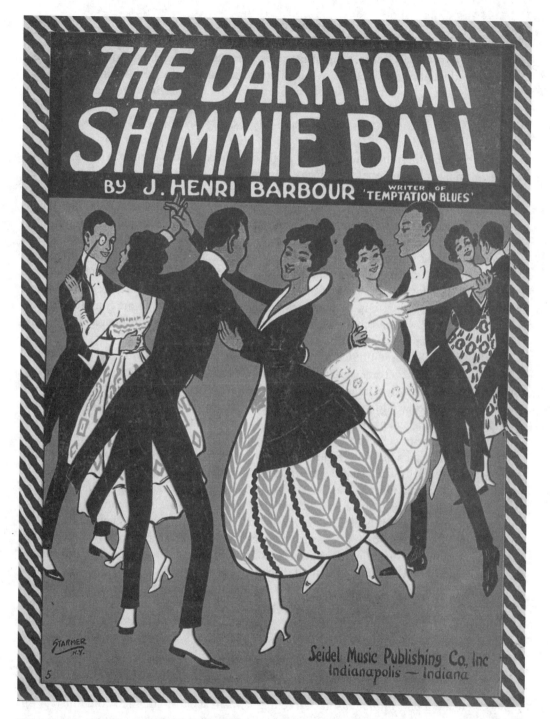

"The Darktown Shimmie Ball" was published in 1919. Couples really did dance a version of the Shimmy in a closed position, as depicted here.

The lines allude to jazz dances of the time, the Shimmy, Walking the Dog, and Ballin' the Jack. Some of the words refer to the importance of the blues and ragtime in the development of jazz, the body shaking or "quivering" central to jazz dance, and the delight of it all. The sexual suggestiveness of the last line reflects a new frankness about the body and how it moves in dance, especially with hip and shoulder shaking to hot rhythms. The dominant metaphor, the wedding, emphasizes the intimate relationship between jazz music and twentieth century social dance. This relationship can hardly be overstated.

THE 1920s

During the 1920s, the black musical again became a vehicle for dance talent, presenting and popularizing many of the dances that we have come to think of as uniquely American. Opening in New York, then touring the country and disseminating sheet music for its hit songs from coast to coast, the black show presented dancers who took older dance material, cast into new forms, and then brought it to mainstream audiences. Major nightclub revues also moved into theatres and contributed to the showcasing of black dances that had come out of the honky-tonks, barrelhouses, jooks, and house parties of the rural South. Among these dances were the Shimmy, Charleston, and Black Bottom. More dances came into the mainstream by way of the dance ballroom, vaudeville, and television—these included the Lindy Hop, Big Apple, Twist and more, and will be treated in the next section. Tap dance blossomed into a variety of new forms, and late in the decade Bill Robinson became the nation's favorite tap star.

The decade began with *Shuffle Along*, which exploded into view in 1921, a smash hit that many say has never been paralleled. Kimball and Bolcom call it "an epoch-making stage work without which much that has been invaluable, original, and viable in American musical theater would probably never have happened."[48] The show had top-notch composing and writing talent. Its music and lyrics were created by Noble Sissle and Eubie Blake and its script by Flournoy Miller and Aubrey Lyles, all four of whom were established vaudeville stars before they joined forces. In 1920, Sissle and Blake, a singer-pianist duo, were playing to white audiences on the exclusive Keith circuit, and had performed at the apex of vaudeville, the Palace Theatre. Miller and Lyles had got their start in college theatricals at Fisk University and had also traveled the Keith circuit. The two duos met at an NAACP benefit in Philadelphia in 1920, where they struck up a friendship and began to talk about how they might put together a black Broadway show. Gradually, they created the script and songs for the show, but none of the four had the money to finance it. All agreed, however, that they would not give up artistic control.

They found some small financial backing and toured the show through New Jersey and Pennsylvania on a shoestring, without enough money to pay for new costumes, sets, travel, food, or lodging. They had purchased used costumes, written songs to accommodate them, and scraped along from venue to venue, always barely meeting expenses and rarely able to pay the cast. Sissle, Blake, Miller, and Lyles all performed in the show—Sissle and Blake in elegant dress, and Miller and Lyles in comic roles for which they wore blackface. The good news was that audiences loved *Shuffle Along*. The jazzy score and songs were a big part of the reason. While mainstream shows maintained old musical formulas audiences were bored with, *Shuffle Along* presented something new.

When the cast finally returned to New York in the spring of 1921, they were $18,000 in the red. They were able to get the 63rd Street Theatre, a decrepit place that had to have renovations before the show could go on. Few reviewers came to see the production, but they wrote praise for its dancing and singing. Alan Dale, for example, called the show "an infection of amusement" and said, "These people made pep seem something different to the tame thing we know further downtown. Every sinew in their bodies danced; every tendon in their frames responded to their extreme energy."[49] More recently, Constance Valis

"I'm Just Wild About Harry" was one of the hits and certainly the most famous song from *Shuffle Along*.

Aubrey Lyles (left) and Flournoy Miller (right) got their start in show business at Fisk University. Lyles, a medical student, found himself in a gym class where he was put into a boxing match with the much larger Miller. Eying each other in the ring, they decided to clown the violence and, as a result, convulsed their audience. Later, they created a comic routine based on a boxing match and used it in *Shuffle Along*.

Hill has written that the show "introduced the most exciting form of jazz dancing that had ever been seen on the Broadway stage. Blake's musical score provided a foot-stomping orgy of giddy rhythms that spanned traditional and early jazz styles."[50]

With a run of 504 performances[51], *Shuffle Along* made instant stars of Florence Mills (a last-minute substitution in the lead role) and sixteen-year-old Josephine Baker, whose comic mugging in the chorus line brought cheers from the audience. The music included the hits "I'm Just Wild About Harry" (which later was the theme song of Harry Truman's presidential campaign), "Love Will Find a Way," "In Honeysuckle Time," and "Shuffle Along." Sissle and Blake, who had almost deleted "I'm Just Wild About Harry," saw it get ten encores a night.[52] And this with an audience that a *Variety* sampling found to be almost ninety percent white.[53]

Jazz dancing to jazz music was the sensation of the show. Charlie Davis' staggering speed and endurance in his tap routine, featuring the Buck and Wing, captivated audiences. Tommy Woods did a slow-motion acrobatic dance, including flips. Bob Williams did a Cakewalk strut, and Ulysses "Slow Kid" Thompson did eccentric dance, Soft Shoe, and legomania. Audiences loved the swinging rhythms, fast-tempo dance, and comic routines. Fiorello LaGuardia enjoyed it all so much he came three times in one week. Because of the city traffic jams had to make the street outside one-way.[54]

The chorus line's high-energy jazz dance and song set an example for other chorines, who in previous white productions had often been glamorous but wooden showgirls. The Stearnses wrote, "The most impressive innovation of *Shuffle Along* was the dancing of the sixteen-girl chorus line. When not dancing on stage, they sang in the wings to keep things moving."[55] The impact on white Broadway was immediate. Producers Florenz Ziegfeld and George White opened special studios and brought in *Shuffle Along* chorus girls to teach white showgirls how to dance to jazz rhythms.[56] Because of the chorus girls, advertising could call *Shuffle Along* "the speediest, peppiest, breeziest, funniest musical comedy" and "the world's greatest dancing show."[57] And partly because of them, chorus dancing on Broadway changed into something jazzier and more energetic.

After its successful run in New York, the production toured for three years, becoming the first of many black musicals to play white theatres across the country. It also made substantial profits, encouraging producers to back future black shows. Finally, it became the gold standard for black shows, the basis on which other shows were judged. *Shuffle Along* had opened doors, made America acknowledge its power, and set a benchmark. It also began a widespread phasing out of segregated theatre seating. By 1930, James Weldon Johnson wrote, "At the present time the sight of colored people in the orchestras of Broadway theatres is not regarded a cause of immediate action or utter astonishment."[58]

Six or eight new black shows appeared very quickly, taking advantage of the attention *Shuffle Along* had attracted. Among the first were *Liza* and *Plantation Revue*, both opening in 1922.

Liza was a hit, running for 172 performances. Eddie Rector was one of its stars, performing a clog waltz. Greenlee and Drayton dressed in top hats and tails to sing while they danced the Virginia Essence. Greenlee and Maude Russell danced the Charleston, the first time it had been presented on the Broadway stage.[59] It did not become popular among mainstream audiences, however, until the chorus boys danced it in *Running Wild*, a black show that opened the next year. A reviewer in the *New York Times* called *Liza* "melodious," mentioned its "fast-moving" chorus, and ended by calling attention to the numerous encores the cast had received.[60] Heywood Broun said, "After seeing *Liza* we have a vague impression that all other dancers whom we ever saw did nothing but minuets."[61]

Above and opposite page: After *Shuffle Along*, **Josephine Baker went to Paris to dance in** *Revue Nègre* **in the Théâtre des Champs Élysées. Her performances there made her a major star. She remained in France for life, becoming a French citizen in 1937. Here, she dances with a partner in the show.**

The *Plantation Revue* was organized by Lew Leslie, owner of the Plantation Club. Leslie was a white man with a penchant for producing black shows. He raided vaudeville, Broadway, and club floorshows for the best black talent, and was known to pay high salaries. During the long run of *Shuffle Along*, for example, Leslie persuaded Florence Mills and her husband U.S. Thompson to entertain at his club late in the evening after their performance in the theatre. By the next year, he had Mills under contract at three times the salary she had made in *Shuffle Along*. Her friends knew, however, that the salary was not what had won her over. She had also received a generous offer from the Ziegfeld Follies, but accepted Leslie's because it would give her a chance to help break color barriers on Broadway.[62]

When the *Plantation Revue* opened, it had Florence Mills as its star, a series of out-

standing black acts from the Plantation Club, and other top black talent. The dancers included Palmer and Kelly, who did a Class Act, a flashy dance routine they performed in top hats and tails, as well as Lou Keane and U.S. Thompson.[63] One reviewer summarized the variety of acts this way: "They've taken the negro musical show from the Plantation Restaurant, added a string of vaudeville numbers, and put it all on at the Forty-eighth Street Theatre...."[64]

After running for 35 performances[65], Leslie's show was revised and enlarged for a tour of England. The new version, renamed *Dover Street to Dixie*, played at the Pavilion Theatre in London and toured Europe, gaining international attention for Mills. The next year, she starred in another Leslie production in New York, *From Dixie to Broadway* (1924) with her husband, U.S. Thompson. Other cast members included the popular and talented tap dancer Johnny Nit, as well as Maud Russell, Willie Covan, Lou Keane, and Shelton

In this picture, Florence Mills sits between an unknown man on the right and her husband, U.S. "Slow Kid" Thompson, on the left.

Brooks. Like other black shows of the twenties, Mills' vehicles brought black dance and music to broad audiences and helped develop tap dance into a fine art.

After *Shuffle Along*, Miller and Lyles parted from Sissle and Blake to create *Runnin' Wild* (1923). Its company included Miller and Lyles themselves, a number of the cast members from *Shuffle Along*, singer Adelaide Hall, and dancers Tommy Woods, George Stamper, Mae Barnes, and Lavinia Mack.[66] The production played to enthusiastic audiences, touring first and then opening in New York in late October.[67] Reviews were favorable, and the catchy songs got encores.

The Charleston quickly spread to England and Europe. This young couple was dancing the Charleston in the Netherlands.

The female chorus line from *Runnin' Wild* reflects the tastes of casting directors on Broadway and in nightclubs. Young women with light skin had the best chance of being chosen. These chorus girls were enormously successful onstage, led by the dancer in the middle, Elizabeth Welch.

As good as all this was, though, it wasn't the best part of the show. The real stars were the chorus boys, The Dancing Redcaps, who danced the Charleston to "the simple accompaniment of hand-clapping and foot-stamping, the way it had been danced for many years in the South."[68] James Weldon Johnson later wrote that "The effect was electrical.... Such a demonstration of beating out complex rhythms had never been seen on a stage in New York."[69] The performance was intoxicating, and audiences who had ignored the dance when they saw it onstage in *Liza* now found ways to learn its steps.

During the height of the Charleston's popularity, the *New York Times* reported that some black domestic workers were being hired partly on the basis of their ability to teach the dance to their employers.[70] Dance instructors swiftly worked up the steps and began charging a fee to teach them. Sergei Marinoff's School of Classic Dancing of Chicago offered a course in the dance in 1925, noting, "All of its principles are directly opposed to ballet rules."[71] Indeed, the dance was performed with bent torso, knees, and elbows.

An old southern dance featuring fast polyrhythms, orientation to the earth, and angularity, the Charleston dated back to at least the turn of the century among African American dancers. Noble Sissle recalled learning it in Savannah, Georgia in 1905, and James P. Johnson said he saw it when he played at the Jungles Casino in New York City in 1913.[72] The Whitman Sisters said they used it in their show in 1911.[73] Even more interesting, it bears a striking similarity to an Asante ancestor dance that was still being performed in Africa in the 1930s. Anthropologist Melville Herskovits filmed the Asante dance in 1931, called it "A Perfect Charleston,"[74] and archived the film.

While Miller and Lyles were working on *Runnin' Wild*, Sissle and Blake created a show they first called *Bamville* and then renamed *Chocolate Dandies* (1924). With the

The garter box reads, "The Charleston Leather Garter is made of choice quality flexible leather in twenty-five fashionable colors; is well fitting and designed to merit your preference." In the mid-1920s, hemlines were rising, and it was important to wear an attractive garter below the knee during an evening of dancing. On the left side of the box are examples of the strenuous activities the garter is meant to withstand, including the kick of the Charleston.

affluence *Shuffle Along* had brought them, the two partners decided they would no longer work on a shoestring. They hired a cast of 125, engaged Charley Davis to train the dancers, bought lavish sets and costumes rivaling those of *Ziegfeld Follies*, and staged a horse race with three real horses on a treadmill. Like a number of other black shows of the period, *Chocolate Dandies* had a story line about the yearning for riches and the struggle to get along. The elegant, expensive gowns and suits, along with the artistic backdrops, were part of a series of fantasy scenes dreamed by the main character, who sleeps through much of the show and wakes at the end.

The show toured outside New York before opening in the city in the autumn of 1924. The stars were Sissle and Blake themselves, Lottie Gee, comedian-dancer Johnny Hudgins, Josephine Baker, who continued to be loved by audiences, dancers Charlie Davis and Bob Williams, and the chorus line, which was praised by critics. The show ran for 96 performances and grossed as much per week as *Shuffle Along*, but the high expenses Sissle and Blake had incurred were a drag on profits. Financially, it was a failure, but its dance was exciting, and Johnny Hudgins was a hit.[75]

Opening in 1927, *Africana* was a short-lived but important show produced by Earl Dancer. Following the pattern of Lew Leslie, he put together a revue that would incorporate tried and true black talent and routines from nightclub and road show acts. The show featured Ethel Waters, who had become successful in vaudeville for her dancing and singing. *Africana* brought her to the attention of theatregoers in New York and proved that she was star material. She later wrote, "It was a good, fast show and gave the theater-going ofays of Broadway their first long look at me…. *Africana* had a good run and afterward we took it on the road, playing the Midwest cities and closing in St. Louis with a bang."[76] In addition to a Cakewalk strut, two dances were keynotes of the production: the Shimmy and the Black Bottom.

The young and beautiful Waters danced the Shimmy, which she had long performed

In the early morning hours of July 4, 1925, the Pickwick Club in Boston was filled with about two hundred people dancing the Charleston. The vibrations produced by the acrobatics were too much for the aging building, and it collapsed. More than forty people died in the wreckage, and others were seriously injured. This photo shows the ruins as police, fire fighters, and volunteers search for sixteen people trapped inside and still alive.

in her various acts, and sang "Shake that Thing." She also danced the Black Bottom and sang "Take Your Black Bottom Outside." The Two Black Dots (Taylor and Johnson) performed a tap Black Bottom routine.

By this time, both the Shimmy and the Black Bottom had been around for a while. Vaudeville performer Coot Grant had seen the Shimmy danced by patrons of her father's honky-tonk around the turn of the century. The body movement of the Shimmy is a shaking of the shoulders and sometimes of the hips as well. Stearns and Stearns wrote, "the Shimmy was performed in the South with hair-raising quivers and shakes."[77] Black composer A. J. Piron's "I Wish I Could Shimmy Like My Sister Kate" (1922) conveyed the idea in the line, "Shake it like jelly on a plate ...,"[78] and the song "Minnie, Shimme for Me" (1918) directed the dancer to "do that lovin' shiveree."[79]

When Sophie Tucker published "Ev'rybody Shimmies Now,"[80] it signaled the dance's transition into mainstream popular culture. In 1922, Gilda Gray introduced the dance in Ziegfeld Follies. She tried to claim she invented it, which few believed, but she did help make it popular. Tucker was a white vaudeville headliner who (like many others) found it profitable to use music and dance from black sources. She also traveled with picks (a shortened form of "pickaninnies"), black children who could sing and dance. Picks added dazzle to an act. After getting such an early start in show business, many picks later became stars in their own right. Tucker scouted for young black talent, as well as for song and

Ethel Waters. This photo was taken in the late 1930s, about a decade after *Africana.* Courtesy Library of Congress.

dance material, by visiting black clubs and theatres. She helped carry black songs and dances across the country, but like other cover artists, often did not reveal their sources. Mae West also sang and published sheet music for "Ev'rybody Shimmies Now." In spite of the title, the Catholic Archbishop of Ohio had condemned the dance in 1921.[81]

By the 1930s, the Shimmy had become a couple dance. This development was part of its entrance into mainstream culture and its enjoyment by whites. In the process, the form lost some of its Africanist characteristics—the loose and flowing articulation of the shoulders and pelvis, the slightly forward tilt of the torso, and performance either as a solo or by a group. In mainstream culture, it conformed to European characteristics—movement of the torso as a single unit, a more vertical stance, and a closed-couple format.

Said by some to have been named after a black section of Atlanta, the Black Bottom was an old African American social dance. Black composer Perry Bradford had produced sheet music for it as early as 1907, and it had been presented in black vaudeville for two decades by performers in Whitman Sisters shows, Waters herself, and many others. Waters wrote that the dance came from Nashville: "This memorable backside-wriggling number got its name from the toughest section in town," she said.[82] "The Original Black Bottom Dance," published in 1926, gave instructions for the dance:

> Hop down front and then you Doodle Back,
> Mooch to your left and then you Mooch to the right
> Hand on your hips and do the Mess Around
> Break a Leg until you're near the ground
> Now that's the Old Black Bottom Dance.[83]

To Doodle is to slide, the Mooche is "a sort of shuffle, combining rubberlegs with rotating hips," and Break a Leg is a hobbling step.[84] When black dancer Buddy Bradley demonstrated the Mess Around for *The Dance* magazine in 1928, he put his hands on his hips, kept his feet still, and moved his hips in a circle.[85] A 1930s dance book laid it all out a little more clearly:

> The Black Bottom ... is a stamp step, with added emphasis by the gyrations of the torso.... Take three quick alternating stamps with both feet, starting with the left ... the knees are slightly bent when the stamp steps are taken, and on the third step, the body leans forward from the waist, the shoulders moving alternately.... The left shoulder is pushed forward.... The right shoulder is pushed forward, and the body straightens.... Repeat.... [86]

Dance instructor Betty Lee isolated the essential elements of the dance: stamping steps, "the proper swing of the body," knee swaying with the knees held together, and shuffle steps, done in an exciting, unusual rhythm.[87] All these characteristics are Africanist, and indeed, many among the public were aware of the black origins of the dance. Caucasian producer George White, who presented the Black Bottom in his show *Scandals*, published sheet music for it that contained the words, "Ev'ry high-brown gal and her bon-bon buddy/Go down where the flats are muddy, / To do a step that will soon be renowned. /They call it Black Bottom."[88]

Afterward, White tried to claim he had invented the Black Bottom as well as the Charleston. Will Marion Cook responded quickly in the *New York Times*, writing that the dances "came from the Cotton Belt, the levee, the Mississippi River, and are African in inspiration.... The 'Charleston' has been done in the South, especially in the little Islands lying off Charleston, S.C., for more than forty years to my knowledge." Cook added scornfully, "It is doubtful if Mr. White even saw a 'Charleston' until he attended the final rehearsals of 'Runnin' Wild.'"[89] It was only one more example of love and theft—attempted theft, anyway.

The dances were wildly popular among the young, and swiftly made the leap across the Atlantic. One 1927 tourist book that guided men through the dangers and fascinations of Paris, for example, described Florence's, a black-managed club in Rue Blanche, Montmartre:

> Princes, Lords and Dukes come here and love it. "Frisco" pulls them right out of their chairs, no matter how blazing their coat of arms; and he drags them out into the middle of the floor and they Charleston and Blackbottom and do everything he tells them to do; and in return they plaster 100 franc notes all over his perspiring face; and then everybody in the place, rocks the walls with a joy-thunder that rumbles like a dynamite explosion in a subway.[90]

London, Paris, Berlin, and other European cities loved the Africanist dances. As a result, there were numerous foreign-language versions of music for the Shimmy, Black Bottom, and Charleston. A *New York Times* article reported that in Madrid the "stately Fandango" had been replaced with the Black Bottom.[91]

Like other jazz dances, the Shimmy crossed the ocean. This French sheet music for the Shimmy was published in 1921.

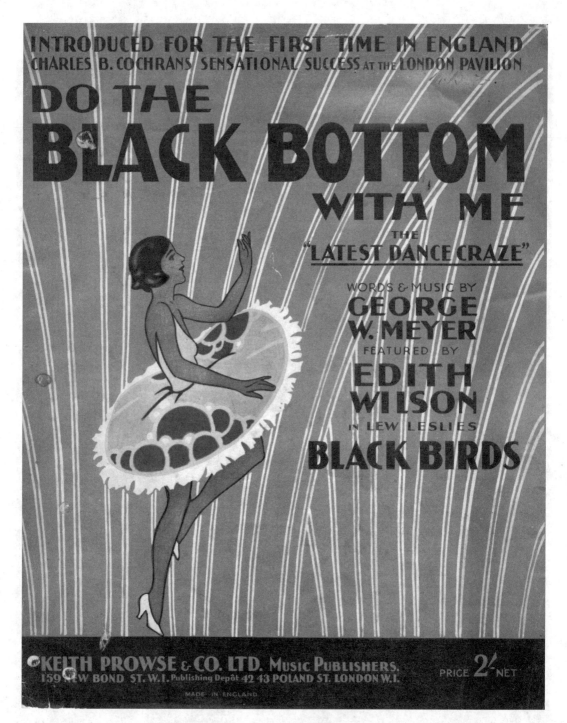

This sheet music references the performance by black entertainer Edith Wilson in Lew Leslie's *Blackbirds*. Notice that the music was printed to be sold in England.

In 1927, Arthur Murray made news by giving a Black Bottom dance lesson via transatlantic telephone to Santos Casani, Principal of the Casani School of Dancing in London. For fifteen intense minutes, Murray counted time while an assistant stamped out the steps on a wooden box and a Victoria played near the phone. The lesson allowed Casani to be the first to introduce the dance to London, all for a cost of $425, mostly for the phone call.[92]

This German Shimmy music was published in Berlin.

Not all was rosy with regard to the new dances, though. Some conservative people found them unacceptable and offensive. Dance instructors set themselves up as judges of the dances, and ministers and politicians tried to ban them. A World Congress of dancing masters in Paris announced it would "purify" the Charleston, adding, "The negro dance is immoral and not fit for good society."[93]

During the period, there was a constant stream of complaints that the music and dance would corrupt morals. In 1920, the Rev. Dr. John Roach Straton went undercover into New York restaurants to gather evidence about illegal drinking and "vulgar dancing … hip-movement dancing" such as the Hootchi-Kootchi and the Shimmy, before he gave his long exposé story to the *New York Times*.[94] In 1921, evangelist M. F. Ham published a booklet called *Light on the Dance*, in which he condemned contemporary dances and in one illustration showed dancers dropping off the dance floor downward through the red light district and potter's field into the flames of hell.[95] Ordinances were enacted against the jazzy dances in New York, Pittsburgh, and other places, leading to police officers' forcing shimmy dancers out of dance halls or arresting young women for performing the forbidden steps. In New York City in 1919, the controversy led to a new entertainment in Brighton Beach: "Jimmy Hussey … with Flo Lewis, William Worsley, and Six Shimmy Cops."[96]

Lew Leslie produced the first *Blackbirds* revue in 1926, starring Florence Mills. It played in a Harlem theatre for six weeks before the cast took it to Paris and London, where Mills became an international celebrity. By this time, Josephine Baker was a star of major proportions in Paris. Baker had come to France with a show called *Le Revue Negro* in 1925 and decided to stay, making her home there for the rest of her life. As Reynolds commented, she was "Paris' latest sensation," with lead billing in French revues and her own night-club.[97] She had married a count and lived in luxury. Yet years later, in 1935, when she returned for a visit to New York, she was turned away from the St. Moritz Hotel because of her color. Moreover, the hotel told Baker's Italian husband and French maid they could stay without Baker.[98] Even in the fifties, the humiliating segregation continued. Baker canceled a performance in Atlanta in 1951 because she could not, even with the intercession of leading black citizens of the city, secure accommodations at a first-class hotel.[99] It was no wonder that many African Americans chose to live abroad.

Paris applauded Florence Mills as well, and her revue was held over for sixteen weeks.[100] She then moved on to London, where the magazine *The Sketch* did a two-page spread of photos of the show in October, 1926. The accompanying text commented, "The show is proving one of London's biggest successes, and the dancing, singing, and comic turns are altogether entrancing."[101] Two of the pictures showed Mills tap dancing with Johnny Nit and Clarence Robinson doing a dance routine with the chorus line. In September, the *New York Times* reported that the Prince of Wales had come to see Mills.[102] Actually, he came to see "Little Twink's" performance at least twelve times.

It was Florence Mills' last big revue. Feeling exhausted and sick, she went to Germany for a rest before returning to the U.S. in September, 1927. Shortly afterward, she checked herself into a hospital for an appendectomy. Although the hospital announced that the surgery had gone well, Mills died within the week of complications. Her funeral was one of the largest and most star-studded New York had ever seen. The love and respect

Opposite page: **In Rev. Ham's booklet** *Light on the Dance*, **we see a graphic illustration of his perception of the dangers of the jazz dances. Dancers fall directly off the dance floor into a red light district, where the hounds of disease, suicide, and insanity attack them. From there, the sinners fall into death and then into the flames of hell.**

Top: In this series of photos, a very young Joan Crawford demonstrates the steps of the Black Bottom. *Bottom:* The Black Bottom Club was in New York City.

people felt for her had to do not only with her talent but also with her humility and her commitment to breaking down racial barriers. Juanita Stinnette of the vocal team Stinnette and Chappelle collapsed of grief while trying to sing the specially composed "Florence" at the service,[103] and she was only one of many who fainted that day in the emotional atmosphere. Inside the church, there was one enormous mass of roses eight feet high and four feet across attached to a note that read, "From a Friend." The sender was rumored to be the Prince of Wales, who had become a devoted fan during Mills' time in London.

Lew Leslie's *Blackbirds of 1928* opened to unenthusiastic reviews, and three weeks later Leslie brought in tap dancer Bill Robinson to prop up the show. It was the first time mainstream New York audiences had seen Robinson, who was already fifty years old and had long been a headliner in black vaudeville. Robinson's effect was immediate. The show's weekly take jumped from nine thousand dollars to twenty-seven thousand.[104] The reviewers' reactions were just as dramatic, but few were able to articulate Robinson's genius. He did a dance routine tapping up and down a set up stairs that wowed audiences. Yet his dancing was not faster or visually more complex than other dancers.' Still, he achieved a clarity, lightness, and rhythmical perfection and sophistication that were unparalleled. In July, 1928, one perceptive reviewer wrote:

> In his dance on the steps, it becomes clear that syncopation to him is simply a medium for building suspense. He plays with the musical phrase, off the beat until the psychological moment, then with a fine sense of theatrical effect he lands on the accent again as the phrase closes.... And his rhythms are no common jazz rhythms; they are filled with an unexpectedness which appeals to the listening ear and the watching eye.[105]

Robinson's supporting cast included singer Adelaide Hall and Earl "Snake Hips" Tucker. Hall had substantial show business credentials. She had been in the famous chorus line of *Shuffle Along* and in the cast of *Runnin' Wild*. She had also toured with Duke Ellington on the RKO-Keith circuit and recorded "Creole Love Song" with him. In *Blackbirds*, her singing of "I Can't Give You Anything But Love" helped make the song a hit.

Tucker, who was rumored to be from Maryland, was known for doing a dance of hip rotations and belly rolls in his act at Connie's Inn. In *Blackbirds*, he impressed many spectators with this torso dance and shocked a few. All in all, the show was one of the biggest black hits of the 1920s, running for 518 performances.

The critics saw Robinson again in *Brown Buddies* (1930) with Adelaide Hall, and slowly gained a better understanding of his art. They noted that he had the showmanship to make audiences watch his feet and appreciate what they did. He danced high up on his toes, making his taps brilliantly clear and clean. His rhythm was perfect, and his taps, laid down in varying pitches, made their own percussive music. "Dancers come and dancers go," wrote Robert Benchley, "they twist their bodies and they work their feet to a double, triple, and even quadruple tempo in an attempt to do something new to the old-fashioned tap." He continued, "But Bill Robinson just goes right ahead—one-two-three-four-one-two-three-four—in the regulation beat, slow measured, and indescribably liquid, like a brook flowing over pebbles ... and satisfies every craving for rhythm."[106] Robinson also had the personality to connect with audiences. This, coupled with his skill and artistry, made him the best known black tap dancer of the twentieth century, and his success opened doors for countless other black dancers who followed him. *Brown Buddies* ran for 113 performances.

Blackbirds of 1930 opened with a star-studded cast that included Ethel Waters, Buck and Bubbles, Jazzlips Richardson, and the Berry Brothers. Buck and Bubbles were seasoned and talented dancers. Buck did eccentric dance, while Bubbles did incredibly fast

This store display drew on the popularity of the Black Bottom to sell bow ties. Courtesy National Afro-American Museum and Cultural Center.

and improvisatory tap steps that other dancers found impossible to steal. The Berry Brothers were a brilliant Flash Act. They performed stunning soft shoe acrobatic routines in elegant dress. Jazzlips Richardson was an excellent eccentric dancer. Despite these very effective cast members, the show ran for just sixty-two performances. On October 23, 1930, Brooks Atkinson wrote that the dance was superb, but it was not enough. "The

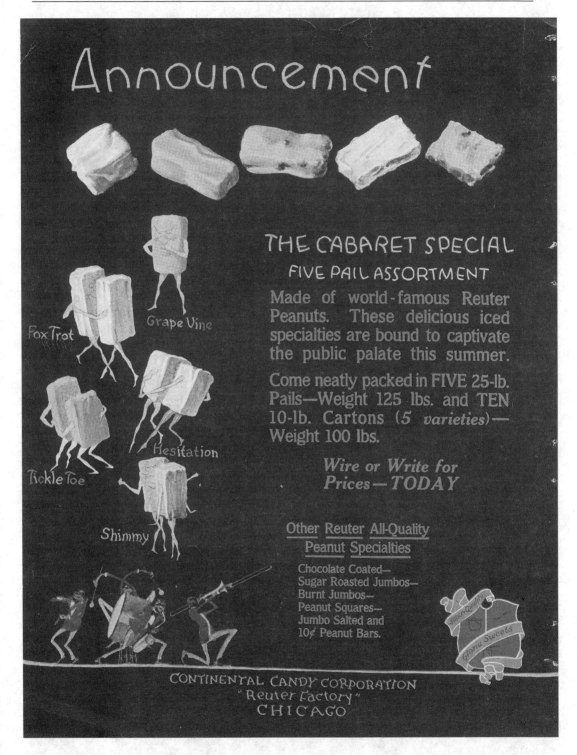

In a 1920s ad, pieces of candy perform the Shimmy and other trendy dances to music created by a black jazz band.

This photo of Bill Robinson was taken in 1933, when he would have been 55 years old. Courtesy Library of Congress.

diminutive black gals have hot feet; the buck dancers are whiling dervishes," he wrote, but "the material is slender."[107] The road show version was unable to draw audiences, and Ethel Waters had to drive some of the stranded and broke cast members home in her own car.

It was one of the last notable black revues before the Depression clamped down on Broadway. During the preceding decades since the turn of the century, the black musical had grown up and away from minstrelsy and achieved success. It had gained maturity and presented African American stars to enthusiastic audiences. Furthermore, during its flowering, the genre had given the world a new kind of social dance whose characteristics still seem eternal.

7

Variety

In the 1890s and early 1900s, the old minstrel shows were passing away, and new forms of entertainment were taking shape, including vaudeville and black musicals. Some of the greatest black dancers avoided working in musicals, though, because the pay was poor. The best money was in vaudeville—programs of entertainment offered at theatres across the country. In vaudeville, entertainers usually played a circuit, a series of bookings at a string of affiliated theatres, such as the Keith-Albee circuit (founded about 1885), the Pantages circuit (begun in 1902), or the Orpheum circuit (founded in 1887), which were white structures run by white management. Then there was the Theatre Owners Booking Association. Abbreviated TOBA and often nicknamed Toby time, this was the black vaudeville circuit set up by Sherman Dudley in the mid teens. Memphis theatre owner F.A. Barrasso had organized a smaller black circuit in 1907, predating TOBA.[1]

Through working a circuit, an act avoided the difficult task of contacting theatres individually to create a road schedule. The circuit management took care of that, and what would otherwise be a logistical nightmare was largely avoided for both sides. Individual theatres offered two to five shows per day, with perhaps eight to fifteen acts and a running time of about one and one-half hours per show. Within these programs, audiences found a variety of entertainers—from singers and dancers to jugglers and acrobats to trained animals and mind readers. Variety was what vaudeville was all about.

Arranging the acts on the program for maximum entertainment value, advertising them effectively, and making the business work economically was the job of management, and it included the circuit management, the theatre management, and the entertainers' management, if any. Black entertainers sometimes could not afford personal agents or could not trust in their fairness. Even the biggest black stars could be and were taken advantage of by their agents. On the other hand, some black dancers, especially women tap dancers, suffered from lack of representation. After a long career in show business, black dancer Cholly Atkins commented, "There were always some excellent women tap dancers who put everything else aside and worked at it real hard, but it appeared—to me— that most of them never had proper representation as far as agents were concerned."[2]

Vaudeville fell into categories of quality and compensation; there were small time, medium time, and first class theatres in the various circuits. Less skilled or younger performers began in the small time and made low salaries, sometimes as low as $20-$75 per week. But even this was good compared to wages in other available occupations. In a time when white families lived on perhaps a thousand or fifteen hundred dollars a year, and most blacks were relegated to the lowest of menial jobs with pay far below white standards, there were many who dreamed of making it into show business. At the medium level, the acts did better financially and had better working conditions. At the top, in the rarified Orpheum Circuit, there were sumptuous houses where big stars like white singer Sophie Tucker could command adulation, special treatment, and weekly salaries that ranged

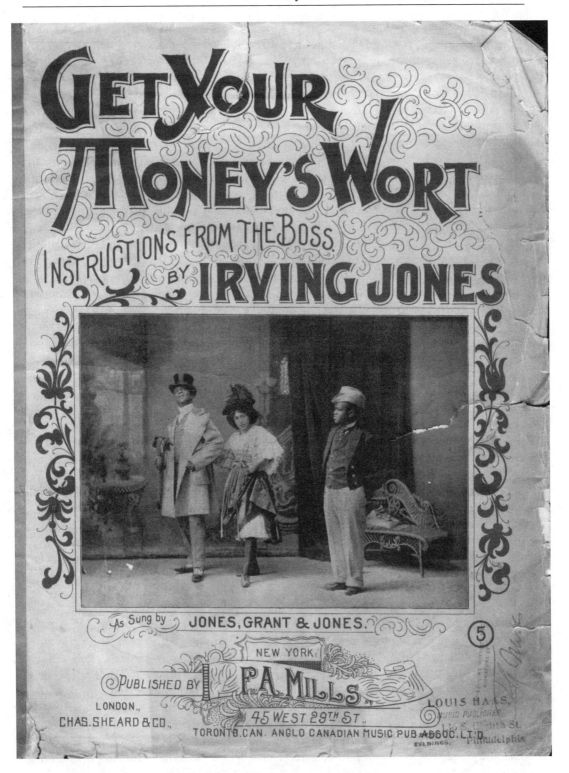

These African American actors were in a stage show about 1897. The man and woman on the left look as if they are taking the first step of a Cakewalk. The illustration is from the cover of the 1897 sheet music "Get Your Money's Worth."

into the thousands of dollars. The acme was the Palace Theatre in New York City. A vaudeville entertainer who played the Palace had arrived. During World War I, only three black acts played at the Palace. They were Bert Williams, Bill Robinson, and Greenlee and Drayton.[3] On the toughest circuits, less respected acts played one-nighters for the lowest pay, while on the high class ones, stars were booked into the best houses for weeks at a time.

Vaudeville had rules, and individual performers obeyed them or else. Those who did not could be blackballed from an entire circuit, suffering enormous consequences not only to income but also to career. On the Keith-Albee circuit, theatre management handed down judgments that could be traced back to Mr. Keith's and Mr. Albee's personal values and mutual determination to make vaudeville a family medium. If an act contained any risqué or blue material, the entertainers would be notified to cut it from the show. If there were resistance, the act would be barred from the theatre and could be dropped from the circuit. With stakes so high, whatever their bitterness over these demands, entertainers met them. When the first vaudeville houses began in the 1880s, it had been an uphill battle to convince middle class families, both black and white, that dancers and actors were respectable. As the decades passed, though, families began to patronize vaudeville, and its biggest names gained positive press and large followings among ordinary people. In black vaudeville, a major early traveling show, the Whitman Sisters, exercised constant vigilance to assure an image of morality and a long-term relationship of trust with audiences.

The predominantly white circuits skimmed the cream of black vaudeville, but the practice was limited by unwritten rules. No more than one or two black acts could be offered on any mainstream theatrical bill, and once these slots were filled, the door closed to other black performers, no matter how much better they were than the white acts already engaged.

The vaudeville theatres, however, were only part of American variety entertainment. Black dancers and performers played at nightclubs, resort restaurants, private clubs and parties, social gatherings in the homes of the wealthy, carnivals and circuses, amusement parks, town halls, and county fairs. Many played such venues all year long or found jobs in them for the summer after coming off a season of vaudeville touring. Black singer-dancer Tom Fletcher, for example, remembers playing in the New York City area. "We never had to worry about work in the summer," he said. "There were colored shows at all the summer resorts and beaches. Coney Island had three theaters with colored shows.... Then there were North Beach, Bergen Beach and South Beach on Staten Island." He adds, "In small towns, the street car company engaged performers to play the open-air theaters they had at the end of their lines, and which they operated to help lure passengers to take rides."[4] Fletcher recounts getting jobs with traveling shows, entertaining guests at the Vanderbilt mansion at 57th and Madison, and teaching the Cakewalk to visitors to the Newport summer home of the wealthy Mrs. Stuyvesant Fish.[5] During his long career, Fletcher entertained President Franklin Roosevelt and presidents-to-be William McKinley, Theodore Roosevelt, and Calvin Coolidge at private parties, and at various times played at Delmonico's, the Waldorf, and the Yale, Princeton, and Harvard Clubs.[6]

Although few in number, there were also resorts that catered to an affluent black clientele, and these hired black entertainers. In St. Louis, for example, the Amytis Theater was part of a larger complex that housed a recreation hall and a hotel, "making it somewhat

Opposite page: **Walker and May were successful comedians and dancers, despite the fact that Walker was blind.**

WALKER & MAY (Charlie & Ida).
America's Premier Coloured Comedians and Dancers.
WALKER, the Great Blind Comedian

This picture from about 1900 shows a group of people in Dayton, Ohio, on a picnic outing. Included in the picture are members of a black band who have provided the entertainment.

of an African American resort" where entertainers could find room and board. Since blacks were routinely excluded from white-run hotels, this was a welcome option. Booked into this venue in 1935, adagio[7] dancers Harold Norton and Margot Webb were featured as the only act on the bill. Gottschild writes, "they attended a reception and coffee hour with audience members—described by Webb as the African American bourgeoisie of St. Louis."[8] Other black resorts dotted the Midwest, such as the Idlewild in Michigan, which brought in black entertainers for guests during its heyday from the twenties to the fifties.[9]

In New York City, there were small theatres playing to black audiences, along with the larger mainstream theatres where one might see both black and white entertainers. At Keith's Alhambra, the young Ethel Waters, just breaking into show business herself, saw "the standard Negro acts that had been playing the white time for years," and these included "Bill (Bojangles) Robinson, Moss and Frye, the dancing Dotson," and major white performers like Belle Baker, Sophie Tucker, Blossom Seeley, and Eva Tanguay.[10]

Receiving lower salaries than white acts, black dancers often worked more than one kind of venue at once, double booking themselves into varying venues and formats, for a range of audiences. In 1937, for example, the young Nicolas Brothers (Fayard would have been about 23, and Harold 16) worked both at the Cotton Club and in the Broadway musical *Babes in Arms*.[11] They kept up the habit over time, working the matinees and evening shows of a variety New York theatres while performing in the midnight and 2 a.m. shows at the Cotton Club. In 1940, the duo could be seen doing five acts a day at the Roxy Theatre with Carmen Miranda and her Latin band while also doing two acts in the evening at Club Zanzibar.[12]

Some black dancers traveled to Europe for bookings, where they were often better treated and more highly paid than at home. Perhaps the greatest example was Josephine Baker, who transformed herself from a lowly chorus girl in *Shuffle Along* into the toast of Paris. A mega-star for half a century in Europe, Baker died in 1975. At her funeral, Carlo Ponti was heard to say to his wife Sophia Loren, "Take a good look, Sophia, at something you've never seen before and will never see again: the burial of a star who was also a queen."[13]

Other black stars found more temporary escape into the less racially prejudiced overseas climate. In 1926, Bill Robinson sailed for an extended stay. He opened at the Holborn Empire Theatre in London, and then visited France where he and his wife Fanny spent time with Florence Mills and her husband U.S. Thompson. Mills was performing in Paris at the time. When Ethel Waters visited Paris in 1929, she found Valaida Snow working there, and the Berry Brothers and Peg Leg Bates dancing in *Blackbirds of 1928* at the Moulin Rouge.[14] In 1936, the Nicholas Brothers went to London to be part of *Blackbirds of 1936*.[15] Norton and Margot traveled to Paris in 1937 with the cast of the *Cotton Club Revue*.[16] In 1947, the Four Step Brothers sailed on the *Queen Mary* and played the Lido Club in Paris for six months. Introduced to jazz during World War I by James Reese Europe's 369th Infantry "Hell Fighters" all-black band, Paris had a longstanding appetite for jazz music and jazz dancers, especially tap dancers. Flash McDonald of the Step Brothers said, "They called us 'claquette' dancers, and we didn't think they would understand. We didn't think they'd like it.... But they went for it!"[17] In 1948, the class act Coles and Atkins traveled to London to appear at a variety theatre and then traveled around to bookings in the provinces—Manchester, Dover, Bristol, and Blackpool—before making an appearance on British TV.[18]

The vast majority of black dancers, however, were in regional variety, working the vaudeville theatres, nightclubs, and other small venues across the nation, where individuals and teams created specialized routines that distinguished them from other acts. They practiced long hours to perfect their presentations and entertain their audiences. Through the harsh competition, the never-ending demand for more and more originality, and the yearning to be the best, they brought African American theatrical dance to new heights, adding new sub-genres to classical jazz dance and exerting a profound shaping influence on mainstream dance. Black entertainers' dance moves, for example, were widely copied by white dancers who had the skill to imitate them, and studios at which white performers were tutored by black dancers could be found not only on Broadway[19] and in Hollywood but also around the country

Tap dance dominated the period, but it was simply the largest branch of a tree that could be labeled classical jazz dance. Other branches included flash, acrobatic, eccentric, and chorus line dance. There was also adagio dance, a form brought to graceful perfection by Norton and Margot, who based their act on Europeanist ballroom dance and ballet, although Norton also did neo-African dance. Their elegant performances challenged period prejudices, for white audiences frequently expected black dancers to "get hot" in sensual displays of exoticism. All these forms were part of African American variety in the first half of the twentieth century.

Top: These musicians and dancers, photographed around 1920, made a living by traveling with a circus or carnival. The two women dance on the platform to encourage spectators to buy tickets to the show. *Bottom:* Black dancers frequently formed one of the shows to be seen at a traveling circus. This show's banners advertise both a version of the Georgia Minstrels (on the left) and an "Old Plantation Show" in continuous performance (center and lower left).

THE WHITMAN SISTERS

Before there was TOBA, there were the Whitman Sisters. The daughters of an African American minister, Mabel (b. 1880), Essie (b. 1882), Alberta (b. 1888), and Alice (b. 1900), were destined to shape African American vaudeville with their strong personalities and visionary management methods. Like many entertainers before and after them, they got their start on the church circuit. The three older sisters sang, danced, and played the guitar while their father preached. Mabel and Essie accompanied their father on an evangelical tour, and according to the *Washington Bee*, the sisters were giving concerts in churches "to overflowing houses" in 1908. By this time, though, they had also branched out into secular performance venues. With a song and dance skit created for them by Will Accoone, an experienced writer for musical comedy productions of the period, the two older sisters toured the South in 1899 under the name Danzette Sisters, chaperoned by their mother Caddie Whitman.[20]

Subsequently, Mabel and Essie were signed by a Mr. Lehman, manager of the Orpheum Theatre in Kansas City, to the Orpheum and Kohl & Castle circuits, to travel with a chaperone. They appeared on these circuits with major white acts, and also went abroad, where they probably played in theatres in Britain and France. According to family stories, they even gave a command performance before King George V of England.[21]

The Whitmans had a number of advantages. First, they were so fair skinned as to be able to pass for white, and this made them more acceptable on white vaudeville circuits. Darker performers had a difficult time breaking into high-level white vaudeville, no matter how skilled they were. In fact, U.S. "Slow Kid" Thompson said of the Whitmans, "they sometimes worked as a white act."[22] Second, the sisters were extraordinarily talented singers and dancers, and without this talent they could not have broken into high-class vaudeville, either. Finally, their family and social background were important. They had been brought up in well-mannered, educated middle class black society, where they learned how to interact graciously with a variety of people and where they acquired confidence in both their artistic and intellectual abilities. In this context, moreover, they gained a keen sense of the importance of respectability and the public relations effort needed to secure it. As Ethel Waters pointed out later, middle class blacks often considered show business people to be "not much better than cattle."[23] In Lexington, Kentucky, while working for a carnival, Waters had to sleep in a stable. "The colored people in Lexington," she said, "wouldn't let carnival show girls into their homes, so we couldn't get a room."[24]

The Whitman Sisters helped change that through their personalities and the power they wielded in the business. Early on, although fresh from success in mainstream vaudeville, they nevertheless chose not to continue working on white circuits. Instead, in 1904 the three older sisters formed their own road show company. Alice joined them after Caddie died in 1909.[25] The company, called The Whitman Sisters' New Orleans Troubadours, played to African American audiences and presented African American talent. Under Mabel's iron hand, the troupe achieved successes beyond those of other black companies. The Whitman Sisters was the only major black company, for example, managed by a black woman. It also became a synonym for the highest quality entertainment, and over the years it nurtured some of the best of black singing, dancing, and acting talent. It created its own stage shows with names like *Stepping Some*, *Spirit of 1930*, *Rompin Through*, and others, and launched them with aplomb. It booked itself to large audiences throughout the South, first through its own efforts and then as a part of the TOBA circuit. The company lasted

Alice Whitman and other members of the Whitman company perform onstage in 1937. Alice was generally acknowledged as one of the best female tap dancers in the country. Courtesy Library of Congress.

for forty years, and the sisters remained together, with one or two small exceptions, for the entire four decades.

Moreover, the Whitman Sisters commanded respect on a personal level wherever they went. They attended church in the towns they played, contributed lavishly to the collection plate, and strategically mentioned their father, a nationally known black poet and minister, as well as the children they had taken under their wing to nurture and educate. These children, the picks who sang and danced in their shows, were sometimes described as "friendless and homeless orphans" the sisters had taken in and were trying to provide for according to God's commandment.[26] In this way, they built a reputation as strong, moral, trustworthy black women. Their speeches on morality were not mere empty words, either. They insisted on good behavior from their troupe, and kept the young people in their care safe.

Catherine Basie, wife of Count Basie, was with the troupe for a time. She told Marshall and Jean Stearns:

> Any mother could tell you that if your daughter was with *The Whitman Sisters*, she was safe. Sister May [Mabel] telegraphed my mother and got her consent to take care of me. We couldn't drink or smoke, and each of the young girls had to travel by car with one of the sisters—they wouldn't let us ride in the bus.[27]

MORE LOW-DOWN DANCING

Buddy Bradley Shows Additional Real Negro Steps

By ELISE MARCUS

(At left)
Sugar Foot Strut, an original Buddy Bradley dance. It combines eccentric dancing and hip-motion, coupled with a strut. The body is stiff from the waist up; heel-step on the beat, toe-step off. The knees are bent, but straighten on the heel step. Three of these, then two fast with sliding hips. Tap and strut steps may be mixed in

(At right)
St. Louis Hop. Hop forward on both feet spread; then give a stamp with each foot

Louisiana Mess Around. Hands on hips. Rock on heels, hips moving in a circle. This keeps the center regions of the body moving, while the rest must remain quiet

Heebie Jeebies. This is a spasmodic placing of the hands all over the body in an agony of perfect rhythm. The more suggestive, the better the effect

Washington Johnny. Body is to be held absolutely rigid. Take short jerky steps, meanwhile moving the head up and down in the same rhythm

NASIB PHOTOS

Virginia Essence. Step with left foot and bring right up with left. Step back with right, and turn whole body in half-circle. Repeat this with right foot stepping first

Mooch. Shuffle forward with both feet. Hips come first, feet follow. Be sure not to lose the rhythm

In 1928, when Buddy Bradley was asked to demonstrate some African American steps, he chose the Virginia Essence, the Louisiana Mess Around, and the Heebie Jeebies, among others.

This photo of a dance event was probably taken in the 1920s.

Moreover, the constantly refreshed supply of young talent required good management and careful training, which it received in abundance. Louis Williams said, "The Whitman Sisters stood for something … they knew talent when they saw it and gave hundreds of dancers their first big break."[28]

Among the young people trained by the Whitman Sisters were dancers who later became stars. Jeni Legon, who danced with Bill Robinson in *Hooray for Love*, joined the company when she was fourteen and a half.[29] She said, "When you joined the Whitman Sisters, you went with them, you worked with them, and you just learned—that was all."[30] Leonard Reed and Willie Bryant danced for the sisters as well. "They were by far the greatest incubator of dancing talent for black shows on or off TOBA," Reed said.[31]

Joe Jones, Louis Williams, Earl "Groundhog" Basie, Alice Whitman herself, and Pops Whitman, her son, who became a child star, were all products of Mabel's training and management.[32] Alice was considered by many to be one of the best women tap dancers of the first half of the twentieth century, and Pops was "one of the first great acrobatic tap dancers, a master of cartwheels, spins, flips, and splits—swinging with the rhythm."[33] Later, such dancers were called flash acts.

One youngster the Whitman Sisters did not take in as a pick, despite errors in the scholarship to the contrary, was the legendary Bill Robinson. George-Graves, for example, identifies the Master Willie Robinson employed in the Whitman troupe around 1908 as Bill Bojangles Robinson.[34] At the time, though, Bill Robinson (who was born in 1878) would have been thirty, far too old to have served as one of the picks in the show, who were typically between six and fifteen years old. Instead, Bill Robinson got his first big break around 1892 when, at age 14, he was hired to be part of the show *The South Before the War*. As the show traveled along the eastern seaboard, Robinson served as one of about a dozen picks for headliner Mayme Remington. He kept the job for only a year because

AMY STANLEY
And her Troupe of Four

GENUINE SOUTHERN

PICK= A NINN IES

REAL PLANTATION DARKIES !

Songs Dances Capers
OF THE
SOUTHLAND!

Earl & Waters	Mac=Connell
In a One-Act Comedy, the	**YODLER**
Life Insurance Agent	**IMITATOR**
FAMILY THEATRE	AND Comedian
Mon. Tue. Wed. APRIL 18,19,20	LATEST AND BEST
MATINEE PRICE ⸰ ⸰ 10 Cents	FOREIGN and DOMESTIC
EVENING ⸰ 10 and 20 Cents	MOTION PICTURES !

The "genuine southern" picks who traveled with Amy Stanley performed songs, dances, and "capers."

of his age.[35] The Whitman Sisters show did not come into existence until more than a decade later.

In 1908, Bill Robinson was married and was a member of the vaudeville team Robinson and Cooper. Moreover, for much of 1908, he was spending his spare time fighting a wrongful charge of armed robbery for which he was arrested in March. In his trial, which took place several months later, he was incorrectly found guilty and had to use the influence of his friends to secure a new trial, which occurred in December. He was then finally acquitted, and his accusers were subsequently indicted for perjury. Shortly afterward, in January, 1909, he went back on the road for an engagement in Albany and one the following week in New York City.[36]

The Whitman Sisters' management decisions give us insight into their impressive characters. They defied, for example, the general rule that only the lightest-skinned girls should be chosen for the chorus line. Instead, the troupe included all colors of dancers. Jeni Legon noted, "The Whitman sisters had fixed the line so we had all the colors that our race is known for. All the pretty shading—from the darkest darkest, to the palest of pale."[37]

Furthermore, Mabel and her sisters would not stand for bad treatment based on racial prejudice. "Once," write Marshall and Jean Stearns, "when the act was about to play the Regal Theater in Chicago, the management decided to pay them less than the agreed-upon amount. May walked across the street to the Metropolitan Theater, which lacked a stage, had a new stage built, opened with a different show, and ruined the Regal's business for two weeks."[38]

George-Graves provides a similar anecdote, which highlights Mabel's determination not to knuckle under to racist compensation practices:

> Samuel Hay tells another story of the Whitman Sisters teaching a lesson to the racist white owner of a high-class theater. Right before a performance, the sisters heard that the owner would not pay the agreed-upon price because it was equal to what he paid his white acts. Knowing that their acts were better than the white companies,' Mabel demanded the agreed-upon amount in advance. The owner offered a compromise, but Mabel told him that they would not play for him for any amount of money and left.[39]

It seems likely that the sisters turned their backs on white vaudeville in part because they wished to serve African American audiences and in part because they desired to retain control over their artistic and economic destinies and avoid suffering the indignities forced upon black entertainers in white vaudeville.

THE THEATRE OWNERS BOOKING ASSOCIATION

As early as 1907, there were about 1,400 black performers in show business.[40] Black show business continued to grow over the following decades in the wake of the Great Migration, during which thousands of blacks left their sharecropper existence in the South and moved to northern cities like Chicago, Detroit, and New York. Harlem became a burgeoning center of black population and black arts and culture. New urban theatres began to emerge to serve the entertainment needs of these relocated African Americans, just as theatres in cities across the South served black clienteles there. By 1922, there were more than 360 black theatres across the U.S., booking about 600 acts.[41] Most of these were small venues serving small to medium sized communities.

Owners of some of the largest of these theatres organized themselves into the The-

HILL TWINS
Age 4
"Fox Follies 1930"

Tap, Clog and Strut   Sing and Harmonize

OX ford 8733   Also Box   RI chmond 2575

The Hill Twins were four when this picture was taken in 1930. It appears on the advertising or booking card for their act.

Clarence "Snowball" Whittier tap dances with a hat and cane. Courtesy National Afro-American Museum and Cultural Group.

atre Owners Booking Association, thereby forming the black vaudeville circuit. In 1921, TOBA included nearly 40 theatres across the South, West, and North.[42] *The Chicago Defender* published a regular column, "TOBA Doings," and through it readers followed the news of their favorite stage entertainers just as people do with film and rock stars today. The circuit peaked in the mid twenties, when it included more than fifty theatres serving weekly audiences of 30,000.[43] Most of the circuit's theatres, however, were not black-owned. In 1921, only 31 percent of the more than 300 theatres inside and outside TOBA serving black audiences were owned and managed by blacks.[44] Some of the smaller houses were not open every day or even every weekend, and many gained a portion of their revenue from being rented out to church conferences, high school graduations, and other events and gatherings.

Most performers on the Toby circuit worked seven days a week and did three to five shows per day. Pay was less for black performers than white, and in the twenties it hovered around $30 per week. Later, in the 1930s, a high quality act like Norton and Margot might get $150 per week (for both members of the duo), but from this amount they had to pay for expensive musical arrangements, custom-made costumes, and publicity photos.[45] In the heyday of black vaudeville, moreover, pay promised was not always the same as pay collected. Theatre owners occasionally attempted to cheat individual performers in a number of ways. Or house managers might claim that ticket sales were insufficient to support the agreed-upon wages and try to negotiate a lower amount. Ethel Waters remembered that a theatre manager in Louisville paid her at the end of one week in pennies, most likely because he felt she would not count the thousands of coins to check the total amount. Waters did count them, though, to find that she had been underpaid by ten dollars.[46]

Dishonest treatment was so widespread that Mabel Whitman discussed it in an interview with the *Baltimore Afro-American* in 1929. She said, "The trouble with this game is a set of unscrupulous owners and managers...." She gave as an example "a certain owner" who had told her, "I have been losing money all year and I have to get out of the red on your engagement here. Therefore I won't pay you what you want. You have a family company. You don't need money because you all work and live together. Come in at my price or stay out." Mabel noted, "Well, I stayed out" and listed some of the expenses that would make it impossible for her troupe to work for the manager and break even financially.[47]

Entertainers who worked for a unit like the Whitman Sisters had a better chance of getting paid fairly, although sometimes whole companies were stranded far from home when their management ran out of money. A unit was a company that could fill the entire bill at a theatre's shows for the week. Most units contained between twenty and forty entertainers. Gottschild describes a unit this way:

> The basic component of the traveling unit was the big band. The master of ceremonies introduced the program and was also a performer or musician in the show. Frequently it was the bandleader or a comedian-dancer who filled this slot. The entire cast joined in a big choreographed opening number and the grand finale, with the chorus line dancing as backup for the featured acts (although the unit tours going to the West did not include chorines). The opening number presented the theme of the show and often had a special song written for it, as did the finale.[48]

In between the opening and the finale, various acts performed, including tap dancers, vocalists, comedians, and the featured and top billed performers. "From featured acts to atmospheric background, dance inflected the entire show," Gottschild writes. "In general," she adds, "a unit remained in each theater in each town for a week at a time."[49]

Theatres in the South were segregated, with blacks seated in the balcony in white theatres and the reverse in black theatres. Whites, however, could sit in the orchestra section on "whites only" nights in black theatres. Segregation in theatres was only one facet of racism. Throughout the South, TOBA entertainers risked encountering racial violence. While working at a theatre in Atlanta owned by Charles P. Bailey, Ethel Waters narrowly escaped being beaten and jailed. After she quarreled with Bailey, a black backstage worker told her that she could expect trouble. Having heard that Bailey had beaten Bessie Smith and had her thrown in jail, Waters gathered her costumes together and tried to get out of town, only to find that the railway office had already been notified not to sell her a train ticket. Then she noticed that police were watching her rooming house. She spent the night praying and watching out her window. In the early morning darkness, when the police left their posts for a few minutes to go for coffee, she was able to slip away and catch a ride on a farmer's wagon out of town. Through this harrowing experience, she lost her props and costumes and barely escaped physically safe and sound. The emotional trauma was more lasting.[50]

The Deep South was not the only region of the country where entertainers encountered racism. Less violent forms were common in the North and West. In various guises, it persisted across the country through the twenties and thirties into the fifties and beyond, affecting all of variety entertainment. Bill Robinson, for example, was often barred from riding passenger elevators. Like Bert Williams before him, he rode freight elevators uncomplainingly. He also waited until all white customers had left the restaurant car on a train before he entered it. When Sammy Davis, Jr. played in Miami in the fifties, he found that

Dance team Nip and Tuck in 1948.

there was a curfew on the beach for blacks and that cabs were not permitted to carry blacks across the bridge from Miami to the beach.[51] Davis began to refuse to work at clubs and hotels where racial prejudice was practiced, and his stance helped integrate Miami Beach nightclubs and Las Vegas casinos. Atkins and Coles could not get a room in a Las Vegas hotel on the strip in 1955 when they played at the Flamingo, but were able to get rooms there in 1958 when they returned for another booking.[52]

Between shows and on any days off, black entertainers often did not go out, even for meals. In most cities, African Americans could not get served in white-owned restaurants. It was difficult to shop, for although black customers sometimes could purchase clothes in department stores, they were frequently not permitted to try them on. It was a time when African Americans had trouble purchasing theatre tickets and could not obtain seating in a white nightclub, even if the floorshow were all black.[53] Many black entertainers instead sent out for food and spent the time between shows playing cards.

Despite its flaws and very real dangers, TOBA continued to attract black performers who yearned to be stars. It was simply the best booking opportunity many dancers had, and through it some rose to modest success and even stardom. Toby time began to decline in the twenties, though, with the coming of movies. Bookings became harder to get, and orchestras, once a staple of every theatre, were let go when talking pictures became common. Many white entertainers took advantage of the situation by seeking work in the movies, where doors were closed to most blacks. African American acts, because they were less expensive, filled some of the places white vaudevillians had left for another two decades.

THE LARGER WORLD OF BLACK VARIETY

Early in the twentieth century, many black entertainers got their start in show business as picks. Willie Covan and his brother Dewey, who spent their early childhood in Chicago, worked around 1908 as part of an act called Cosie Smith and Her Six Pickaninnies.[54] Other well known black performers who began as picks included Coot Grant, Dewey Weinglass, Luckey Roberts, Archie Ware, Eddie Rector, Lou Keane, and Toots Davis.[55] Margot Webb, who lived in Harlem in her middle-grade years and early teens, remembered traveling to New Jersey on weekends to work as a pick in musical comedy theatres there.[56] Both Margot Webb and Lena Horne worked as chorus girls at young ages.

Black show business—including TOBA and other variety venues—proved a haven to some children trapped in dire poverty or in dysfunctional family situations. Bill Robinson, for example, ran away from his grandmother's home at the age of eight, probably in 1886, riding the rails to Washington, DC, where he did odd jobs and stole early morning deliveries of milk and bread off porches to feed himself until he was able to get a job as a pick. Because of his independent, hand-to-mouth childhood, Robinson never attended school. He could not write his name until taught by his wife Fanny. He learned music by ear and learned his lines by having others read them to him. Perhaps because he honed his memory skills so carefully, he was said never to forget a face or name.

He did not get a reputation as a dancer until around 1900, when he won a dance contest in New York City. A show called *In Old Kentucky* was playing in Brooklyn and holding its regular Friday Buck and Wing dance contest in the theatre. One of the stars of the show was Harry Swinton, considered by many at the time to be the best dancer in the country. Each contestant took a number, and Swinton is said to have avoided the competition by taking a low one. Dancers performed in numerical order, and those who did their routines early were more quickly forgotten by the audience and the judges, and thus ruled out through no fault of their own. A higher number and a later spot were considered better for those who wanted to compete seriously. The Buck and Wing dancers of Brooklyn were tough to beat, and a gentleman might be forgiven for bowing out. Robinson won against the local talent, although he had not really competed directly against Swinton. From the account of

the event, it is clear that little had changed in dance contests since William Henry Lane. The execution judges still sat under the stage, while the time judges sat in the wings, and the style judges sat out front.[57] For the judges under the stage, the music beaten out by the dancer's feet was still a key standard by which his skill was measured.

When the competition was over, Robinson had earned a reputation as a Buck and Wing dancer. As most who knew him could attest, he was painstaking in his work, and so it is unlikely he rested on his laurels. Over time in bookings across the country, Robinson showed that he could lay down taps not only with perfect timing, but also in varying pitches, making his famous stair dance a work of beauty. In it, he moved up and down a small set of stairs in the middle of the stage:

His stair dance, when perfected, involved a different rhythm for each step—each one reverberating with a different pitch—and the fact that he had a special set of portable steps enhanced his claim to originating the dance. By the spring of 1921 it was a standard part of his act....[58]

Because he could tap out pitch as well as maintain exact rhythm, his feet created a distinctive jazz sound.

Furthermore, his taps were clean and crystal clear. He brought tap up onto its toes in a swinging rhythm, distinguishing it from older buck dance—in which the feet were worked close to the floor in sliding and scuffing steps—and giving it a new feeling of lightness and elegance. Part of his secret was his mastery of old-fashioned wooden-soled shoes:

They were split-clogs, ordinary shoes with a wooden half sole, about three eighths of an inch thick, and a wooden heel slightly higher than the leather heel on a street shoe. The wooden half sole was attached to the leather sole from the toe to a point behind the ball of the foot and thereafter was left looser to permit flexibility ... he wore out twenty to thirty pairs a year.[59]

Bill Robinson called attention to what he was doing with his feet by simply looking at them himself.

Robinson's shoes harked back to the wooden-soled shoes slaves had worn and danced in a century earlier.

He also had the showmanship to make audiences recognize and appreciate what he was doing on stage, in contrast to many other dancers, whose virtuoso routines went unappreciated by clueless reviewers and theatregoers. For example, Robinson led spectators to watch his feet by the simple expedient of watching them himself. He had excellent comic timing, a great singing voice, an appealing personality that won over his audiences, and the ability to train those who danced with him

This Bill Robinson Hair Dressing shows Robinson doing his trademark stair dance.

to perform to his own perfectionist standards. He was the first black dance star familiar to national white audiences, and his work opened doors and increased opportunities for black dancers in a variety of entertainment genres.

In addition, Robinson had spent years building relationships to help him avoid racist confrontations. Having lived on the streets as a child and teenager, and having faced unjust armed robbery charges, he knew the importance of making friends with the police. When he came to a new town, he went first to the police station to register his gun—a gun was important to any African American of the time who had to fear sudden racist violence—and to get to know the officers. Often, he gave them free tickets to his shows, and throughout his life he gave benefit performances for policemen and firemen killed in the line of duty. And because he never forgot a face, he was adept at picking out police and firemen in the audience and introducing them when his show began. His actions paid off—in a touchy situation, the police could generally be depended upon to help him rather than harm him.

Robinson's soft heart was legendary, and one of his concerns was always African Americans who had been arrested. Rae Samuels said, "He'd go down to night court, and if anyone had been arrested that had never been arrested before, he'd find out who they were and what they did and he'd get them out. He could talk [the police] out of anything, and he put up [bail] money, too."[60] If Robinson walked past a family being evicted, he would find their landlord, pay their back rent, and buy them groceries, too. He sent money to people who wrote him letters with hard luck stories, although his wife had to read the letters to him. He was known for presenting his friends with sumptuous gifts of expensive jewelry, and he had furriers make up a tiny ermine coat and bonnet for Shirley Temple's baby in 1948.

Robinson gave an almost incredible number of benefit performances that demonstrated his amazing stamina as well as his generosity. Eddie Brown, who appeared in The Bill Robinson Revue over a period of six years, testified that Robinson gave more than five hundred benefits a year, in addition to his multiple paid appearances in shows and at clubs.[61] Ed Sullivan remembered that he "used to be ashamed to call him up so often for benefit shows."[62] Robinson, who made enormous amounts of money in his career, died

In this Chicago cabaret, black dancers entertain a white audience in 1941. Courtesy Library of Congress.

penniless in part because of his giving nature. As Rosetta LeNoire said, it was because he "just loved people."[63] When he died in 1949, an estimated 32,000 people filed past his body as it lay in state in New York City and, and, celebrities from entertainment, sports, and politics jammed his funeral service.

While Robinson was perhaps the best representative of tap dance in the first half of the twentieth century, other black dancers were developing other genres of classical jazz dance on the variety stage. Ethel Waters was mistress of several older black social dances that became stage dances and then crossed racial lines to become social dances performed by whites at parties and in nightclubs. The first of these was the Shimmy. By the time Waters was seventeen (in 1917), she could do the dance with professional expertise. "I had developed into a really agile shimmy shaker," she wrote. "I sure knew how to roll and quiver, and my hips would become whirling dervishes."[64]

She gained her first employment as an entertainer, though, not as a dancer, but as a blues singer in a Philadelphia saloon, then in a Baltimore theatre earning ten dollars a week performing in an eggshell white satin dress purchased "at a rummage store."[65] She followed up with jobs in traveling shows outside TOBA, including a carnival. In the carnival tent, dancing was important. "We shimmied," she said, "only for the special delight of the men who paid their dimes to see us."[66] The next step was Harlem, where she performed at the Lincoln Theatre and in nightclubs. One of her featured acts was her "Shim-Me-Sha-Wabble" number, in which she sang and danced the Shimmy:

"The Shim-Me-Sha-Wabblers' Ball" (1918) was one of the earliest Shimmy songs, before there was a shared sense of how the dance's name should be spelled. Apparently, though, a sense of decorum led the publisher to show the dancers in ballet-like poses.

"Shim-Me-Sha-Wabble," the big shimmy song, had just come out. When the boys played that I'd put my hands on my hips and work my body fast, without moving my feet. There was never anything vulgar about my fast and furious wrigglings. Even in towns where other girl performers were stopped from shimmying by the local bluenoses, no one objected to my doing it.[67]

She also shimmied in a show in Atlantic City, where the Shimmy had been banned. But that did not stop Waters' performance. "After looking over the [Shimmy] I did the authorities said it was artistic and decent," she wrote, "and that I could go ahead and shake to my heart's content."[68] There, in a club called Rafe's Paradise, Waters' show attracted the big names in black show business. Bill Robinson, Florence Mills, and Bert Williams came to see her sing and dance.

When she returned to the TOBA circuit, she sang "Shake that Thing" for her closing number and danced for the encore.[69] By the 1920s, she had made the jump to white circuits such as Keith and Orpheum, where she sang and danced the Shimmy, the Black Bottom, and eccentric steps, adding in a comedy routine, too, for $750 per week. At a relatively young age, Ethel had achieved a level of success many other black performers could only dream of. Some of her material became part of the musical *Africana* in 1927. Waters, who is generally recognized primarily as a jazz singer, was also a superb dancer, and her interpretations of vernacular African American dances helped popularize them among white audiences.

Other black dancers made up their own comic and eccentric dance acts that combined acrobatics with tap or other forms. These individualistic blends, presented with skill and audience appeal, allowed dancers to get and keep jobs in venues across black variety entertainment. Jigsaw Jackson, for example, did a routine in which he kept his face on the floor in the center of the stage while his feet tapped in a circle around his face in perfect rhythm.[70] In his routine, Rubberlegs Wilson performed legomania with high kicks and moves from the Shimmy, Boogie Woogie, Camel Walk, and other dances.[71] Cook and Brown combined acrobatics, tap, vernacular social dance steps, and comedy to create a routine that audiences loved. Brown could drop "into a split, sliding the length of the stage, and bouncing up at the other end thumbing his nose," Stearns said. "It looks like bone-crushing mayhem, but it is actually carefully rehearsed dancing and acrobatics, with tiny Brown emerging triumphant at stage center in the finale doing a wildly satirical version of the Twist."[72]

Most of the members of the Crackerjacks, which varied from four to six performers, were acrobats who used their circus craft to enhance a dance act. The act included several routines. Among them were: a flash tap number involving group precision dance; a solo acrobatic-contortionist dance; and a version of the ancient Old Man act from minstrel shows in which the dancers hobble onstage dressed as graybeards and then gradually cast aside their canes and explode into almost superhuman agility, all in dance rhythm. The Crackerjacks wowed audiences in nightclubs, stage shows, and road shows. Stearns quotes Archie Ware on what made the group so successful. "We weren't just acrobats," he said. "We had an acrobatic *variety* act—we tumbled in different costumes, we tapped, we sang, we danced, we featured lots of comedy—and our act was the fastest and *the first to do it in swinging rhythm*."[73] The team lasted from the twenties to the fifties.

In the 1930s, acrobatics developed into flash dance—a breathtaking combination of acrobatics with tap. Willie Covan, a key figure, was born in 1897. He first attracted attention in the twenties doing a visually beautiful soft shoe with his partner Leonard Ruffin. This was a class act, a routine in which the performers both dressed and danced with eye-pleasing elegance. From there, Willie went on to form a four-person team, including his brother Dewey and their two wives—Willie's wife Florence had been a chorus line dancer

Bill Bailey, older brother of singer Pearl Bailey, was a brilliant dancer. He appeared in a number of films, including *Cabin in the Sky*.

when she married him. The Four Covans' act included jazz dancing without tap, a solo tap routine by Willie, a sequence of nearly incredible acrobatics, and a precision tap sequence by all four members of the troupe.[74] "Our dance was eight minutes," Willie Covan told Rusty Frank. He added, "We headlined white vaudeville."[75] After vaudeville died, Covan spent his time in Hollywood giving private dance lessons to white film stars.[76]

PRESENTS
Anna Mae
WINBURN

SINGING
DANCING
DIRECTING....

WITH
HER OWN
13

- COTTON CLUB BOYS -

The next stage in the development of flash as part of tap routines could be seen in the acts of the Berry Brothers and the Nicholas Brothers at the famous Cotton Club, where both teams performed consistently for several years.

THE COTTON CLUB

During the 1920s, the Cotton Club was a major Harlem nightspot. In the early years— it opened in 1923—it served only white patrons, as did Connie's Inn, also in Harlem. The Cotton Club engaged top quality black entertainers, especially dancers, and maintained a superb chorus line. Despite its discriminatory policies and the stereotypical themes it presented in its shows, the Cotton Club promoted African American talent by showcasing it for white audiences. The lavish, star-studded revues, the swinging jazz broadcast from the club around the nation via radio, and the celebrity patrons made the Cotton Club famous. Movie stars, politicians, and socialites traveled from the affluent neighborhoods of New York as well as from out of town to see the floorshows. Leading New York newspapers sent arts writers to review the opening nights of Cotton Club shows. Imitators of the concept sprang up across the nation.

Whites had gone "slumming" in Harlem for many years before the Cotton Club opened its doors, but prior to World War I, the patrons of the clubs and saloons in the neighborhood were still mostly black. After World War I, in 1919, a new era was triggered by the Volstead Act, which prohibited the manufacturing, transporting, and selling of alcoholic beverages. Mafia-backed "businessmen" entered quickly into bootlegging and looked around for ways and places to sell their products. In 1923, a prominent gangster named Owney Madden purchased a very large, open second floor space in Harlem. Originally intended to be a dance hall, the space was at the time a supper room named Club Deluxe, operated by former heavyweight champion Jack Johnson. Madden wanted to create a nightspot that would be a successful sales outlet for his brand of bootleg beer. He renamed the space the Cotton Club.

The interior was decorated to look like a southern plantation, and the band area, where Duke Ellington and Cab Calloway would later play the piano or dance while they conducted, was set up to look like the pillared front porch of a southern mansion. The décor and the name set the tone, and whites watching the floor show ordered drinks and food from black waiters. "I suppose," wrote Cab Calloway, "the idea was to make whites who came to the club feel like they were being catered to and entertained by black slaves."[77]

Although it employed all-black performers, the Cotton Club admitted only whites. Furthermore, the entertainment was groomed to represent the sensual, risqué themes many whites identified with black culture. Songs contained off-color material, and the chorus girls danced in abbreviated costumes sometimes decorated with fur or feathers to help conjure up an atmosphere of the exotic or the primitive. Artwork on menus and sheet music produced for the shows featured semi-nude girls, and Duke Ellington's "jungle" orchestra produced the expected growls and drumbeats.

Opposite page: **Anna Mae Winburn was a jazz bandleader in the late 1930s directing The Cotton Club Boys, from Omaha, Nebraska. She stayed with the group until it folded in 1940. From there, she went on to direct the first racially diverse, all-female jazz band in the United States, the International Sweethearts of Rhythm. She served as vocalist for the band, as it played for predominantly black audiences in theatres and ballrooms across the U.S.**

CLOVER LEAF BAR AND CABARET

SMALL'S PARADISE, 135th STREET and 7th AVE., NEW YORK CITY

Located at 135th Street and 7th Avenue, Small's Paradise was one of the three most popular jazz clubs in Harlem in the 1920s and 1930s, along with Connie's Inn and the Cotton Club.

These stereotypes only enhanced the patrons' sense of distance from the residents of Harlem. Jimmy Durante, for example, who was photographed at the club with friends, said, "It isn't necessary to mix with colored people if you don't feel like it. You have your own party and keep to yourself. But it's worth seeing. How they step!"[78] The hiring of the chorus line embodied some of the coldness in Durante's statement. Once it was established that the girls were excellent dancers, they were chosen for their physical characteristics. They all had to be very light in color, at least 5'6" tall, and all under 21 years of age. They were "tall, tan, and terrific," as one of the Cotton Club song titles proclaimed. Often choreographed by the talented Elida Webb, the girls were stars in their own right. Having been a chorine at the Cotton Club opened other doors in show business. It was common knowledge that only superb dancers could work there.

The color line in the club was relaxed slightly over the years. Lucille Wilson, later the wife of Louis Armstrong, auditioned at the club. She was attractive, and was a wonderful dancer. But she was dark-skinned. Management was uneasy about hiring her, and did so on a trial basis. If customers didn't like her, she could be let go. But there were no complaints, and she stayed in the line for eight years.[79]

Eventually, some black customers were admitted, as well. Because of Ellington's argument that it was a shame that his friends and the families of performers could not see the show, management gave in. Black customers were evaluated on a case-by-case basis, and usually given the worst seats. And, as Haskins points out, few Harlemites cared "to patronize the new semi-Jim Crow establishment," anyway.[80]

The Cotton Club became known across the country in part because of its radio broadcasts. New York radio stations did a number of remote broadcasts of live black jazz music

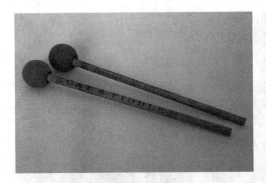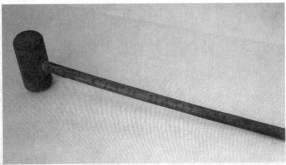

These small hammers were called cocktail knockers, and they were often given as souvenirs by nightclubs, including the Cotton Club. Customers could indicate their appreciation of a performance by using them to knock on the table. The pair is from the Cat and the Fiddle in Cincinnati, while the single knocker is from Club Harlem in Baltimore.

in the 1920s from nightclubs and dance halls like Club Alabam—where Fletcher Henderson and his orchestra, including Louis Armstrong, played—and Harlem spots like the Plantation Club, Savoy Ballroom, and Cotton Club. WHW and CBS broadcast the Duke Ellington orchestra live from the Cotton Club, presenting the music on more than two hundred radio shows between 1927 and 1930.[81] Haskins notes that these broadcasts made both the club and the Duke famous:

> What happened was that the "Cotton Club sound" became a national smash. Before long, nearly every American who had a radio knew of the Cotton Club, and what visions of glamour and sophistication and big-city wickedness that name conjured up in their minds! A trip to Harlem, and to the Cotton Club in particular, became a "must" for every Midwesterner who visited New York City. Tourists from all over the country came flocking uptown.[82]

The broadcasts that fired up listeners' imaginations also helped to spread the concept of Cotton Club imitators across the country, and probably boosted sales of a soft drink brand named Cotton Club.

People in other parts of the country also had opportunities to see the Cotton Club orchestras live. The club's bandleaders toured the nation with singers and dancers for months at a time, performing in both large theatres and in small dance halls both before and after the closing of the Cotton Club in 1940. In September, 1934, in Atlanta, for example, Cab Calloway and his orchestra played at an all-white Election Night dance one evening and at an all-black dance in the City Auditorium the next.[83] Vocalist Dotty Saulters and her husband, dancer Cholly Atkins, both traveled in the Cab Calloway Revue.[84] Duke Ellington often traveled with dancers Bunny Briggs and Baby Laurence.

Initially, the Cotton Club band and even all the waiters, cooks, and busboys had been imported from Chicago, to ensure their loyalty. But Duke Ellington had been hired in 1927, when he was relatively unknown, and Owney Madden had used mob muscle to get him out of his then-current contract with Gibson's Standard Theater in Philadelphia.[85] At first an unknown quantity, Ellington and his band began proving their brilliance immediately. The rest of the entertainment was composed of already-well known black talent. For a time, Lew Leslie staged the Cotton Club shows, which were similar to black Broadway revues. (Leslie was also the creator of the *Blackbirds* revues, which were hits on Broadway and also traveled to England and France.) Later, Leslie was replaced by the equally talented Herman Stark.

This photo captures a Harlem chorus line some time during the late 1920s.

New shows were premiered every six months. As Constance Hill has pointed out, "Opening nights at the Cotton Club were as exciting and important as any on Broadway. The newspapers sent their top columnists, celebrities studded the audience, and the club was filled to capacity."[86] Among these columnists were Ed Sullivan, then a reporter for the *New York Daily News*, Walter Winchell, and Louis Sobol, who reviewed the shows for their readers.[87]

Audiences at the club were able to enjoy the magnificent jazz of Duke Ellington, and in later years, the energetic conducting of Cab Calloway. Of him, Haskins writes, "From the first downbeat to the last note of a number, he was all motion. He waved his arms, he ran back and forth from orchestra to microphone, he danced in a frenzy to the music."[88] Dancers included Ethel Waters, Bill Robinson, the Cotton Club Boys (one of whom was Cholly Atkins), Earl "Snake Hips" Tucker, Florence Mills, Buck and Bubbles, Whyte's Lindy Hoppers, and a host of other stars.

Lena Horne got her first show business job at the Cotton Club, where she began as a chorus girl and moved up to singing. She found, however, that quitting to go on to other jobs was not easy. Haskins writes, "On Lena's last night at the club, both her mother and stepfather confronted the club bosses, who were furious. When verbal persuasion and threats did not work, they beat up her stepfather, pushed his head down a toilet bowl and then threw him out." Lena was then compelled to perform through the evening's shows. Eventually, she and her mother left the club surrounded by a protective circle of chorus girls.[89]

A card advertises the Cotton Club Revue, performing at the London Palladium in 1937. The cast was composed of superb entertainers, and included tap dance, adagio, and Lindy Hop, as well as the classic jazz dance of the Berry Brothers.

Among the greatest dancers to perform at the Cotton Club were the Nicholas Brothers and the Berry Brothers, whose tap and flash acts were visually and musically stunning. The Nicholas Brothers began their classical tap act early. Leonard Reed, a dancer on the TOBA circuit, said he saw them dance with their sister Dorothy at the Lincoln Theatre in Baltimore in 1926, when Fayard would have been twelve and Harold five.[90] In 1932, the 18- and 11-year-old brothers performed in the Vitaphone short *Pie, Pie, Blackbird* with Eubie Blake at the piano. Heat and cooking are the central metaphors of the film. Eubie Blake and his "hot" jazz musicians rise on a platform out of a giant pie onstage, all wearing white chef hats. The two boys enter and toss off beautiful steps, beginning with a classy soft shoe and moving into a Charleston tap routine performed in a challenge format. They take turns topping each other's steps in a routine that "cooks" and gets "hotter" with each boy's performance in turn. The dance, including paddle-and-rolls, trenches, crossovers, and perches, is finally so "hot" that smoke begins to rise up around them and the entire scene bursts into flame.[91]

Constance Hill points out that the performed steps are reminiscent of older buck dancing steps while also looking forward to the higher, lighter steps to come that used more space on the stage.[92] Moreover, the brothers at this point in their careers were already using the soft shoe and challenge format that would show up again and again in their acts. They

The young Nicholas Brothers pose here with Josephine Baker.

were masters of handing off a routine to each other, performing in consecutive solos, and combining these tradeoffs with precision duets, singing, comedy, and acrobatics, always performed in elegant dress with a suave, cool style. The challenge, as Hill notes, was what gave their routines a sense of mounting tension, cooled and balanced by exchanges of verbal wit, as well as a dynamic exchange of rhythm and style, and a sense of ongoing improvisation, all of which entranced their audiences.[93]

They auditioned for the *Cotton Club Parade* of 1932 and received an offer from Herman Stark for $750 per week, substantially more than an offer from Connie's Inn for $500 per week. When the *Parade* premiered in October, the boys again performed soft shoe and challenge solos. To this, they added a finale that Hill describes in some detail: "Their finale, danced to 'Bugle Call Rag,' W. C. Handy's classic composition of 1916 that opened with a high-pitched bugle solo, was an explosion of offbeat rhythms and alternating solos punctuated with superbly timed splits and surprising flips."[94] The routine now included serious acrobatics, and this material made the Nicholas Brothers, still only 18 and 11 years old, not only a classical tap act, but also a flash act.

The Nicholas Brothers, two youngsters amid the lavishly costumed adult singers and dance acts and the skimpily dressed chorus girls, found something of a home in the Cotton Club. They danced there for seven years, from 1932 to 1939, with time out for gigs

Norton and Margot performed elegant ballroom dance with balletic grace.

overseas, in movies, and in vaudeville. During these years, their flash steps became more and more spectacular as they incorporated high leaps, twists, and splits into their tap routines.

During the same period of time, another tap dance act using some flash—the three Berry Brothers (born 1922, 1914, and ca. 1912) were also wowing audiences. The older two brothers, Ananias and James, got their start in the 1920s on the church circuit. They played the Cotton Club in 1929 and, like the Nicholas Brothers, were so successful that they were brought back again and again, essentially using the club as home base while they also completed bookings in other venues. For four years, they returned repeatedly in between playing in *Lew Leslie's Blackbirds*, at Radio City Music Hall, in Europe, and across the U.S.[95] Ananias left the dance duo when he married Valaida Snow, when youngest brother Warren joined it to fill in the gap, and then Ananias returned to make the duo into a trio. Rusty Frank writes that the act was based on the individual skills and personalities of the brothers: "James was the comedian and singer; Ananias was the king of the Strut; and Warren was the solid dancer/acrobat. Together, they combined their talents to form one of the most exciting flash acts known."[96] It was filled with splits, high kicks, spins, a flying somersault, and absolutely split-second timing, all in rhythm to jazz music.

But Warren Berry emphasized to Rusty Frank that the brothers were primarily tap dancers rather than flash dancers. "We never wore tap shoes," he said. "We tapped—but without taps on our shoes." He added, "We always had a lovely description of our act—exotic Soft Shoe dancing, acrobatic Soft Shoe dancing. Flashy, yes. But not really in the flash range. I wouldn't say it was a 'flash act.'"[97]

In 1938, both the acts—The Nicholas Brothers and the Berry Brothers—were booked for the same show at the Cotton Club. The Berry Brothers' spot came at the end of the rather long show (lasting two and one-half hours), when the audience could be expected to be a little tired. Furthermore, the act's chief rivals for the spotlight were scheduled roughly halfway through. The Berry team knew they had to put together a routine that was breathtaking. They decided on an ending—a high, gut-wrenching, twelve-foot leap over the Cab Calloway orchestra onto the stage, landing in splits. It required split-second timing for all three brothers to land together at the same instant. What made the act even more astonishing was that it was never rehearsed. Warren explained, "Now, the whole thing about this act, incidentally, was the fact—between Nyas and Jimmy—that they hated to rehearse."[98]

On the night of the performance, this is how it worked out, in perfect timing and with no rehearsal:

> Just before the end of their act Ananias and Jimmy Berry jumped up on the band platform and then sprinted further up the stairs (followed by spotlights) and took a running leap out, over the heads of the musicians—twelve feet through the air—and down to the stage, landing with their legs apart in a body-rending split on both sides of Warren Berry, who had just snapped out of a twisting back somersault into a split of his own at stage center—*all on the last note of the music*.[99]

Warren added, "as they slid to where I was (I had just completed my Flip-Flop-Twist), we would be up—the three of us—and then do a hand spring, split, up—and bow right on the beat. It was terrific. At that point the people went crazy."[100] No one who had seen it was likely to ever forget it. But this wildly risky and exhausting kind of routine was why the Berry Brothers' act was short (only four and a half minutes) and why acrobatic dancers often did not last long. Over time, the wear and tear on their bodies was too much.

A third pioneering, inimitable dancer who performed at the club was the superb jazz tap star John Bubbles. Bubbles, born in 1902, got his start in show business as part of a

The Berry Brothers pose with hats and canes. From left to right, James, Warren, and Ananias.

child dance act. Aged ten and six, he and Ford Lee Washington formed Buck and Bubbles. They began playing small-time dates but quickly drew attention. Eventually, they skipped TOBA and went directly to the top of white vaudeville, playing the Palace in 1922.[101] Bubbles was a dancer admired by other dancers. With an air of boredom, he tossed off amazingly complex steps that no one else had the skill to steal.

But his greatest accomplishment, one that enshrined him forever in tap history, was originating a new style called rhythm tap. The late Fayard Nicholas described it: "Most dancers only danced on their toes. He brought this heel beat into tap dancin'—rhythm and syncopation! It was really something."[102] In dropping his heel to create additional percus-

In this picture, a young Buck and Bubbles perform together. Bubbles is on the left, and Buck is seated at the piano.

sion on the stage, Bubbles created new accents. Unlike some other dancers who were focusing on flash steps and speed, Bubbles was interested in enhancing the rhythmic sound of tap. He showed how his style of tapping could change the accents of the dance and create a new sound. The legacy of what he created was later called Jazz Tap.

The Cotton Club's flaws must not be permitted to overshadow its achievements, the most important of which was bringing exposure to black dancers who otherwise might never have been seen by white audiences and thus encouraging the development of new forms of jazz dance. The club made audiences aware of the jazz sound of Duke Ellington, not only in New York City, but also throughout the nation. Within its space, new-old dances originating from African American movement vocabulary were introduced—the Susie-Q, the Shag, Truckin,' and others. These dances might have never been seen in mainstream ballrooms, but in part because they drew attention at the Cotton Club, they appeared in Arthur Murray's dance instruction booklets, which were widely purchased and studied.[103]

A race riot occurred in Harlem in 1935, and the Cotton Club moved from the neighborhood in 1936 amid mounting racial tensions, which were worsened by the economic pressure of the Depression. The Club relocated downtown to Broadway and 48th, where it attempted to conduct business as usual. But it lasted there only a few years, in part because of the 1939 federal campaign to collect back taxes, which resulted in court dates and heavy fines for the club's management. Furthermore, Prohibition was over, and the club was no longer important as a way to sell bootlegged liquor. The Cotton Club closed permanently in June, 1940.

MOVIES AND TELEVISION

A number of black dance stars appeared in movies of the period. Bill Robinson worked in features with Shirley Temple, played a servant to Will Rogers in *In Old Kentucky*, danced with Jeni Legon in *Hooray for Love*, played opposite Lena Horne in *Stormy Weather*, and performed a dance sequence in the *Big Broadcast of 1936*. Donald Bogle has called Robinson and Temple "the screen's first interracial couple,"[104] and indeed they were two actors of different races who were able to meet each other on terms of mutual affection and respect. Elsewhere in the screen world, prejudice and stereotypes held sway. Blacks mostly played servants or jungle natives, or did specialty song and dance numbers. The latter were carefully circumscribed so as to be easily removed by southern censors, who did not permit non-subservient images of blacks to be seen.[105] According to *Variety*, servile roles comprised eighty percent of all movie roles for blacks in the 1920s.[106]

Some of the best of black dance talent appeared in specialty song and dance numbers in predominantly white movies. The films *Stormy Weather* and *Cabin in the Sky* (both released in 1943), however, represented a significant step away from the older stereotyped roles African Americans had performed. Both the films were all-black features created by major studios, presenting black stars in roles with character depth and development. Furthermore, each movie included dance by superb black dancers. In a nightclub scene, *Cabin in the Sky* offers up a brilliant tap dance by John Bubbles as Domino Johnson. *Stormy Weather* gave its audiences not only the tap dance of Bill Robinson, but also a dynamite tap and flash number by the Nicholas Brothers.

The Nicholas Brothers' scene was one of the most powerful dance sequences in American film. In a nightclub scene, the brothers leap from table to table, and then tap dance on the stage floor in a series of "spins, cramprolls, turns, and crossover steps" that lead into solos and duets. Next, they land in a back-slide split and jump-split to bring themselves to the first level of the orchestra platform. They leap from one drum-like shape to another, tapping out the rhythms of the music, "moving higher and higher up past the rows of musicians, and criss-crossing each other midair as they jumped." Few who saw the movie could take their eyes off the brothers as they "jumped over the heads

In 1938, Lena Horne made her first film appearance in *The Bronze Venus*. Courtesy Library of Congress.

This dance act probably performed in the 1950s.

of the musicians, skipping lightly from drum to drum until they landed once again on the stage floor."

In the second dancing chorus, they leapt up a flight of stairs, danced with acrobatic moves along a narrow platform above the musicians, and then jumped downward to the top of a piano one level below. From there, they launched into the air over the heads of musicians to land on the stage floor. Then they went back to the stairs, moving up and down them in riveting leapfrogs and splits, finally sliding down curving ramps in full-splits.[107]

The routine received rave reviews, and like the Berry Brothers number at the Cotton Club, was unrehearsed. Fayard commented, "Nick Castle said not to rehearse it, that we knew what to do, so we did it like a rehearsal. And in one take!"[108] Like Warren Berry, Fayard was careful to point out that what he and his brothers did was not simply flash. Instead, acrobatic moves formed part of their tap choreography:

When we tapped, we added a little ballet to it, plus a little eccentric, a little flash, and we used our hands a great deal. With style and grace we used the whole body from our heads down to our toes. And that's why we called our type of dancing classical tap. That's what it is — the lacing together of tap, balletic leaps and turns, and dazzling acrobatics.[109]

To that, we might add that the entire sequence was completed in the inimitable style of the brothers — coolly and professionally, with complete mastery of their art.

Television was another world. In the fifties, black dancers appeared from time to time on variety shows,

This is an early photo of Peg Leg Bates, who is shown with a hat and cane.

although, as Cholly Atkins pointed out, "they also paid very low in the fifties."[110] Coles and Atkins danced on *The Ford Hour*, *The Kate Smith Show*, *The Garry Moore Show*, and *The Milton Berle Show*. The time devoted to the dancers and their routines, however, was minimal. "Producers never wanted more than three minutes," Atkins noted.[111]

Dancer Peg Leg Bates appeared on *The Ed Sullivan Show* more than any other tap dancer—twenty-one times.[112] Bates had lost his leg below the knee to an accident in a cottonseed mill when he was twelve. He immediately set about proving that he could continue his beloved dancing despite his disability. With his peg leg he mastered all the major styles of tap dance. Rusty Frank wrote, "In addition to his top-rate ability as a rhythm tap dancer, Peg Leg Bates was thoroughly accomplished in acrobatics, flash, legomania, and novelty repertoire, all of which he incorporated widely into his dancing."[113]

Bates began dancing in minstrel shows and carnivals, after which he graduated to TOBA in 1922, and in 1926 made the jump to black Broadway, European bookings, clubs, and high-class vaudeville. He created tap steps to work with his three taps (two-legged dancers had four), and his act proved to be enduring, spanning four decades. Through his appearances on *The Ed Sullivan Show*, he became known to mainstream audiences.

The Four Step Brothers also got television work. The group was another tap and flash team, begun in the mid-twenties and lasting into the sixties. The team's members were not really brothers, but friends who enjoyed working together. They began by practicing together in one member's home and at the Hoofers Club and then talked their way into the Cotton Club. They danced there for four years at the same time they worked both black and white circuits. The team replaced members when necessary, and a total of ten dancers belonged to the group over the years. Their trademark was challenge dance, spiced with comedy. Their television appearances included *The Perry Como Show*, *The Ed Sullivan Show*, and *Texas Star Theatre*.

THE END OF AN ERA

As tap was dying out in the 1940s and 1950s, one team tried valiantly to survive. Coles and Atkins were a class act, a team marked not only by classy dress, but also by graceful and sophisticated moves. The duo's routine came to personify the class act, combining precision tap with comedy and singing, for a total of six to twelve minutes onstage. Atkins gave the team balletic moves, and Coles was a brilliant rhythm dancer. Cholly Atkins said Honi Coles "did the same type of things that Bubbles had done, but at much faster tempo ... His dancing was just so complex and so technical, it was hard for the average person sitting in the audience to really understand what he was doing."[114]

Marshall and Jean Stearns described Coles and Atkins as a class act "transformed by additional accents into new rhythmic patterns." The Stearnses wrote, "Relaxed and smiling, Coles and Atkins toss off gliding turns, leaning pull-ups, casual slides, and crystal-clear taps. The suspense is continuous, the execution flawless." Coles and Atkins could work at slow tempo, holding the audience transfixed, or they could incorporate dazzling speed.[115]

The two met before World War II, were both inducted into the Army, and tried to make a living with their act after peace returned. They found it extraordinarily difficult. Coles and Atkins traveled with big bands, including those of Cab Calloway, Louis Armstrong, Charlie Barnet, Lionel Hampton, Billy Eckstine, and Count Basie, through the late forties. They danced in *Gentlemen Prefer Blondes* from 1949 to 1951.[116] In the fifties, when work became thinner, they took their act to theatres, Las Vegas, and television, wherever

A club's jazz combo poses together in front of a painted backdrop.

they could get bookings. Eventually, they had to accept other jobs. Coles became the production manager of the Apollo Theatre, and Atkins began a long career of working with vocal groups, both independently and for Motown. He coached the Cadillacs, the Spinners, Gladys Knight and the Pips, the Supremes, the Temptations, and many more, choreographing them and teaching them performance technique. Like other black dancers who retired from active performance, Coles used his talent to influence a new generation of performers.

What had happened to dry up traditional dance work in variety entertainment? A number of factors played a role. People were moving to the suburbs and found it inconvenient to go to urban theatres for an evening out. Television allowed audiences to see top-notch performers in the comfort of their living rooms. Amusement taxes grated harshly on clubs with entertainment, and to survive, many simply went to small jazz combos and eliminated other performers. Bebop came in, with rhythms and improvisation techniques that made it difficult to dance to. Tap in its myriad varieties fell out of favor. Black dance forms that had been in demand for half a century no longer drew audiences. It was indeed the end of an era.

Raymond King and Jared Crawford create a beat using pots and pans for percussion in *Bring in 'Da Noise, Bring in 'Da Funk*, in 1997. Courtesy National Afro-American Museum and Cultural Center. Photo reprinted by permission of photographer, Michal Daniel.

CONCLUSION

During the first half of the twentieth century, African American variety entertainment broke new barriers and created new forms, while still exhibiting the characteristics of African-based dance. Tap, which dominated the theatrical dance of the period, continued to add jazz percussion to the polyrhythms of its accompaniment, while pushing the boundaries of its form outward into flash elements, eccentric dance, rhythm tap, and more. The great dancers of the period, from Bill Robinson to the Nicholas Brothers to Coles and Atkins, through improvisation and competition, created ever more breathtaking routines.

Moreover, as Ethel Waters' memoirs show, the sense of community between the dancer and black audiences was still strong. When she moved from TOBA to white vaudeville, she immediately felt something was missing in the audience response. After performing her first show in "white time," she said to her partner Earl Dancer: "You know we took the flop of our lives just now. Those people out front applauded us only because they wanted to be polite. Nobody stomped as they always do in colored theaters when I finish my act. Nobody screamed or jumped up and down. Nobody howled with joy."[117] Actually, though, Waters had wowed them. What was missing was the open and vociferous exchange between the performer and black audience that she was accustomed to sharing.

This tradition was also continued by the Apollo theatre as it never was in white-audience venues. The Apollo continued to serve its Harlem audiences with live perform-

ances into the fifties and sixties. Moreover, the theatre featured what the audience pre-
ferred: comedy—the "sharp-tongued, sexually explicit, race-conscious genre that is the
bedrock of African American humor"[118]; dance, which had to be high quality or face the
contempt of the spectators; and competition through its Wednesday night amateur shows,
which over the years brought exposure to Ella Fitzgerald, Sarah Vaughn, Nancy Wilson,
Gladys Knight, James Brown, Lauryn Hill, and other entertainment greats. Throughout
the decades, the Apollo reflected traditional African American entertainment values as no
other venue could.

There was also ongoing communication between African American musicians and
dancers. Not only did their rhythms influence each other, but they also communicated during performance in an improvisatory way. Jeni Legon, for example, remembers her dynamic
challenge exchanges with Fats Waller: "he'd play something on the piano, a rhythm pattern—and I would imitate it with my feet. Then I'd say, 'I bet he can't do this,' and I'd do
one, and he'd answer on the piano. We would do that back and forth maybe for a chorus."[119]
The sense of community and communication was still very much alive.

Tap never really died—it was kept alive for a new generation through the brilliance
of masters like Jimmy Slyde, Buster Brown, Eddie Brown, Honi Coles, Chuck Green, Harriet Browne, Charles "Cookie" Cook, and Fayard and Harold Nicholas. Although many of
the great African American tap dancers found themselves without steady theatrical jobs
for much of the second half of the twentieth century, they were able to transmit their art
to a new generation. They lived to see the formation of tap organizations like the National
Tap Ensemble, Jazz Tap Ensemble, American Tap Dance Foundation, and Manhattan Tap.
Furthermore, new tap stars like Gregory Hines and the young Savion Glover emerged, calling attention to their craft in Broadway shows like *The Tap Dance Kid* (1983), *Black and
Blue* (1989), *Jelly's Last Jam* (1992), and *Bring in da Noise, Bring in da Funk* (1996). *Noise
/ Funk* was a tap history of blacks in America, using percussive foot rhythms to tell a pow-
erful story. It proved that a new generation of tap dancers had the talent and imagination
to take an old art to a new level and give it new form.

8

Grassroots

As the first quarter of the twentieth century ended, African Americans were still suffering from racist stereotypes and brutality, at the same time the black northward migration that swelled during World War I was speeding the growth of black communities in urban areas. Harlem, for example, had the largest black population of any urban neighborhood in the world and was becoming a center for black arts. The development of these arts, including music, literature, dance, painting, photography, and other forms of expression, became known as the Harlem Renaissance. While these gains were being made, blacks were continuing be victimized in lynchings and other racial violence. In 1919, there were 83 recorded lynchings of blacks in the U.S.; in 1920, there were 59; in 1921, there were 59. The Lincoln Memorial was dedicated in 1922, in a segregated event in which African Americans had to stand in a roped-off area behind the white audience. The Ku Klux Klan had grown to about 4.5 million members by the middle of the decade, at the same time Asa Philip Randolph was organizing the black union named the Brotherhood of Sleeping Car Porters, and black newspapers were becoming established in cities across the country. These newspapers called for equality in jobs, education, and other arenas. Carter G. Woodson, leader of the Association for the Study of Negro Life and History, inaugurated Negro History Week in 1926, a tradition that would later become Black History Month. Throughout the nation, African Americans continued to struggle with oppression and to work for equal treatment. The arts were a major arena of this undertaking.

In the struggle, black entertainers, especially dancers, drew on a stream of cultural riches from the past. From the beginnings of black theatrical performance, dance material presented onstage had often come from grassroots sources ultimately indebted to the plantation, early free black communities, and Africa. By the twentieth century, these sources were manifesting themselves in the rent party, street corner, rural or urban club, dance contest and marathon, dance hall, and other places where ordinary people showed off steps. The forms performed there can be loosely labeled *vernacular* dance, defined by Roberts in 1995 as "dance that people create in homes and clubs" and described as "a tremendously significant expressive tradition."[1] Evidence of it was and is everywhere. The star of a local dance hall, for example, might capture attention at a dance marathon. Patrons of a saloon might applaud and reward a busker—someone who entertains and then passes a hat for contributions. Teens might introduce an original dance form at a high school prom. Such informal, fluid situations provided a steady stream of new performance concepts to anyone who saw them, and simultaneously dances onstage and off influenced and cross-fertilized each other.

Often the process was dizzyingly complex, as when an old African American dance exploded on a New York stage as the Charleston, then crossed the footlights again to become a mainstream social dance seen at parties and in clubs, while also being performed by youngsters on street corners for coins from passers-by, and then was glimpsed over and

Above: This couple is enjoying a dance at a party or club, ca. 1940s. *Opposite page:* These two drawings from the *New York Times* show the Charleston as it was being danced on the street corner and onstage in a cabaret. From the *New York Times Sunday Magazine*, August 30, 1925.

over as its steps were incorporated into newer theatrical forms and routines throughout vaudeville and other venues. The *Sunday Magazine* of the *New York Times* for August 30, 1925, in an article called "The Charleston Prances into Favor," emphasized the phenomenon with two illustrations: one of African American boys improvising presentations of the dance on a street corner and one of a professional entertainer performing it on a cabaret stage.

Thus dance moves that had been passed down through generations were revised, recombined, and given new flourishes, ultimately flowering in dozens of ways in both African American and mainstream culture here and abroad. What did not change, however, were the fundamental African American qualities of the dance—the percussion, polyrhythms, and African movement vocabulary on which it was based; the orientation to the earth, use of special objects, pantomime, and frequent circle and line format that shaped its form; and the competition, community, and improvisation that spurred its development. What also did not change was the attention given to the process by its society. Typically, new dances with the ancient characteristics were joyfully embraced by dancers, hotly condemned by moral authority, and enthusiastically written about by the press.

LEARNING TO DANCE AT HOME, MOVING ON TO THE STREETS

Most African Americans learned to dance at home, taught by parents, siblings, and other relatives. As Roberts points out, "intergenerational dancing at home seems to have been a common experience for African Americans of all age groups."[2] While Roberts' study focuses on Philadelphia, his comments apply to communities throughout the nation. He writes that he sees dance as "a dynamic form of African American creative art, constantly changing within proscribed parameters defined by an African American tradition of creative cultural production."[3] We can add that one of the defining and continuing features of this tradition is the enormous value placed on dancing, and the passionate enjoyment of it as a leisure activity.

A few young people who practiced dance moves at home, like the Nicholas Brothers, became professionals who went straight to the theatrical stage and nightclub floorshow. Most others who wanted to be professionals, however, began in humbler ways. Performing on street corners and busking in saloons, cafes, and ballrooms gave many an audience. Bunny Briggs began dancing on the street in 1927 when he was only five years old. A man called Porkchops saw him and asked Briggs' mother permission to take the tiny dancer around to dance halls. "All I did at that time would be the Charleston and the Mess Around," recalled Briggs, and remembers that people would "throw money."[4] In later years after a successful career, Briggs remembered that he "was always an improvisation dancer." He added, "I danced in the streets, I danced in hallways, I danced in hot-dog stands, and I danced for society."[5]

As Frank commented, "Dancing on street corners was an integral part of many a dancer's schooling, and it was not, by any means, casual. There a dancer had to demonstrate bona fide skill to 'survive.'" She explained, "If a dancer could not 'cut it,' there was just no staying on that particular corner. Corners were ranked, and a dancer's goal was to move up to the top corner. It was not easy. There was a tremendous amount of competition."[6]

A mother watches her children dance, ca. 1930s.

LaVaughn Robinson grew up tap dancing on the streets of Philadelphia. Robinson, who learned the time step at home from his mother, said, "In the 1930s, you could walk from one end of South Street to the other and see a different style of tap dancing just about on every corner." Robinson saw competition as the essence of street dance: "Tap dancing had become very competitive. It was like gunfighters. When a dancer would come in town, there was always somebody there ready to challenge him." He added that dancers without much skill started on 25th and South, then worked their way through 21st and 20th where tap dancers were "mediocre." The expert dancers—men and women—held territory around the fourteen hundred block. Where you danced said something about your skill. When you conquered the streets, you could move up to busking, and some of the tips you earned had to go to the musicians in the club or bar you chose to dance in, the people who supported your act with music.[7] Getting seen, achieving recognition, and getting paid—these accomplishments were all part of the informal system that allowed you to advance from amateur status to professional.

DANCE MARATHONS AND THE LINDY HOP

Dancers and their steps also gained exposure through dance contests. Such contests had been around for centuries when the marathon came into being as a new subset of competition. The format was born partly of the 1920s penchant for any expression of novelty or originality that smacked of spunk and fun, and partly of the economic desperation of the Depression. In the 1920s, the contest form was simple; entrants simply danced until exhaustion forced them out of the running. By the 1930s, though, the marathon was a

A busker and his accompanist (in foreground on left with guitar) are performing for contributions, probably in the 1940s.

staged event replete with self-expression, entertainment, and publicity. An advance man arranged all the logistics, gained the support of local authorities, and began a public relations effort.[8] Next, the professional marathoners arrived, many of whom followed promoters from place to place to make some money.[9] Then local dancers, some simply looking for free meals, including coffee breaks with doughnuts, and other amenities, entered the contest. Finally, the paying public was invited in.

As the genre developed, so did the rules and theatrical effects. Couples had to "dance" for forty-five minutes of every hour, although toward the end of the event that could simply mean dozing on your feet as you were dragged around the floor by your partner. The rest periods could be spent changing clothes, eating, getting a shave or hair wash by the barber and beauty shops set up on the sidelines, or getting a massage or manicure. Often, the fifteen-minute break was not enough, and a dancer went back to the floor followed by a manicurist or barber. Contestants had to be judged fit by medical staff, who also treated injuries, especially foot injuries, incurred during the ordeal.[10] The marathon lengthened into a drama. Couples got married during the event. Individuals were brought forward to the microphone to sing or tell their stories for the audience. Promoters organized dancing "sprints," in which already-exhausted entrants could risk huge expenditure of effort to win additional purses. Also, audience members could reward dancers with a shower of coins or offer additional prize money for the best original or specialty dance. All these elements kept things interesting.

Moreover, promoters could exploit any local disapproval of the event for publicity. Sometimes, police tried to make arrests when the marathon extended into Sundays—many local blue laws forbade conducting business or working on Sunday. Martin writes:

When warrants were served to dancers in the 1923 marathon contest in Houston, it was McMillan, the promoter of the contest ... who stepped in to post the bond for the contestants. McMillan was the host, promoter, proprietor, protector, sponsor, and advocate of both the dance marathon event and the individual dancers. In their roles as both proprietors and protectors, men like McMillan commanded a new kind of respect and notoriety.[11]

Casting the event as a struggle between the young and the old, between youth culture and repressive church members or town officials, always drew attention. The marathon typically challenged longstanding moral attitudes by encouraging the new dances, many of which had come from the African American community. These "hot" dances involved shoulder and hip shaking, close embrace, syncopated jazz rhythms, and animal pantomime, as with the Bunny Hug, Turkey Trot, Camel Walk, and Grizzly Bear. When the arbiters of taste and morality condemned the dances, the contestants frequently gained the support of the press, dramatizing the situation to their own advantage and amusement.

The staging, the drama, the publicity, and the focus on novelty all invited the showcasing of original steps. In 1928, a marathon in New York's Manhattan Casino went on for eighteen days. Reporters Walter Winchell and Ed Sullivan, who were working for the New York *Graphic*, covered the event. They added human interest to their accounts by paying special attention to an African American dancer named George "Shorty" Snowden, whose moves were eye-catching. When some audience members offered five- and ten-dollar prizes for the best specialty dance, Snowden responded by spinning his partner outward in a manner that today we all recognize as part of the Jitterbug. In this "break" Snowden did some solo steps. The audience cheered, clearly pleased with having encouraged something new and exciting. The reporters asked Snowden what he had been doing. "The Lindy," he replied, making a clear reference to Charles "Lindy" Lindbergh and his recent "hop" across the Atlantic.[12]

Snowden was an extremely accomplished dancer, a regular at the Savoy Ballroom in Harlem who was known for putting together impressive combinations of steps and performing them with speed and smoothness. The new dance he had demonstrated was something like the Texas Tommy, a dance that had been around for decades and that Ethel Williams had performed in *Darktown Follies*. Perhaps Snowden knew the older dance and had used some of its moves. Some say the Lindy also owed something to the Breakaway, a dance that developed in Harlem in the early twenties, which included both Charleston steps and the classic breakaway move. Whatever the circumstances of its origin, the Lindy included the breakaway, a moment when the couple swung apart and partners inserted their own improvised steps. Through this and other features, the dance combined elements of both European and African dance heritage—couple dance, solo dance, improvisation, orientation to the earth, and swinging rhythms.

The breakaway is a key feature that provides a moment of freedom and self-expression. Gottschild comments, "the Lindy-Hopper or rhythm tap dancer is allowed to insert anything, no holds barred, into her improvisations. Movements that are humorous, imitative, abstract or sober may be juxtaposed, so that the concept of uniformity may be undermined—as long as one keeps the timing and preserves the rhythm."[13] Moreover, this free-flowing creativity made the Lindy into a superb contest dance. The history of vernacular dance for the next thirty years was strewn with posters advertising Lindy or Jitterbug contests.

The Lindy became known as the Jitterbug in 1935, when Benny Goodman and his orchestra played the new swing music in the Palomar Ballroom in Los Angeles. About 4,000 couples Lindy Hopped to the beat, and a news writer called them "jitterbugs." From then on, Lindy Hopping to swing music was called Jitterbugging. The magnitude of the phenomenon became clear in 1938 when 23,400 people jammed Randalls Island to Jitter-

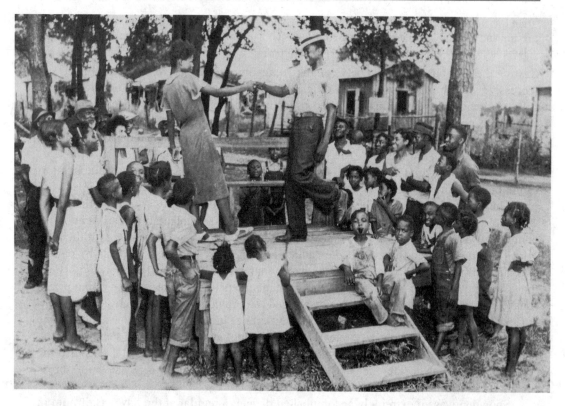

A young couple dances the Lindy on an outdoor platform in Florida, probably in the 1930s.

bug for nearly six hours to 25 swing orchestras, whose musicians had to be protected by police from the overly enthusiastic crowd.[14]

The form reached technical brilliance with the invention of fast, acrobatic steps in places like the Savoy ballroom, at dance contests like the famous Harvest Moon Ball contest in Madison Square Garden, and in the performances of professional dance teams like Whyte's Hopping Maniacs, who appeared on stage and in films in the 1930s and 1940s. McDonagh provides a good description of what a performance of the Lindy/Jitterbug might look like:

> With her right hand firmly hooked into his left and the other lightly draped on his right shoulder, she placed her weight on the balls of her feet, raising her heels slightly. His right hand was touching her waist as they stepped to the syncopated beat that shifted rhythmic emphasis from the normal to the unanticipated counts. A light push from him would send her in a half turn out and away and she would return on the next count. If the push were inward she did a full circle under his raised arm and closed in the familiar starting position. A few torso twists in unison and they were ready for the next "flight" which could be a double turn.... When the Lindy was properly executed the young woman looked like a top with her hair flying out.[15]

When the woman held her right hand behind her back, and when her partner used his right hand to reach around her left side to take her right hand and spin her around, the move was called the Texas Tommy.[16] Thus some of the terminology recalled a source of the dance. There were also "air" steps in which the woman leaped at the same time she was tossed into the air, flying completely over her partner's head or landing on his back before sliding to her feet. Other spectacular aerial steps involved high flips. Interspersed with all this acrobatic movement were the breakaways, moments when the couple was not touching at all, but doing solo steps facing each other—or not facing each other.

This couple is dancing the Lindy or Jitterbug in 1939. Courtesy Library of Congress.

Professional Lindy dancers performed in clubs (including the Cotton Club in New York and the Moulin Rouge in Paris), traveled with vaudeville units, did a show at Radio City Music Hall, and appeared in thousands of smaller venues around the country. Most of the teams who danced in movies and Broadway musicals had Herbert White, head bouncer of the Savoy Ballroom, as their agent. Known as Whitey, he managed more than seventy dancers under such names as Whitey's Lindy Hoppers, The Jive-A-Dears, Harlem Congaroo Dancers, Whitey's International Hoppers, and The Savoy Hoppers. If a director or producer argued with Whitey, Lindy Hoppers disappeared from the set, and no more were available.[17] Whitey's Hopping Maniacs danced at the Cotton Club for six months in 1936, and six teams of his dancers were part of the Broadway show *The Hot Mikado* starring Bill Robinson in 1939. Whitey's Lindy Hoppers performed in the Marx Brothers movie *A Day at the Races* and did a breathtaking routine in the 1941 *Hellzapoppin*,[18] choreographed by famous Lindy Hop dancer Frankie Manning.[19] Very much in keeping with their resourcefulness and independence, the Whitman Sisters traveled with their own team, The Original Harlem Lindy Hoppers.[20]

Newsreels, movies, and other media brought the Lindy/Jitterbug to huge American audiences, and amateurs everywhere took up the dance. Young people jitterbugged at soda fountains, high school dances, and house parties throughout the country. For several decades, "The Lindy became the first step youngsters learned, and it remained the foun-

Above and opposite page: **These accomplished Lindy Hoppers are managing some acrobatics. In the first picture, the girl is being thrown over her partner's back. In the second, they finish with a flourish.**

dation of most of their dancing."[21] Most teens embroidered on the basic steps, adding their own improvisatory touches.

Dance instructors disdained the phenomenon for a time, but in 1941, both the Lindy and the Jitterbug appeared in *Arthur Murray's Dance Book*. The instructions reflected Murray's Europeanist attitudes ("Dance as though your body were floating through air. Keep

head and shoulders high and always on the same level.... Don't bend your knees...."[22]), but the Jitterbug and Lindy sections revealed his attempt to keep up with the times, showing young people swinging their shoulders, articulating their pelvises, and snapping their fingers. By 1947, even the American Agriculturist Reader Service was prepared to admit the dance had come to stay. Its booklet *How to Do the Latest Dance Steps* did not explain the Lindy until the last few pages, and placed the Foxtrot, Waltz, Tango, Rumba, and Samba before it—but the author provided a complete rundown of the steps, with photos of the breakaway.[23] In 1942, the *New York Times* reported that members of the New York

Instruction booklets for the Lindy Hop proliferated during the 1930s and 1940s. In them, illustrations like this one gave learners an idea of how the dance was supposed to look when it was performed correctly.

Society of Teachers of Dancing in their October meeting had decided to stop ignoring the dance and begin teaching it.[24] They had finally realized that they had to embrace the Jitterbug or become irrelevant.

As Stearns and Stearns point out, conservative styles of dancing never again dominated the American social dance scene. By the 1950s, the Jitterbug had adapted to rock 'n' roll music, and the breakaway seemed to have largely disappeared.

THE RENT PARTY, JOOK, AND DANCE HALL

The black feature film *House Rent Party* (1946) provided big-screen examples of Jitterbugging. It also called attention to a black cultural phenomenon, the rent party. As African Americans migrated northward, they faced housing discrimination. For most blacks, the result was that they paid significantly higher rent than whites for much lower quality housing. If a black urban family faced the end of the month without money to pay their rent, they might host a rent party, also called rent shouts, rent socials, or Saturday night functions. In exchange for an admission fee, a family provided music, food, and drink to guests. The profit helped pay the rent, and the party became a setting for the informal improvisation that marked black social music and dance.

In Harlem, a hand-lettered sign tacked up on the street or a message sent around with a local numbers runner might invite neighbors into a rent party where the piano might be played with brilliance by an as-yet-unrecognized genius. Fats Waller, for example, earned money playing piano at rent parties in Harlem in his early years. Waller and Calabrese write that the music (overwhelmingly, it was piano music) was the most important part of the entertainment, especially when there were two pianists who competed to see whose playing was best: "it wasn't the food or liquor that attracted crowds to a social, it was the music and the fierce competition that existed between the pianists. That's what you paid your two bits for, to see James P. outdo Willie The Lion, or Luckey Roberts cut up Eubie Blake."[25] The rent party was also a place to dance, a place where people could show off new steps to the finest music. With Harlem clubs overflowing with whites from downtown, the rent party was one of the last bastions of all-black social life in New York.

Rent parties were not confined to Harlem. Roberts interviewed people in Philadelphia who remembered rent parties at mid-century.

> The most common type of house party that individuals remember from their parents' era were rent parties. Louise Boggs remembers her parents giving rent parties during World War II and notes that, during the 1940s, "Every weekend they [different people] had a selling party in the home." She also shares a personal experience of sponsoring a house party necessitated by financial need: "And I know when I came here, in the 50s, my roof was bad, and I had to have a house party to get the couple hundred dollars...."[26]

Rent parties or pay parties could arise from economic need of various sorts, or could simply be a way of financing an entertainment for one's friends or one's children's friends.

Another social dance venue, found mostly in the South, was the jook, a rural black-owned bar or club where working class blacks could gather to eat, drink, socialize, play cards or dice, and dance. Zora Neal Hurston wrote, "Musically speaking, the Jook is the most important place in America. For in its shoddy confines has been born the secular music known as the blues, and on blues has been founded jazz. The singing and playing in the true Negro style is called 'jooking.'"[27] In the late 1800s and early 1900s, the music in jooks was likely to be provided by traveling blues musicians, ragtime pianists, local amateur talent, or a victrola.

The work *jook* probably comes from the Bamana work *dzugu* meaning "wicked' or "bad."[28] Hazzard-Gordon adds, "Jooks, honky-tonks, and after-hours joints are secular institutions of social interaction and entertainment, usually associated with some quasilegal activity such as liquor sales or gambling," and "*jook* is a more general label, since the honky-tonk and the after-hours joint may be classed as types of jooks."[29] As time passed and the black middle class came into being, the word also reflected the negative attitude toward jooks held by some blacks. Middle class blacks were much more likely to embrace

This poster for *House-Rent Party*, an all-black feature film, shows people dancing at a rent party. The movie was released in 1946. Courtesy Library of Congress.

A jook in Belle Glade, Florida, photographed in 1941. Courtesy Library of Congress.

and internalize white social attitudes, while less educated and less well-to-do blacks were more likely to express and preserve African values, especially regarding dance.

The jook helped preserve older African American social dances and provided a place for the development of new ones. Early in the twentieth century, dances performed in a jook might include the ones Coot Grant remembered seeing in her father's honky-tonk at that time—the Slow Drag, Fanny Bump, Buzzard Lope, Fish Tail, Eagle Rock, Itch, Shimmy, Squat, Grind, Mooche, and others.[30] When blacks migrated northward, they took the jook with them. One of Katrina Hazzard-Gordon's informants said of pre–1917 Cleveland, "There were no barbecue joints or storefront churches or jook joints up here until all these Negroes came from down South."[31]

In urban areas, the migrants also found the dance hall and made it their own. While dance halls could be found in cities across the American landscape, the example *par excellence* was the Savoy Ballroom in Harlem.[32] Stearns and Stearns comment incisively that "the Savoy's influence was all pervasive and conclusive. Harlem, with its rapidly increasing population from the deep South, had the talent and the tap-root connections with a dance tradition that could nourish a fine art."[33]

The Savoy billed itself as "the home of happy feet," and its steady patrons tended to be excellent dancers. It could be found in a huge second-floor space (200' x 50') between 140th and 141st Streets. During the three decades of its existence, from 1926 to 1958, it produced a variety of new social dance forms and became a focal point for dance lovers, including visitors to New York, who came to watch and then carried new dances back home

These young people are dancing in a jook in Clarksdale, Mississippi, in 1939. Courtesy Library of Congress.

with them. It was the place to hear the best of the best live swing music, including the magic of Chick Webb, Count Basie, Cab Calloway, and Duke Ellington. John Briggs summarized, "Nearly every name band of the late Twenties, Thirties and Forties ... played at the Savoy."[34] Although about 250 big bands played the Savoy over the years, it kept the Chick Webb Orchestra and later Al Cooper's Savoy Sultans as house bands. The Savoy also elicited the most superb performances of the fine bands it hosted, holding battles of the bands on its big double bandstand, just as it held dance competitions.

The floor there was busy every night, including Sunday. Saturday night was the most crowded, known as "square's night" because so many outsiders came to see and be part of the dancing. If you were serious about dancing, Tuesday night was the best. Labeled the "400 Club," it was for dancers only, at reduced admission. For many in attendance, dance was their hobby, their artistic expression, their passion. Shorty Snowden, for example, was there five nights out of seven.[35] John Martin, dance critic for the *New York Times*, wrote an article reviewing social dances in 1943. Of the Savoy, he said:

> For real spectator excitement there is probably nothing within hailing distance of the Savoy Ballroom in Harlem, especially on a Tuesday night when the Four Hundred Club is in session ... movements are never so exaggerated that they lack control, and there is an unmistakable dignity.... There is a remarkable amount of improvisation and personal specialty mixed in with the Suzy-Q and familiar Lindy Hop figures; some of it is acrobatic and strenuous, some of it superficially erotic, and all of it full of temperament and quality.[36]

This is the Count Basie Band playing at Chicago's Savoy Ballroom in 1941. The Chicago Savoy opened in 1927 and served the predominantly African American area between 23rd and 63rd Streets, sometimes called the Harlem of Chicago. The ballroom was a popular nightspot and featured the best in live music. Courtesy Library of Congress.

The ballroom represented the interest in and quality of, dance in its neighborhood, Harlem. Its dancers, moreover, were of all ages, from the young to the old, and all took pride in their steps.

Inside the Savoy, a number of chairs faced the bandstand, underlining the vital role of the band in the dance. Musicians and dancers both spoke of the electricity that connected them there. For them, every number was a conversation, often bringing out the best of both. But if dancers were not satisfied with the music, a crowd would collect in front of the bandstand, clapping out the rhythms people wanted until the band responded. This mutually demanding interaction between the musician and dancer is quintessentially African, harking back to the drummer-dancer relationship still visible in West Africa.

THE BIG APPLE

The Big Apple originated in an African American nightclub by the same name in Columbia, South Carolina, in the mid 1930s.[37] Dancers formed a circle, raised their arms high, and moved in a counterclockwise direction. A caller spoke the directions, and dancers responded, often with steps from other dances such as the Lindy, Shag, and Truckin.' White dancer Betty Wood, who was once a member of a professional Big Apple troupe, remembered seeing the dance for the first time. She said that in 1930, when she was sixteen, she and friends visited the club, calling it "a juke joint," where the dance was being

SAVOY BALLROOM —— Lenox Avenue and 140th Street —— · NEW YORK

This undated postcard shows the chairs facing the bandstand in the Savoy Ballroom in New York City's Harlem.

performed. During those times of racial segregation, whites could not dance with blacks, but could be admitted to a balcony as spectators. In 1937, Betty entered and won a contest to become one of a team of dancers for a traveling Big Apple show that went on tour, playing Roxy theatres across the country. Furthermore, Betty claimed that her friend Billy Spivey, who was with her in the club, revised the dance he saw, creating many of the characteristics of the dance we know today as the Big Apple.[38]

Betty's date of 1930 is probably early, for other accounts indicate whites saw the dance in the club around 1936. Betty and her friends, moreover, were not the only whites to imitate the dance. A group of university students from Charleston saw it, too, and began showing it to classmates at their school dances. From there, it spread up the eastern seaboard and then across the country. It is now difficult to tell if Spivey made any substantive contributions, or if they survived as part of the dance. He was not the only one to be remembered in such a role, either. Arthur Murray sent a dance instructor to take a look at the dance. When he learned in detail what the dance was like, he drafted patterns for teaching it and named some of its steps. His actions resulted in some historians' claims that he had a hand in inventing it, too, but this sort of thing is nothing new in African American dance history. At any rate, the Big Apple helped catapult the Arthur Murray studio into a chain of dance studios.[39]

The *New York Times* reported on new craze, noticing, "The chief attraction of the dance is that individual couples can take the floor and show off their fancy steps, retreating into the circle of spectator-participants as others replace them. In other words, everybody can cut a slice of the big apple."[40] To go to the center of the circle and perform a step was "to shine." It was a moment when a couple obeyed the directions of the caller and simultaneously had a chance to show off their own improvisations on a standard step.

Dancers are having fun doing the Big Apple in the original Big Apple club. The photo was shot from above, probably because whites were permitted only in the balcony.

Within a few months, the dance had arrived in another Big Apple, and a *New York Times* reporter wrote an account of it in a pictorial feature:

"Swing high—swing low!" shouts the master of the revels, as a group of dancing couples, responding to the urge of a hot band, "truck" into a semiformal circle and start a slow, rotating shuffle around the floor.... "Get your girl and take a twirl!" The couples swirl out individually, "shaggin" and shouting with glee.... "Double stomp and cut the apple!" Youthful feet click the floor; peppy hands clap in rhythm.... "Heel the apple!" They heel it.... A clarinet squeals, a trombone sears the air. Up goes the tempo as the dancers whirl faster, excitement mounting to a crescendo. And then, on a nod from the leader, the music comes tumbling down and the dancers rush panting into a huddle with a heaven-reaching chorus of "Praise Allah!"[41]

From this description, the influence of the Ring Shout is clear. Moreover, a range of African American dance characteristics were certainly present, including the rhymed phrases of a Square Dance caller (harking back to black callers of the dance in colonial times), the syncopated rhythms of swing music, as well as circle formation, communal performance, and individual improvisation.

Stage magazine reported on the dance in its October issue.[42] There was a photo of the dancers in the Big Apple Night Club, where whites had first seen the dance. The writer described the form in terms of stereotypes that had been around for at least a century. "The music (from a Nickelodeon) comes out loud and hot," the article said. "They [the dancers] form a circle, a circle that swirls with a rhythm known only to the black man, a hottentot jumble of syncopation, religion, and sex." Whites were still enthusiastically appropriating black dances, which they then described as somehow primitive and sexual.

Arthur Murray included three of the component dances right away in his *Let's Dance*

Above and opposite page: This group of illustrations from a how-to booklet show the Big Apple as well as some of its component dances, the Shag, the Susie-Q, and Truckin.'

FIG. 13

FIG. 8

of 1937 (the Susie-Q, Truckin,' and the Shag). He included the Big Apple and two of the component dances in his new edition of *Arthur Murray's Dance Book*, published in 1938. His booklets, however, reflected the ongoing love-hate relationship whites had with black dance, for Murray seemed to single out the Big Apple dances with hints that they were less sophisticated than the traditional ballroom forms. Big Apple steps appeared near the end of the book, and they were demonstrated by couples in street clothes rather than in the evening wear shown for the other dances in the books. The text explained the component dances as "parlor stunt" dances rather than ballroom dances.[43]

The Big Apple spread quickly throughout the mainstream, especially to the young. In April, 1938, fifty Big Apple dance teams, each of which had been voted the best by their high schools and colleges, were awarded Big Apple jackets by none other than Arthur Murray himself.[44] New York apple growers held a Big Apple contest and photographed the dancers around a pile of apples.[45] Numerous New Year's dance parties that ushered in 1938 featured the Big Apple, and the Roosevelt children danced it at the White House.[46] The form, however, was also associated with youth protest and crime. There was a student strike in Kearny, New Jersey, and one of the demands of the rebellious teens was the right to do the Big Apple at school dances.[47] In other news, a gang of six boys who had been arrested for stealing and stripping cars said they did it to get money to spend in dance halls where they could do the Big Apple.[48]

The Big Apple did not last long in the mainstream—a few years at most. What it showed, though, was that African-based dance characteristics were not only still vibrant in the African American community, but also that they continued to appeal powerfully to non-blacks. Like other Africanist dances that had become national crazes, the Big Apple was created by black dancers, enjoyed in the African American community for a time, then seen and adopted by whites (some of whom laid claims to inventing at least part of it), and quickly taken up by people across the country.

TELEVISION DANCE FOR TEENS

By the mid-fifties and early sixties, the dance venue that reached both the most eager and the most far-flung audiences was the television dance program, like *Teenarama Dance Party* and *American Bandstand*. *Teenarama Dance Party*, produced and broadcast on WOOK-TV in Washington, DC from 1963 until 1970 and hosted by Bob King, was among the early shows directed to black teens with an emphasis on dancing, and WOOK was the first black television network. Although WOOK was a local station, the teen dance show hosted black recording artists when they were in town—Marvin Gaye, James Brown, The Temptations, The Marvelettes, and Martha Reeves and the Vandellas. The program was part of a genre that was exploding into popularity across the country.

American Bandstand, predominantly white in its studio audience, was hosted initially by Bob Horn on a local station in Philadelphia. Horn, a popular disc jockey from WFIL radio, kicked off the teen dance show in 1952, when it was called *Bob Horn's Bandstand*.

At first, the show was nothing more than a series of early music videos featuring vocalists of the time, like Bing Crosby, Patti Page, and Frankie Laine. This format was not particularly successful, though, so station executives agreed to bring "a bunch of kids into the studio to the dance to the latest records."[49] When Horn left the show, Clark became its host. Clark's personality and the show's format struck a chord in mainstream teen culture, and Clark began to market *Bandstand* to ABC. It went national on August 5, 1957, broad-

This cigarette advertisement draws on the popularity of black music and dance to sell the product.

cast on 67 stations and by year's end to four million homes from coast to coast.[50] Suddenly, white American teens saw their reflections on television, and the effect was magical. Arlene Sullivan—a regular on *Bandstand*—said, "Nothing I did was different than what kids were doing in their own basements. But maybe that's why we were so popular. We were them, and they were us."[51]

From the late fifties through the sixties, what most teens danced to was rock 'n' roll, which absorbed African American music characteristics in its strong beat, offbeat accents, and polyrhythmic complexity. The accompanying dance genre included variations of the Jitterbug—today known as swing. The swing steps used by most of the regulars could be seen on the television screen by teens everywhere. Dance historian Kurt Lichtman writes:

> The most common Bandstand-style swing **seen on camera** was a 6-count pattern employing two *tap-steps* followed by a *rock step,* and a distinct "lift" on the taps. The TRIPLE STEP pattern was essentially unknown to the American Bandstand TV cameras! Sure, there were probably some kids doing a triple-step pattern on Bandstand, but the cameras weren't on them for any significant amount of time. And uptempo rock and roll doesn't lend itself to triple-steps for the average person, neither then, nor now.[52]

Many of the "new" dances seen on the show came out of the African American community, and most contained movements recycled from older African American dances.

Through the television dance shows, a whole generation of white teens learned African American dances in their own living rooms, often as they watched African American musicians and vocalists. The station and its host were conscious of race issues, both in the music and the audience. As Dick Clark explained about the racial integration of *American Bandstand*'s audience, "Look, it was just too painfully obvious that rock 'n' roll—and by extension *Bandstand*—owed its very existence to black people, their culture, and their music."[53]

Before *Bandstand*, most popular music charts were segregated. But when the show played rock 'n' roll records by black artists, many of them achieved such mainstream popularity (thus was the power of *Bandstand*) that they crossed over onto "each of the then-segregated popular, rhythm-and-blues, and country-and-Western charts at the same time."[54] It was a moment in musical history, for prior to the show, rock 'n' roll had been villainized across the country as a corrupter of the nation's youth. As Dawson comments, "Anything associated with black culture was tinged with sin, a loss of inhibitions, a slide into the primitive."[55] Clark's wholesome good looks and the sincerity and good manners he projected helped make the music seem acceptable to people who had condemned it mainly because of its black roots. The effect was accelerated and broadened when imitators of *Bandstand* sprang up across the nation.[56]

Clark also brought the recording artists themselves—from Bo Diddley to Little Anthony to Mary Wells to the Shirelles to Chubby Checker—onto the show to lip-synch their songs as young people danced to the music. Teens who appeared before the camera were almost entirely from the Philadelphia area, and they included both the *Bandstand* regulars who were excellent dancers and ordinary kids who came down to the studio and stood in line to gain entrance, wearing the required tie (for boys) or skirt-with-blouse or dress (for girls). The dances they did over time included the Slop, Chicken, Bop, Twist, Frug, and many others.

The show's racial policies, however, were not quite as liberal in practice as Clark made them sound. The teens shown dancing on camera were typically all white, and many dances that were passed off as inventions of the white regulars had in fact black sources. It was love and theft all over again.

Chubby Checker demonstrated the Twist on the Ed Sullivan Show twice, in 1961 and 1963. Photo reprinted by permission of Michael Ochs Archives at www.michaelochs.com.

Clark had pointed out that, when black teens were invited in to dance on the show, it was daring for the times:

> It's no surprise that Bandstand was an exclusively white show from its beginnings with Bob Horn in 1952 to 1957. When Tony and I made the decision to bring in black dancers, no one had told us we had to, and we didn't make a big deal out of it. We found some black teenagers who wanted to dance on the show and invited them to the studio. The black guys danced with black girls and the white guys danced with the white girls—network television wasn't ready for anything more at that point.[57]

Nevertheless, if one thumbs through the old 1950s film frames in *Dick Clark's American Bandstand* or *The History of American Bandstand*, it's difficult to find images of black teens. Dawson confirms this when he writes, "Black kids were rarely if ever seen on 'American Bandstand' in 1959–60."[58]

Roberts adds, "Despite the importance of *American Bandstand* in the history of popular dance and music in the United States, many African Americans in Philadelphia remember *Bandstand* primarily for its racist policies and practices."[59] Roberts also quotes informants who remember either being excluded from the show after it went national or being ignored by the camera. Philadelphians Mary Richardson and Regina Lyons remembered being turned away "any number of times" before being permitted into the studio. When they did get in, they recalled, "Nobody ever saw us on camera, because the cameras never focused on any of us. We were there dancing."[60]

A group of high school students dance the Twist in a baggage car on a train in 1962. A horn player and a drummer are visible in the foreground of the picture. Courtesy Library of Congress.

Another show accessible in Philadelphia and based in Wilmington, Delaware, was *The Mitch Thomas Show*, aimed at black audiences. Roberts interviewee Donna Brown said, "And that was something for the Black kids to really identify with. Because you would look at *Bandstand* and we thought it was a joke."[61] Roberts notes, "*The Mitch Thomas Show* became a showcase for African American dancers and dance styles. Some of the individuals who remember this show credit it with being an important source for learning new dance steps."[62]

There is also evidence that some of the dance steps the regulars brought onto *Bandstand* as their own were really taken from black dancers. Kurt Lichtmann, who teaches swing dance and ballroom dance at Cornell University, says:

> New moves and new dances, such as *The Strand* and the *Bop*, "debuted" on Bandstand. Where did these dances come from? Here we have a continuation of the same old story that has grated on black dancers since the '20s. With a few exceptions, white teens, attending integrated school dances, "adapted" the moves from black teens, introducing the moves on Bandstand as their own (The '50s Bandstand crowd was 98% white).[63]

Dawson concurs. He writes that in a 1993 film documentary several former Bandstand regulars "sheepishly confessed to copying dances such as the Strand at black clubs and then tacitly being encouraged by the 'American Bandstand' staff to execute the new steps on-air and claim them as their own inventions."[64] One informant said, "We had to say we made it up," and others agreed that this was indeed the case. The consensus was that "Dick Clark didn't want to hear about them picking up new dances from black kids in West Philly."[65]

Clark also shaped the presentation of the Twist. Chubby Checker's first television performance of the song and the dance was not on *Bandstand*, however, but on the Saturday evening prime time *Dick Clark Show* on August 6, 1960. Checker not only lip-synched the song, but also gave the TV audience its first Twist lesson. "Just pretend you're wiping your bottom with a towel as you get out of the shower and putting out a cigarette with both feet," he advised.[66]

Despite his visibility, Checker was not the first to record the song. Hank Ballard and the Midnighters had recorded it in November, 1958, in Cincinnati, Ohio. The recording had made it to number sixteen on the *Billboard* R&B chart, and Ballard remembered both blacks and whites dancing to it on a Baltimore dance show called *The Buddy Deane Show*. The new Twist was a lot like the one seen in Baltimore, and later in Philadelphia, but there was a difference. The one Chubby Checker demonstrated on television had less hip and shoulder movement and came across as more wholesome.

The Baltimore version of the Twist had already turned up on *Bandstand*. Evidently, Clark felt it was too sexy for mainstream audiences:

> In his book *Rock, Roll and Remember*, Dick Clark recalled.... "I saw a black couple doing a dance that consisted of revolving their hips in quick, half-circle jerks, so their pelvic regions were heaving in time to the music. The white kids around them watched, fascinated. Some started to imitate the dance." Clark said he told the cameramen to keep away from the couple because their moves were too suggestive for the show.[67]

Clark asked the couple what dance they were doing, and they responded, "The Twist." He also noticed the dance was catching on, with more kids dancing it on the next show.

Perhaps Clark felt he needed to step in to control the development of the dance. Perhaps he wanted to promote the dance and the song, but wanted to avoid any moral backlash that might arise from the sexier hip movement. Perhaps he was leery of Ballard's tendency to off-color lyrics. John A. Jackson wrote of Clark, for example, that "The last thing he was about to do was place himself in a position whereby he could be accused of promoting a dance as controversial as the twist, sung by a group with as bawdy a reputation as the Midnighters."[68] Perhaps Clark remembered that he had set Ballard up to appear on *Bandstand* three times, and Ballard had failed to show each time. And Clark may have remembered a singer who was very, very good at doing impressions of other vocalists, a chubby guy named Ernest Evans. Evans had put together a novelty record for Dick Clark that served as his Christmas card to friends in 1959. Clark may well have influenced Cameo's decision to have Evans record "The Twist."

Whatever the chain of causation, six months or so later, Evans (by now singing as Chubby Checker, a name dreamed up by Clark's wife that was a sort of imitation of the name Fats Domino) recorded "The Twist" for Cameo/Parkway, doing "a stunning job imitating Ballard's squealy baritone."[69] The tamer version of the dance he did, despite later negative press coverage of it, was acceptable to television audiences.

It's impossible to measure to what extend Clark may have manipulated the form of the dance he introduced on his program, but his showcasing of the song and dance catapulted Checker into national stardom. Not only did the song become a mega-hit and spin

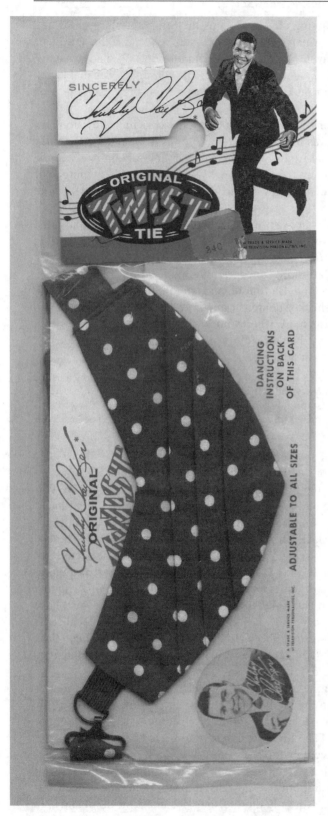

off a number of other Twist hits, but the dance also caught on as no other rock 'n' roll dance ever had before. Maybe it was because the dance was so easy to do, or because the timing was right, or because Checker's personality was so engaging. Whatever the reason, the Twist converted the middle class, the middle aged, and the conservative as well as the young.

McDonagh points out that "adults who had been tapping their feet under the table for years, actually discovered they could do this new dance." It was easy to learn:

The body twists first to the left as the left knee twists inward. A weight shift to the other foot and same grinding motion of the ball of the foot is repeated as if one were actually snuffing out a cigarette butt. For variety, a little kick is added now and them. The arms are kept up close to the chest, punching out and pulling back with the corresponding twists of the body.[70]

There was no leading and following—couples didn't even touch, but rather simply danced individually while facing each other. Nor did anyone move around the dance floor. Partners twisted in a single spot, and their separation made individual flourishes and improvisations easy. The ties to Africa were strong and visible, despite the mainstream's generally stiff torso.

Celebrities took up the dance, and the somewhat seedy Peppermint Lounge in New York City attracted them by the dozens. Elizabeth Taylor and Richard Burton, Zsa Zsa Gabor, Judy Garland, and the Duke and Duchess of Windsor all stopped by

Left and opposite page: **The packaging for this "Twist" tie includes pictures of Chubby Checker, as well as instructions for the dance on the back.**

to Twist. The Lounge's band, Joey Dee and the Starliters, recorded a new Twist song named after the club, "The Peppermint Twist," and it was an instant hit. Even Jackie Kennedy was spotted doing the Twist at the Lounge.

But while the dance was being performed enthusiastically in the U.S. and abroad, it was being attacked just as energetically. Parents, politicians, and foreign regimes condemned it as physically and morally unhealthy. Even a brief glimpse at *New York Times* headlines and quotes suggests the magnitude of the backlash: "Eisenhower Discerns a Decline in Morality: Decries Modern Art and Twist in Talk at Library Dedication" (May 2, 1962); "The Twist: 'It's Not a Dance'" (Geoffrey Holder, December 3, 1961); "Risk in Twist Cited by Surgeon" (December 3, 1961); "Twist Danced at Metropolitan as Director Watches in Dismay" (May 21, 1961); "Saigon Regime Bans Songs for Twisting (April 2, 1962); "Soviet is Seeking a Twist Antidote" (April 5, 1964).

Aficionados ignored the criticism. More spin-off songs were recorded, and Checker himself hit the charts with "Let's Twist Again" and more than two dozen other songs. He also starred in two feature films, *Twist Around the Clock* and *Don't Knock the Twist*. What was it about the dance that made it so popular? It was both old and new, easy and hip. Best of all, for once, nearly everyone could dance.

More television dance shows followed *Bandstand*, and most depended heavily on Africanist music and dance. *Shindig*, premiering in 1964, was hosted by Jimmy O'Neill. Its guests were a who's who of rock 'n' roll greats such as the Supremes, Chuck Berry, Jackie DeShannon, the

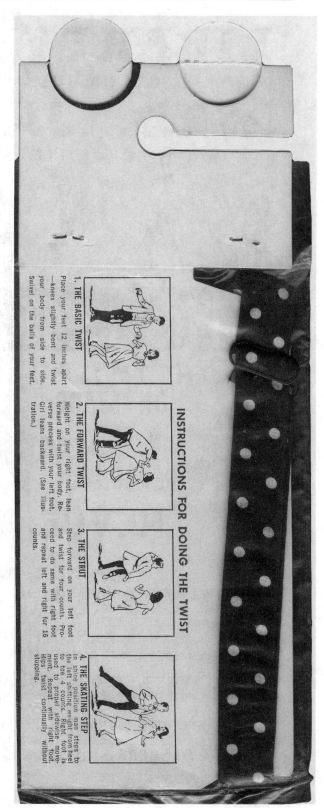

The advertised event indicated that the ancient tradition of competition was still very much alive.

Beatles, Little Anthony and the Imperials, Mary Wells, Smokey Robinson and the Miracles, McCoys, Rolling Stones, Hollies, Marvin Gaye, Cher, Righteous Brothers, Dave Clark Five, and more. It also featured dance by the Shindiggers. *Hullabaloo*, first airing in 1965, presented some of the earliest disco dances, such as the Frug, Jerk, Swim, Monkey, Mashed Potatoes, and Watusi.[71] *Soul Train*, beginning in 1970 and long hosted by Don Cornelius, also gained huge followings among TV audiences for performances by soul, R & B, jazz, gospel, and hip hop vocalists, as well as the group of regulars who danced to the music as it was being performed. Sometimes called the "Black American Bandstand," *Soul Train* ended every show with its signature line dance. *Solid Gold*, premiering in 1980, was hosted by Dionne Warwick during its first season. The weekly show featured songs on the Top 10 charts, along with the Solid Gold Dancers. Many people remember the once-per-year two-hour January *Solid Gold* specials counting down the top one hundred songs of the year. All these programs brought contemporary African American music and dance into the living rooms of families across America.

DISCO

For those of us who were adults when disco came into fashion, memories of it include images of dance palaces with DJs and light shows, orchestral music with an uptempo beat, diva Donna Summer, and the moment in *Saturday Night Fever* when John Travolta poses in a white suit with one arm pointing skyward. But these images reveal little about the music's origins. The disco sound emerged in black, gay, and Latin underground clubs such as New York's Salvation, Sanctuary, and The Loft in the very late sixties and early seventies, with sources in black and Latin music traditions by way of funk, soul, and salsa.

The word *discothèque*, from which came both the name of the music and the clubs where it was played, was French for record library and reflected the use of recordings rather than live musicians. One of the most important elements of the new style was the DJ or disc jockey, whose role quickly changed from simply playing records one at a time to using mechanical and electronic means to mix pieces of music, modifying them and making new arrangements and reinterpretations of existing songs and sounds. Using two turntables with pitch control, a mixer, a drum machine, and headphones, the DJ created the remix, a new version of the music that matched beats, segued from one song into another, and changed them all. Reighley sums this up by saying of DJs, "Their eclectic, mercurial collages embody our multitasking modern mind-set."[72]

The DJ phenomena in disco and rap cross-fertilized, as discos in Manhattan and dance events in Bronx schoolyards shared techniques. Reighley points out:

> In the Bronx, rap innovators like Kool DJ Herc, Afrika Bambaataa, and Grandmaster Flash expanded the musical abilities of two turntables and a mixer. Cutting back and forth between isolated snippets of sound with lightning-fast dexterity and physically manipulating the surface of the record against the needle to generate unfamiliar bursts of noise, they transformed slabs of vinyl into fresh creations. Meanwhile, at Manhattan discos, club jocks like Francis Grasso created inspired programs of interlocking songs and even began simultaneously layering passages from different records.[73]

Both kinds of DJs were pioneering a new sound, a sound that broke away from traditional live music combos, emphasized the electronic capabilities of the times, and drew on the Africanist traditions of improvisation, overlaying beats, and unusual or rasping effects.

The music had a driving, continuous 4/4 beat with about 110–130 beats per minute.

The DJ mixes sound to create a unique new arrangement of music for dancers. Photographer Amitai.

This beat dominated vocals in extended songs that allowed long intervals of dancing. As Jack and Kathleen Sims Villari wrote, "Basically, disco music combines strings and big-band effects to come up with foot-stomping, hip-bumping, happy music that almost forces you to get up and move."[74] John-Manuel Andriote adds that it was "frequently likened to the big-band sound of the thirties because of its lively rhythm, brassy horns, and textured sound."[75]

Disco lyrics often spoke of the need to dance or to love, of the submergence of the will to the beat or to a lover. Hughes remarks of this beat, "As the lyrics of disco songs make clear for us in a characteristically redundant way, the beat brooks no denial, but moves us, controls us, deprives us of our will. Dancing becomes a form of submission to this overmastering beat."[76] The disco club became an escapist world, a way to unwind for workers everywhere, a place where dancers set aside their worries and surrendered to the music.

By 1975 disco was widely popular. Among its stars were the Jackson 5, Barry White, the Commodores, Patti LaBelle, Van McCoy, Gloria Gaynor, and Donna Summer. McCoy's "The Hustle" and Summer's "Love to Love You Baby" were standards in the disco clubs where the music came from DJs and a fantasy world was created with special effects such as changing patterns of lights and colors, mirrored and faceted balls suspended from the ceiling to reflect and fragment light, smoke machines and dry ice, and dance floors illuminated from underneath.

The first important disco dance to emerge was the Hustle, taking its name from the Van McCoy hit song. Peter Shapiro finds the song both "strangely rhythmless" and "inescapable and inevitable, the kind of record that crawls under your skin, subliminally taking root ...,"[77] and his comments reinforce the enthrallment motif of many disco dance

Disco and Hustle patches like these ornamented dancers' clothing.

songs. The Hustle was a partner dance, a return to touch dancing with a smooth, sophisticated look. The dance drew on the old box step as well as Latin forms, as dancers assumed a vertical posture and tilted their pelvises backward rather than forward. The man led, the woman followed, and both dressed up for the occasion. Disco dance floors were filled with women in soft, frilly dresses and high heels responding to the touches and moves of men in three-piece suits or snug pants and flowing shirts.

The dance was perhaps most indebted to the Lindy, with constant opening and closing of the couple format, spinning the woman away from and back toward her partner. The Hustle was danced in four rather than six counts, though, and there was a hint of posing and stomping that was more Latin than Lindy. The Hustle was exciting and romantic all at once, and the movies made it more so, especially *Saturday Night Fever*. As Barry Walters pointed out, "the quintessential mainstream disco image" became "a white-suited John Travolta hustling his girl around a lit disco floor."[78]

The Hustle was a line dance as well as a partner dance, with partners performing the same steps as they danced together in a row with other couples. People moved across the dance floor in a line—or in multiple parallel lines. Partners' feet traced geometric figures such as squares, circles, or triangles, as they slid, swiveled, and turned their bodies in unison. In addition to the Hustle forms, there were also the Bump, Bus Stop (a line dance done by individuals rather than partners), Continental, Disco Duck, Freak, and Disco Swing.

Disco included pantomime, as the Bump showed, with partners bumping their hips together on the beat, and improvisation, with every couple inserting its own freestyle moves. Furthermore, competition was important. In *Saturday Night Fever*, the lead characters won a disco competition, and such competitions sprang up everywhere, including foreign countries. A variety of cups, medals, and ribbons were awarded to winners, most of whom were accomplished in athletic routines.

At the height of the craze in the late seventies, there were disco clubs in every city, and most successful recording artists had released a disco album. One of the clubs was the three-level Harlem World at 116th and Lenox in New York City, where Eartha Kitt, D.J. Hollywood, and Dr. Jekyll and Mr. Hyde came to party.[79] There were also Studio 54 further downtown, Club 747 in an old airplane in Buffalo, the Trocadero in San Francisco, and the Warehouse in Chicago. Celebrities like Princess Caroline of Monaco danced in European discos till dawn. In 1978, the disco industry grossed $8 billion, there were more than 10,000 disco clubs in the U.S., and *Cornerstone* magazine estimated that 37 million

Americans had danced in one during the previous year.[80] The same article said the phenomenon was an expression of the average person's need for fantasy: "as one discophile

put it, 'I need fantasy in my life. That's what most people are looking for these days.'"[81]

Over time, disco faded, like other trends, but it never disappeared. New York's top radio station, WKTU, became a disco oldies station, and the 2005 movie *Roll Bounce* dramatized the fad of roller disco—roller skating to disco rhythms. Also in 2005, Madonna released *Confessions on a Dance Floor*, an album that vividly recalls the disco era and her own musical past. Ordinary people still disco in clubs, on cruise ships, and at house parties. Disco continues to be a dance genre enjoyed by thousands of people.

This disco medal was awarded to a winning couple in England in the early 1970s.

HIP HOP

When New York photographer Martha Cooper began shooting graffiti on subway cars in Brooklyn train yards, she became aware of it as a street phenomenon, a folk art in which black and Latino young people in marginalized areas were able to express their ideas and personalities. It was a time when the city was nearly bankrupt, many of the kids' neighborhoods were scarred with rubble from demolished buildings, gang emblems were thrown up on some of the walls still standing, and crime was escalating. "When I began trying to catch graffiti on trains in 1980," she said, "the South Bronx was a wasteland. Shops were shuttered, buildings were boarded-up, and there were entire blocks of vacant lots."[82] In this setting, families struggled to stay safe, and kids searched for something to do with their time.

Cooper's long-time interest as a photographer was capturing art in its cultural context. Her ethnographic perspective guided her to probe the backgrounds and motivations of the graffiti writers. She realized that the art, although despised by many New Yorkers as vandalism and considered a criminal act by police, was a way for young people to shape and call attention to self-images. Each artist created a logo-like name or handle that he or she drew and ornamented with spray paint on the cars. The trains then became moving canvases of the teens' individualized expressions. A writer named WICKED GARY explained, "We were always told to go and be productive members of society, but we didn't have a lot of options so we created an identity through our alter-egos and we went out and asserted that identity."[83]

Furthermore, the artwork was a positive activity in a shadowed and dangerous world. BAN 2 commented:

> You always heard, "Why are you doing this?" or "You are too old to do that." At least I was not doing heroin or smoking crack. At least we were not robbing anybody. We were not really committing crime. This is art taken to a subway level. Being on the streets is boring, so graffiti gave us a whole new world to get into where we could express our feelings through a can of paint.

Examples of graffiti in New York City. Reprinted by permission of photographer, Mark Jawdoszyn.

> There sure is no crime in that. We did not have jobs, we barely went to school, we had single-parent homes, stuff like that. At least graffiti gave us something to do.[84]

KASE 2 added, "Graffiti can save someone's life because it takes you away from being a drug addict or runnin' around in the ghetto with other drug addicts. It's a feelin' when people got a good common sense of doing something or working something together."[85]

Cooper documented the writers in the train yard late at night, capturing and preserving the process of creating a painting. She also ran alongside them when the police arrived or the trains pulled out, visited their homes to see the piece books in which they sketched new artworks, and invited them to her home to look at slides.

One night, covering a story at the police station, she learned that graffiti was not the neighborhood kids' only art. They also danced. Sally Banes wrote about the event in the *Village Voice*:

> Chico and Tee and their friends from 175th Street in the High Times crew were breaking in the subway and the cops busted them for fighting.
> "We're not fighting. We're dancing!" they claimed. At the precinct station, one kid demonstrated certain moves: a head spin, ass spin, swipe, chin freeze, "the Helicopter," "the Baby."[86]

The dance was fast and acrobatic. It emerged that it was also competitive, with "crews" of young people battling each other for their t-shirts. The dance competitions could substitute for gang violence, provide bonding within crews, and push the dancers to new heights of originality and athleticism.

There was a moment in the dance sequence when the dancer improvised, signaled by the drum in an African way, and it was labeled with the time-honored word *break*: "As the beat of the drummer came to the fore, the music let you know it was time to break down, to free style."[87] The accompaniment was rap music: "The cadenced, rhyming, fast-talking epic mode of rapping, with its smooth surface of sexual braggadocio, provides a perfect base for a dance style that is cool, swift, and intricate."[88] Furthermore, the crew was a context of mutual respect and equality, and crew members encircled and affirmed the performers as they took turns dancing. Youngsters of all ethnic backgrounds could gain acceptance in crews for their abilities and their commitment to the art. A crew chose its name to reflect the personality and ideals of its members.

Today, we know the dance form as break dance or breaking or b-boying, named for the break beats in the music as the DJ creates a remix. The dance form's sources date back to the seventies. Nelson George writes that "The first break dancers were, according to old schoolers, ... street gang members who danced upright, had names like El Dorado, Sasa, Mr. Rock, and Nigger Twins, and were overwhelmingly African American."[89] Many of these breakers showed off their moves in streets, parks, and clubs in return for monetary donations from their audiences. They were part of a long, long tradition of black street dance.

But even before the breakers, there were other kinds of Hip Hop dancers. In the late sixties and early seventies, at the same time disco was growing, Hip Hop was developing. There was a dance called the Good Foot, for example, based on James Brown's song by the same name, and it included freestyle drops and spins. Dancers went down on the beat and came back up on the beat.

And we must not forget popping and locking. Soon after Don Cornelius premiered his *Soul Train* television show, he began bringing in street dancers to show their stuff on national television. One of the groups was the Lockers, a dance team put together by Don Campbell, who had invented The Campbellock. Sally Banes described their style this way:

Crazy Legs practices some moves on a base of cardboard, during the period 1979–1984. Photographer Martha Cooper. Reprinted by permission of MZEE Productions.

> Wearing outrageous uniforms of knickers, striped socks, thick-soled elaborate shoes, and fancy hats, the Lockers flapped, leapt, jumped, danced on their hands, and scoo-be-dooed to music by the O'Jays, Sly and the Family stone, James Brown, and Joe Tex. They did foot stomps and chants, mimed killing roaches with well-aimed slaps of the hands on the floor.[90]

It was an improvisatory form, punctuated by "locking." Locking involved old-fashioned freezes, called locks, when the dancers became immobile in poses. The body "locked" for an instant and then unlocked into fast movement. The poses, as the name suggests, were a central feature of the dance. Popping is a separate style in which segments of limbs are isolated, muscles are flexed, and body parts are snapped into new directions and shapes continuously, all to the beat, creating a jerky motion that is yet graceful and aesthetically pleasing.[91]

At the same time, Michael Jackson was moonwalking, and people were dancing the Robot, in which they imitated the jerky moves of a robot (imagine the body language of C-3PO in *Star Wars*). The Electric Boogaloo or Electric Boogie brought together Locking, the Robot, and the traditionally smooth, clear communication of the mime. Dancers appeared to be passing electricity through their bodies and into each other, all the while moving arms and shoulders in a smooth, controlled way. Other mimetic forms included the Egyptian or King Tut and the Puppet.

When breaking began on the East Coast, locking, popping, and the Electric Boogaloo were gaining popularity on the West Coast, and when Cooper learned about breaking, it was already old in the kids' estimation. They were moving onto roller disco. Nevertheless, they were willing to show Cooper and her colleagues, including filmmaker Henry Chalfant, how they danced.[92]

Banes reported that there was a standard structure to the 10–30 second action-packed performance each crew member gave. First, there was an *entry*, a "stylized walk into the ring for four or five beats to the music." Then there was a segment of *footwork*, "a rapid, circular scan of the floor by sneakered feet while the hands support the body's weight and the head and torso revolve slowly," followed by the *freeze*, "a stylized signature pose, usually preceded by a spin," and finalized by the *exit*, "a return to verticality and to the outside of the circle."[93] The freeze was usually the dancer's moment to show off original moves, to inject humor, and to challenge and insult his opponents in a mimetic way. Breakers or b-boys named their freezes and took ownership of them.

The African American elements of this street form clearly include community, polyrhythms, competition, improvisation, pantomime, and percussion. The crews also carried with them large pieces of cardboard or a roll of linoleum to cushion their bodies from the abrasive pavement and help them achieve fast spins. These special objects harked back to the shingles black dancers had carried nearly two centuries earlier. The cardboard, though, enhanced speed and safety rather than the sound of the dance. Like the street dancers before them, the b-boys used dance to gain honor and achieve a position in the community. They improvised to challenge competitors and establish their own individual records of achievement.

Furthermore, their dance was simply one part of a larger culture we now call Hip Hop. Hip Hop included rap music, dance forms (breaking, popping, and locking), the DJ-ing that was itself an art, graffiti, and clothing styles. "It was the era," George remembers, "of the mobile disc jockey, when guys with crates of records and big speakers would roll into a public park and, for nothing but the pleasure of publicly rocking two turntables, play for hours."[94] Poor neighborhoods could not afford to hire bands, so the DJs used records. In their spare time, DJs searched through record stores, thrift shops, and friends and relatives' collections for interesting sounds, the perfect bits to remix for exciting dance music.

Clothing was distinctive, reflecting the wearer's self-image, but also making a cultural statement. Cooper points out that in prisons, belts and shoe laces are confiscated, "resulting in sagging pants and sneakers without laces," and says that the prison practice became a fashion statement on the streets.[95] Hooded shirts protected dancers' heads and shoulders during spins. White gloves came from mimes, and called attention to dancers' hands in dances like the Electric Boogaloo. Most important of all was wearing comfortable, loose clothing that facilitated dancing.

Cooper, Banes, Chalfant, and others had wanted to document a cultural phenomenon, but when they did so they changed it. By studying it and calling attention to it, they focused a new energy and public response around it. Canvases created by some of the writers soon filled a small art gallery, breaking was demonstrated in three films, and Rock Steady Crew began performing in clubs. Instead of fading as its practitioners moved in a new direction, breaking swiftly became a national and international happening, seen by everyone on television, in the movies, in advertising, in how-to books purchased at bookshops, and in live performances. Twenty years later, we remember breaker Crazy Legs not only from Cooper's book, but also from his film performances, his dance tribute to the Nicholas Brothers at the Kennedy Center, and his winning of the Bessie Award for choreography. Break dance has entered the mainstream. Breaking, locking, and popping are all current and vibrant forms, with some dance groups performing all three. Hip Hop dance has devoted fans in nearly every country around the world, from Japan to Iceland to Italy, and performances have moved forward into new styles and standards.

Spider (Cliff Lyons) of the Dynamite Rockers launches off a pyramid of crew members in Queens, New York, in the early 1980s. Photographer Martha Cooper. Reprinted by permission of MZEE Productions.

Two crew members practice moves on a cardboard base in the early 1980s, to music from a boom box. Notice that the boom box supports two cans of spray paint. Photographer Martha Cooper. Reprinted by permission of MZEE Productions.

An Ohio State University student executes a head spin on campus. Courtesy *The Lantern*, OSU's student-run campus newspaper. Photographer David Heasley.

STEP SHOWS

The step show is an African American performance art first developed within fraternities and sororities in historically black colleges and universities. It is a group or unison form incorporating dance steps, singing, chanting, percussive clapping, and dramatic elements. The steppers communicate not only their commitment to, and pride in, their group, but also something of their group's history or character. The societies step in competition with each other, exhibiting signature steps and styles, community solidarity, percussion, polyrhythms, improvisation, use of special objects, line formation, and a host of other African American performance characteristics.

Lisa Yarger provides a brief picture of a stepping routine by the Mu Zeta chapter of Alpha Phi Alpha Fraternity:

> … the steppers spread out across the floor and begin a vigorous dance routine to the beat of recorded hip hop music. Jumping into the air, the young men kick one leg up to chest level and clap their hands under the raised knee. Crouching forward, they take giant steps from side to side, alternately sweeping their arms in front of their chests and pounding clenched fists toward the ground. Throughout the entire performance, the steppers wear the gold Pharaonic headdresses.[96]

Performers may also present extended clapping and patting routines or acrobatics, and they frequently speak or chant in unison to convey the values or history of their organizations.

The step show is an expression of shared pride and spirit, also involving education of any-one in the audience who had not previously understood what a particular sorority or fra-ternity stood for.

Step shows are thus about identity, and traditionally involve new pledges who are expressing their commitment to the organization. The origins of stepping lie deep in the history of African American higher education. Howard University was the site of the for-mation of five of the nine black Greek letter societies, and others were formed elsewhere, including Alpha Phi Alpha at Cornell in 1906. The impetus for such organizations may come from the African American mutual aid societies, which offered financial, social, and other kinds of support to a people systematically excluded from the mainstream.[97]

Citing the first initiation of Alpha Phi Alpha, which took place at the Masonic Hall, Fine writes:

> This close association with an African American Masonic society, even to the point of borrow-ing their ritual clothing, suggests that early fraternities and sororities may have modeled some of their rituals on those of other secret societies of the time. Because mutual aid societies were known for their competitive drill teams, as Malone observes, it is possible that the black Greek-letter society tradition of marching on line, from which stepping likely evolved, may have been borrowed from such societies.[98]

By the 1940s and 1950s, the sororities and fraternities were marching or parading in lines, sometimes appearing to sing or chant as they moved together. They also often carried the symbols of their society, such as dog-related items for the Omegas and Egyptian head-dresses for Alpha Phi Alpha. By the 1960s and 1970s, stepping was clearly visible in Howard photographs of Greek groups.[99]

Stepping is also about competition, as each team strives to be judged the best. The competitive format has spurred high levels of creativity and audience appeal. In the past, step teams also engaged in "cracking," or verbal mockery of other groups. As Fine points out, cracking can also be carried out nonverbally "by parodying the steps or style of another group."[100] Cracking has become less common in recent years, however, because it is now seen as creating tensions and ill will that are ultimately divisive.[101]

The originality of the teams and their deeply held appreciation of the African Amer-ican cultural past has led them to include in their choreography a wide variety of elements from counterclockwise circular movement to social dance steps to acrobatics to rap music to tap dance. As Malone comments, "Critics who dismiss this dance genre as undergrad-uate folly fail to recognize its cultural richness and the vitally important role it plays as a carrier of Black traditions in song, music, dance, and language."[102] These elements are com-bined with a variety of allusions to current pop culture and entertainment material.

Teams also include their own signature steps and special objects. The AKA sorority, for example, may close its routine with a trademark step, "This is a Serious Matter," which "includes intricate footwork, complex and percussive hand clapping, and a call-and-response chant...."[103] Phi Beta Sigma may close with a step that is performed blind folded. Kappas are known for "their flashy and skillful cane work."[104] Operating simultaneously with this expression of team unity is a sense of community with the audience, which responds with cheers, shouted comments, and applause. In this way, the audience becomes an active participant.

Stepping has moved beyond the historically black college campus to a wider audi-ence. It has been seen in films such as Spike Lee's *School Daze* and on television. Step-pers performed at President Clinton's first inauguration festivities. Elizabeth Fine calls attention to The First National Conference on Stepping, held in 2001, and to community

Top: A line of Iota Phi Thetas moves in unison at an Ohio State University step show. Photographer Sarah Glass. *Bottom:* Two alumni Phi Beta Sigmas work through a synchronized hand clapping sequence at an Ohio State University step show. Photographer Sarah Glass.

An alumnus of Phi Beta Sigma completes a routine at an Ohio State University step show. Photographer Sarah Glass.

programs that use stepping as a positive activity for young people.[105] Step shows at Ohio State University have drawn large and appreciative audiences of people from diverse ethnic backgrounds. The step show is yet another way for broad audiences to enjoy a genre of African American dance and the deep and broad tradition from which it comes.

CONCLUSION

African American vernacular dance showed itself both resilient and influential throughout the twentieth century, giving us new dance forms and new dance venues. Black vernacular dance, in fact, transformed the mainstream by enchanting, educating, and converting audiences to dances as various as the Lindy Hop, Big Apple, and break dance. Black dancers drew attention to themselves on street corners, in dance contests, in ballrooms, on television, and on college campuses. Once ostracized and avoided, black dance forms became the choice of celebrities and royalty, gaining news coverage and generating a stream of how-to books and videos. In the process, African American vernacular dance became mainstream American dance—the dance of all Americans. It expresses us, entertains us, and involves us in a never-ending cycle of change and renewal, while at the same time continuing to be a broad stream of inspiration and source material for theatrical dance.

Notes

CHAPTER 1

1. See Porter's letter to Professor Beth Dillingham, 5 August 1969, in Porter's unpublished papers at the New York Public Library. There he writes, "Some of them, in particular, spoke the particular brand of plantation English, with an unusual number of African words, known as Gullah." Porter also notes, "When I was in Nacimiento [Mexico], 1942–43, there were two praise or prayer houses … I attended services one morning in the one still in use. The meeting consisted of singing spirituals, prayers, and a concluding 'ring shout' or circular dance." He adds, "The service was similar to, although on a smaller scale than, the service I had attended in the most conservative of the three Baptist churches in the Seminole Negro community of Brackettville [Texas].…" Paulina Del Moral notes in her *Tribus Olvidadas de Coahuila* (Gobierno del Estado de Coahuila /Consejo Nacional Para La Cultura y las Artes, 1999), 128, that she gathered testimony that the Mexican ring shout songs are still sung in English. Her informant said, "Nada más había las iglesia que era de las señores grandes de color, pero rezaban en inglés." Also, "Sus alabanzas in inglés eran muy bonitas; sus cantos muchos eran tristes y muchos eran alegres; era la religión de ellas."

2. Mechal Sobel, *The World They Made Together: Black and White Values in Eighteenth-Century Virginia* (Princeton: Princeton University Press, 1987), 5–6.

3. John Thornton, *Africa and Africans in the Making of the Atlantic World, 1400–1680* (Cambridge: Cambridge University Press, 1992), 183–192.

4. Peter Kolchin, *American Slavery, 1619–1877* (New York: Hill and Wang, 1993), 42.

5. Lee Warren, The Dance of Africa: An Introduction (Englewood Cliffs, New Jersey: Prentice-Hall, 1972), 2.

6. Warren, 6.

7. Quoted by Henry John Drewel and Margaret Drewel, *Gelede: Art and Female Power Among the Yoruba*. (Bloomington: Indiana University Press, 1990), 7.

8. Stephen Pern, *Masked Dancers of West Africa: The Dogon* (Amsterdam: Time-Life Books, 1982), 90.

9. To gain a sense of the excitement and color of the dance, as well as the art it generates, see the VHS tape *The Art of the Dogon*, based on the collection of the Metropolitan Museum of Art and on footage shot in Mali. Home Vision Entertainment, 1988.

10. Web Site discussion of the exhibition *Genesis: Ideas of Origin in African Sculpture*, presented by the Metropolitan Museum of Art from November 19, 2002, through July 6, 2003. http://www.metmuseum.org/special/Genesis/origin_more.htm.

11. John W. Blassingame, *The Slave Community: Plantation Life in the Antebellum South* (New York and Oxford: Oxford University Press, 1972), 29.

12. *Harper's Weekly*, June 2, 1860.

13. Mel Fisher Maritime Heritage Society Web Site. See http://melfisher.org/lastslaveships/slaveships.htm and http://www.melfisher.org/lastslaveships/intro.htm.

14. Terry Harnan, *African Rhythm, American Dance: A Biography of Katherine Dunham* (New York: Alfred A. Knopf, 1969), 57–96.

15. Lists and discussion of African dance characteristics can be found in a variety of sources. See, for example: Marshall Stearns and Jean Stearns, *Jazz Dance: The Story of American Vernacular Dance* (New York: Da Capo Press, 1994), 14–15; The *Making of a Mosaic: An Introduction to the Music and Dance of the Americas*, National Dance Institute Artistic Supplement, 62;

Doris Green, "Traditional Dance in Africa," in *African Dance: An Artistic, Historical, and Philosophical Inquiry*, ed. Kariamu Welsh Asante (Trenton, New Jersey: Africa World Press, Inc., 1996), 13–28.

16. For a discussion of angularity, see Peter Wood, "'Gimme de Kneebone Bent': African Body Language and the Evolution of American Dance Forms," in *The Black Tradition in American Modern Dance* (Durham: American Dance Festival, 1988), 7–8. Wood points out that "Many West Africans believed that straightened knees, hips, and elbows epitomized death and rigidity, while flexed joints embodied energy and life."

17. Omofolabo Ajayi, *Yoruba Dance* (Trenton, New Jersey: Africa World Press, 1998), 35.

18. Ajayi, 36.

19. Margaret Thompson Drewel, *Yoruba Ritual: Performers, Play, Agency* (Bloomington: Indiana University Press, 1992), 23.

20. Henry John Drewel and Margaret Drewel, 8.

21. Pern, 16.

22. Pern, 122.

23. Sana Reynolds, "The Human Need for Privacy: How Individualist and Collective Cultures Use Personal Space." Presentation at Association for Business Communication Conference, October 27–30, 2004.

24. See Leonard Goines, Program for *Dance Black America*, April 21–24, 1983, presented by Brooklyn Academy of Music, 10.

25. Alan Lomax, *Folk Song Style and Culture* (New Brunswick, New Jersey: Transaction Publishers, 1994), 258.

26. Peter Buckman, *Let's Dance*, 66.

27. Carol McD. Wallace, Don McDonagh, Jean L. Druesedow, Laurence Libin, and Constance Old, *Dance: A Very Social History* (New York: Metropolitan Museum of Art and Rizzoli International Publications, 1986), 18.

28. Brenda Dixon Gottschild, *Waltzing in the Dark: African American Vaudeville and Race Politics in the Swing Era* (New York: St. Martin's Press, 2000).

CHAPTER 2

1. In 2004, The National Underground Railroad Freedom Center (NURFC) opened in Cincinnati, Ohio. The new facility houses, among other exhibits, a complete, authentic slave pen built in 1830 and transported from Mason, Kentucky. Because a much larger tobacco barn had been built around and over the log structure, the pen survived in good condition, allowing NURFC to disassemble and rebuild it in a dedicated exhibit space. Readers may read more at the museum's website, or see a picture of the slave pen by going to http://en.wikipedia.org/ wiki/National_Underground_Railroad_Freedom_Center#Slave_pen.

2. See Walter Johnson, *Soul by Soul: Life Inside the Antebellum Slave Market* (Cambridge, MA: Harvard University Press, 1999), 23.

3. Ira Berlin explores the complexities of this truth in his *Many Thousands Gone: The First Two Centuries of Slavery in North America* (Cambridge and London: Harvard University Press, 1998).

4. Drew Gilpin Faust, "Slavery in the American Experience," in Museum of the Confederacy's exhibition catalogue *Before Freedom Came: African-American Life in the Antebellum South*, ed. Edward D. C. Campbell, Jr. and Kym S. Rice (Charlottesville: University Press of Virginia, 1991), 12–13.

5. Ira Berlin, 146.

6. Art Rosenbaum, *Shout Because You're Free: The African American Ring Shout Tradition in Coastal Georgia* (Athens, Georgia: University of Georgia Press, 1998), 1.

7. Among the most prominent were the following: a) Laura Towne, who traveled to St. Helena Island in 1862, during the Civil War, and started a school there. She stayed for thirty-eight years, devoting her life to educating former slaves and their children. See *Letters and Diary of Laura M. Towne*, ed. Rupert Sargent Holland (Cambridge: Riverside Press, 1912). b) William Francis Allen, Lucy McKym Garrison, and Charles Pickard Ware, who worked together to transcribe and publish in 1867 a landmark collection of slave songs, with music. See *Slave Songs of the United States* (Bedford, Massachu-

setts: Applewood Books, 1996). c) Lydia Parrish, who lived for a time on St. Simon's island coaxing local African Americans into demonstrating their songs and dances for her. Her versions of these songs, along with descriptions of dances and commentaries on their African roots may be found in her *Slave Songs of the Georgia Sea Islands* (Athens, Georgia: University of Georgia Press, 1992). Parrish's book was first published in 1942. In her sound recordings of the songs, she was aided by Lorenzo Dow Turner.

8. John Atkins, *A Voyage to Guinea, Brazil, and the West Indies* (London, 1735), 53. Quoted in Dena Epstein, *Sinful Tunes and Spirituals: Black Folk Music to the Civil War* (Urbana, Illinois: University of Illinois Press, 1977), 5.

9. Berlin, 146.

10. Edward Ball, *Slaves in the Family* (New York: Ballantine Books, 1999), 102.

11. William S. Pollitzer, *The Gullah People and Their African Heritage* (Athens and London: University of Georgia Press, 1999), 88–89.

12. See Fanny Kemble, Letter to the Editor of the London Times. In *Journal of a Residence on a Georgian Plantation, 1838–39* (Athens, Georgia: University of Georgia Press, 1984), 356. Kemble was an acclaimed and educated British actress who married Philadelphian Pierce Butler, owner of a cotton and rice plantation in the Sea Islands. Kemble's first serious exposure to slavery came during a visit to this plantation, whose horrors appalled her. She became an immediate antagonist of slavery.

13. Kathleen Deagon and Darcie MacMahon, *Fort Mose: Colonial America's Fortress of Freedom* (Gainesville: University Press of Florida, 1996), 17.

14. *South Carolina Slave Laws Summary and Record.* See http:// www.slaveryinamerica.org/geography/slave_laws_SC.htm.

15. Parrish, xiv.

16. *McIntosh County Shouters: Slave Songs from the Coast of Georgia.* Smithsonian Folkways Recordings. Folkways F4344 1984. This CD contains a broad selection of traditional shout songs.

17. Towne, 20.

18. William Frances Allen, *Diary, 1863–1866 II.* Unpublished manuscript, State Historical Society of Wisconsin. Entry for December 25, 1863. Quoted by Epstein, 284–85.

19. John Lomax and Alan Lomax,

Folk Song, U.S.A. (New York: Duell, Sloan & Pearce, 1947), 335.

20. W. M. Connell, "A South Carolina 'Shouting,'" *The Illustrated American* (September 19, 1896), 395.

21. Epstein, 233.

22. John Watson, *Methodist Error or Friendly Advise to Those Methodists who Indulge in Extravagant Religious Emotions and Bodily Exercises* (Trenton, New Jersey, 1819). Quoted in Ann Taves, "Knowing Through the Body: Dissociative Religious Experience in the African- and British-American Methodist Traditions," *Journal of Religion* 73 (April, 1993), 215.

23. W.E.B. DuBois, "Of the Faith of the Fathers," in his *Souls of Black Folks* (New York: Pocket, 2005). Go to http://www.pagebypagebooks. com/W_E_B_DuBois/The_Souls_o f_Black_Folk/index.html to see the full text online.

24. Boston *Weekly News-Letter*, October 15–22, 1730. Quoted by Herbert Aptheker, *American Negro Slave Revolts*, 6th ed. (New York: International Publishers, 1993), 181.

25. Captain Basil Hall, *Travels in the United States.* Quoted in Parrish, 21–22.

26. Frederick Douglass, *Life and Times of Frederick Douglass: His Early Life as a Slave, His Escape from Bondage, and His Complete History to the Present Time* (Hartford, Connecticut: Park Publishing Company, 1881), 70.

27. Bess Lomax Hawes, *The Films of Bess Lomax Hawes*, 6. This booklet serves as notes for the four films Hawes made of African American dance. See the text of the booklet at http://media-generation.com/ Films/Bess/master.pdf#search ='the%20films%20of%20bessie%2 010max%20hawes.' Hawes' footage of the Georgia Sea Island Singers was shot on 35 mm film on a sound stage in Los Angeles, and a DVD of this work and the other three films is available from media-connection. com.

28. Letter from Wendell Phillips Garrison to William Lloyd Garrison II, Dec. 2, 1868. Unpublished manuscript, Smith College Library. Quoted in Epstein, 340.

29. Lines taken from Parrish, 88.

30. Bruno Nettl, *Music in Primitive Culture* (Cambridge: Harvard University Press, 1972), 72. Reprinted from a 1956 edition.

31. Hawes, 7.

32. National Historic Landmarks. See the web page about the Stono River Rebellion landmark at http://tps.cr.nps.gov/nhl/detail.cfm?

ResourceId=1488&ResourceType=Site.

33. Parrish, 85.
34. Parrish, 55.
35. Robert W. Gordon, "The Negro Spiritual." In Augustine Smythe et.al., *The Carolina Low Country* (New York: Macmillan, 1931), 199.
36. *Ibid.*
37. Quoted in Rosenbaum, 125.
38. "I'm Flying High," by Thomas L. Mack. J. C. Groene & Co., Cincinnati, Ohio, 1886.
39. Sterling Stuckey, *Slave Culture: Nationalist Theory and the Foundations of Black America* (Oxford University Press, 1988), 87.
40. Letitia Burwell, *A Girl's Life in Virginia Before the War* (Dahlonega, Georgia: Crown Rights Book Company, 2003), 163–64. Reprinted from 1895 edition by Frederick A. Stokes Company, New York.
41. Parrish, 10.
42. Bishop D. Payne, *Recollections of Seventy Years*, ed. C. S. Smith (Nashville, AME Sunday School Union, 1888), 253–54.
43. See Taves, 203.
44. Taves, 205.
45. Parrish, 17–18.
46. Parrish, 35–36.
47. See discussion in John Michael Spencer, "Rhythm in Black Religion of the African Diaspora," *Journal of Religious Thought* 44 (Winter/Spring, 1988), 67–82.
48. Frances Butler Leigh, *Ten Years on a Georgia Plantation Since the War: Electronic Version*, first edition (Library of Congress/Ameritech National Digital Library Competition, 1998), 60. See http://docsouth.unc.edu/leigh/leigh.html
49. Stuckey, 12.
50. James Weldon Johnson, *The Book of American Negro Spirituals* (New York: Viking Press, 1925), 32–33. Quoted in Rosenbaum, 41.
51. Hawes, 4.
52. Thomas Wentworth Higginson, *Army Life in a Black Regiment* (Boston: Houghton Mifflin, 1900), 23–24.
53. Ibid. See http://www.gutenberg.org/dirs/etext04/army110.txt for a full-text copy of the book.
54. Rosenbaum, 64.
55. Parrish, 71.
56. Hawes, 10.
57. John F. Szwed and Morton Marks, "The Afro-American Transformation of European Set Dances and Dance Suites," *Dance Research Journal* 20 (Summer, 1988), 33.
58. See Epstein's note, 159.
59. The Lenjengo dance can be viewed in the film *JVC Smithsonian*

Folkways Video Anthology of Dance /Music of Africa (1990). 30 video cassettes with booklets.
60. Parrish, 111.
61. Parrish, 111.
62. Melville Herskovits and Frances Herskovits, *Rebel Destiny: Among the Bush Negroes of Dutch Guiana* (New York: McGraw Hill, 1934), 330. Quoted in Hawes, 8.
63. Hawes, 8.
64. Quoted by Hawes, 8.
65. Hawes, 9.

CHAPTER 3

1. Sterling Stuckey, *Going Through the Storm: The Influence of African American Art in History* (New York: Oxford University Press, 1994), 54.
2. Genevieve Fabre, "Pinkster Festival, 1776–1811: An African-American Celebration." In *Feasts and Celebrations in North American Ethnic Communities*, ed. Ramon Guiterrez and Genevieve Fabre (Albuquerque: University of New Mexico Press: 1995), 13.
3. Alice Morse Earle, *Colonial Days in Old New York* (New York: Charles Scribner's Sons: 1896), 195.
4. See the version in Geraldine R. Pleat and Agnes N. Underwood, "Pinkster Ode, Albany, 1803," *New York Folklore Quarterly* 8 (1952), 32.
5. Stuckey mentions New York, Albany, Troy, Kingston, and Poughkeepsie (57–59).
6. Figures taken from New York State Department of Economic Development, State Data Center, *Population of New York State by County, 1790 to 1990* (July 2000), and from A. J. Williams-Myers, *The Long Hammering: Essays on the Forging of an African American Presence in the Hudson River Valley to the Early Twentieth Century* (Trenton, New Jersey: Africa World Press, 1994), 86.
7. Stuckey, 57. Stuckey cites James G. Lydon.
8. Colonial Albany Social History Project. http://www.nysm.nysed.gov/albany/population.html. Accessed June 12, 2005.
9. Earle, 196.
10. Pleat and Underwood, "Pinkster Ode, Albany, 1803," 33. See also Dr. James Eights, "Pinkster Festivities in Albany Sixty years Ago." In John Munsell, *Collections on the History of Albany*, vol. 2 (Albany 1865), 325.
11. Eights, 325.
12. Pleat and Underwood, 34.
13. Shane White, "Pinkster: Afro-

Dutch Syncretization in New York City and the Hudson Valley," Journal *of American Folklore* 102 (1989), 70.
14. Stuckey, 62.
15. White, "Pinkster," 70.
16. White, "Pinkster," 71.
17. White, "Pinkster," 68 and 72.
18. Pleat and Underwood, 37–41.
19. James Fenimore Cooper, *Satanstoe* (New York: Burgess and Stringer, 1845), 65.
20. Eights, 326.
21. Eights, 326.
22. White, "Pinkster," 69.
23. Cooper, 62.
24. Cooper, 60.
25. Quoted by Shane White in "'It was a Proud Day': African Americans, Festivals, and Parades in the North, 1741–1834," *Journal of American History* 81 (1994), 19.
26. See Hubert H. Aimes, "African Institutions in America," *Journal of American Folklore* 18 (January-March 1905), 18. In writing of New England customs, Aimes remarks, "Not long after the Revolution the Negro population began to decrease, owing to the removal of slaves to the South...." Also, Shane White, in his "Proud Day" article, p. 34, notes, "Rumors, in New York in 1801, that a Madam Volunbrun was about to dispatch twenty slaves to the South caused a volatile crowd of several hundred blacks to gather outside her house. Force had to be used to disperse the blacks...."
27. Earle, 198.
28. North Carolina Office of Archives and History in association with The University of North Carolina Press, *The Way We Lived in North Carolina*. http://www.waywelivednc.com/1770–1820/plantersslaves.htm. Accessed on 3/3/05.
29. See Elizabeth A. Fenn, "'All Dance, Leap and Play': Jonkonnu, Slave Society, and Black Dance," *American Dance Festival 1988: The Black Tradition in American Modern Dance* (Durham, North Carolina: American Dance Festival, 1988), 9.
30. Harriet Jacobs, *Incidents in the Life of a Slave Girl, Written by Herself* (Cambridge: Harvard University Press, 1987), 277–278.
31. Dougald Mac Millan, "John Kuners," *Journal of American Folklore* 39 (January-March, 1926), 53.
32. Mac Millan, 54.
33. For quotes from a number of period accounts, both before and after the Civil War, see Richard Walser, "His Worship, the John Kuner," *North Carolina Folklore Journal* 47 (2000), 97–110.
34. Walser, 102.

35. See Fenn, 10, for a similar version.

36. Walser, 106.

37. *Pulse of the Planet*, a radio program funded in part by the National Science Foundation and the National Endowment of the Humanities, as well as the DuPont Company, December 2, 2003, Program 3067.

38. Ibid., December, 2001.

39. Edward Long, *This History of Jamaica* (London: T. Lowndes, 1774), 424. Quoted by John W. Nunley and Judith Bettelheim, *Caribbean Festival Arts* (Seattle and London: St. Louis Art Museum and University of Washington Press, 1988), 47.

40. Both accounts quoted by Fenn, 9.

41. Sir Hans Sloane, *A Voyage to the Islands of Madera, Barbados, and Jamaica*, Vol. 1 (London: B.M., 1707), 46–48. Quoted by Nunley and Bettelheim, 47.

42. Janet L. DeCosmo, "Junkanoo: The African Cultural Connection in Nassau, Bahamas," *The Western Journal of Black Studies* 27 (2003), 247; Robert Dirks, "Slaves' Holiday," *Natural History* 84 (December, 1975), 84.

43. Samuel Wilson, "Saint George and John Canoe," *Natural History* 12 (1991), 24–25.

44. For a photo of a contemporary Pitchy-Patchy costume, see Jane Maxfield, "Millicent Matthie's Pitchy Patchy," *Arts & Activities* (January 1995), 33.

45. Scholar Robert Farris Thompson remembers seeing an Egungun character in vegetable fibers. See Nunley and Bettelheim, 51. They cite a personal communication with Thompson in 1976.

46. For a full discussion of the Mocko Jumbie and his probably African forebears, see Robert W. Nicholls, "The Mocko Jumbie of the U.S. Virgin Islands: History and Antecedents," *African Arts* 32 (Autumn 1999), 48–61.

47. Nunley and Bettelheim, 62.

48. DeCosmo, 246.

49. Nunley and Bettelheim, 54.

50. Robert Dirks, "Slaves' Holiday," 82.

51. Dirks, 82–84.

52. Dirks, 88–89.

53. Quoted by Nunley and Bettelheim, 72.

54. See DeCosmo, 249.

55. DeCosmo, 249.

56. DeCosmo, 252.

57. "Plans in the Island Colonies," *New York Times*, December 25, 1938, 116. For similar articles, see "Parade at Nassau," *New York Times*,

December 26, 1937, 130, and Catherine Mackenzie, "Bermuda and Nassau Beckon," *New York Times*, December 29, 1935, xxi.

58. Nunley and Bettelheim, 63.

59. Nunley and Bettelheim, 69.

60. Henry Bacon McKoy, *Wilmington, N.C.: Do you Remember When?* (Greenville: Keys Printing, 1957). See pp. 141–145.

61. Connecticut State Library, "Connecticut's 'Black Governors,'" at www.cslib.org/gov/blackgov.htm.

62. Aimes, 15.

63. Hartford Black History Project, "Emerging from the Shadows," at http://www.hartford-hwp.com/HBHP/exhibit/03/1.html.

64. Webster Brooks, "Connecticut, the Birthplace of Democracy in America," symposium presentation at The Africa Meeting House in Boston, July 24, 2004.

65. For a list, see Hartford Black History Project.

66. See "Black Election Day in 18th Century New England," on About.com at http://afroamhistory.about.com/library/weekly/aa09030la.htm.

67. Earle, 201–202. Earle adds, "The 'Black Governor' was elected on the week following the election of the white Governor, usually on a Saturday."

68. Connecticut State Library.

69. Brooks.

70. See Aimes, 18. Aimes quotes Stuart in *Hartford in the Olden Time*.

71. Jane De Forest Shelton, "The New England Negro: A Remnant," *Harper's New Monthly Magazine* 88 (March, 1894), 537.

72. General training days also took place in southern colonies such as Georgia and Virginia, but this study will focus on the New England General Training because of its association with a black holiday.

73. Telfer Mook, "Training Day in New England," *The New England Quarterly* 11 (December, 1938), 676.

74. *Turns of the Centuries*, an exhibit mounted by Memorial Hall Museum, in Old Deerfield, Massachusetts. You may see some of the exhibit content at www.americancenturies.mass.edu. There is, for example, a woodcut called *Southern View of Deerfield*, showing the town common, where the town militia would have mustered on Training Day. Accessed 3/15/05.

75. Mook, 685.

76. Mook, 680.

77. White, "Proud Day," 21.

78. Mook, 682.

79. Franklin Butler Van Valkenburgh, *Grandpa's Letter to his Chil-*

dren: Being the Story of a Boy's Life in a Country Village from 1835 to 1847. Available at http://www.navvf.org/grandpapa/g-pa-part18.html.

80. See *A Chronology of African American Military Service from the Colonial Era through the Antebellum Period* at http://www.ufphq.com/aams.htm.

81. See Jeffrey Kerr-Ritchie, "Rehearsal for War: Black Militias in the Atlantic World," *Slavery & Abolition* 26 (April, 2005), 1–33.

82. White, "Proud Day," 18.

83. White, "Proud Day," 18.

84. Guy C. McElroy, *Facing History: The Black Image in American Art 1710–1940* (San Francisco and Washington: Bedford Arts, Publishers, in association with The Corcoran Gallery of Art, 1990), 39.

85. Fred Mather, *In the Louisiana Lowlands*, Chapter VI, printed in *Forest and Stream: A Journal of Outdoor Life, Travel, Nature Study, and Shooting* 51 (October 29, 1898), 345ff. Mather's book was serialized in the magazine.

86. John Cabell Chenault, *Old Cane Springs: A Story of the War Between the States in Madison County, Kentucky*, rev. and suppl. Jonathan Truman Dorris (Louisville: The Standard Printing Company, 1937), 42–50. Entire passage reprinted by Roger Abrahams, *Singing the Master: The Emergence of African American Culture in the Plantation South* (New York: Pantheon Books, 1992), 287–293.

87. Marion Harland, *The Story of a Long Life* (New York and London: Harper and Brothers, Publishers, 1910), 146.

88. James Battle Avirett, *The Old Plantation* (New York: F. T. Neely, 1901), 140–146. Full text of this account, based on events in North Carolina in the 1850s, is provided by Abrahams, 233–238.

89. Letitia M. Burwell, *A Girl's Life in Virginia Before the War* (New York: Frederick A. Stokes Company, 1895), 131.

90. Mather, 345ff.

91. Burwell, 132.

92. Mather, 345ff.

93. Chenault, reprinted in Abrahams, 290.

94. Francis Fredric, *Slave Life in Virginia and Kentucky* (London: Wertheim, McIntosh and Hunt, 1863), 47–51, reprinted in Abrahams, 239–242. See p. 240. Mary Terhune, writing under the pseudonym Marion Harland, remembered the pile as "a mighty pyramid." See her autobiography, 145.

95. Burwell, 131.

96. Harland, 146.

97. Abrahams, 125–126. He cites Marry Ross Banks, *Bright Days on the Old Plantation* (Boston: Lee and Shepherd, 1882), 122–123.

98. David Barrow, "A Georgia Corn-Shucking," *Century Magazine* 24 (1882), 874.

99. Barrow, 874.

100. Mather, 345ff.

101. Quoted by Barrow, 875.

102. Rev. C. Thornton, *An Inquiry Into the History of Slavery* (Washington, D.C.: William M. Morrison, 1841), 122. Reproduced by Abrahams, 204–207. For the song quoted here, see pp. 206–207.

103. Barrow, 876.

104. Celia M. Benton, "Corn Shuckings in Sampson County," *North Carolina Folklore Journal* 24 (1974), 131–139.

105. Benton, 134.

106. Abrahams, 18.

107. Abrahams, 309.

108. Barrow, 878.

109. Mather, 345ff.

110. Mather, 345ff.

111. Barrow, 878.

112. George Washington Cable, "The Dance in Place Congo," *Century Magazine* 31 (February, 1886), 519.

113. Lynne Emery, *Black Dance from 1619 to Today*, 2nd ed. (Princeton: Princeton Book Company, 1988), 156. See also Jerah Johnson, *Congo Square in New Orleans* (New Orleans: Louisiana Landmarks Society, 1995).

114. See Jessie Gaston Mulira, "The Case of Voodoo in New Orleans," in *Africanisms in American Culture*, ed. Joseph E. Holloway (Bloomington: Indiana University Press, 1991), 40.

115. National Park Service web site, "Congo Square." See www.nps.gov/jazz/Armstrong%20Park_congo_square.htm.

116. Johnson, 34.

117. Emery quotes Latrobe regarding these numbers. See Emery, 159.

118. Christian Schultz, *Travels on an Inland Voyage through the States of New-York, Pennsylvania, Virginia, Ohio, Kentucky and Tennessee, and through the Territories of Indiana, Louisiana, Mississippi and New Orleans*, vol 2 (New York: Isaac Riley, 1810), 197. Facsimile edition.

119. Cable, 422; Emery, 158–159.

120. Henry Didimus, quoted by Rudi Blesh and Harriet Janis, *They All Played Ragtime* (New York: Knopf, 1950), p. 83.

121. Emery, 164.

122. Père Labat, *Nouveau Voyage Aux Isles de l'Amerique*, trans. Anthony Bliss, vol. 2 (The Hague, 1724), 52. Quoted by Emery, 21–22.

123. Quoted by Emery 22–23.

124. For a discussion of this issue, see Julian Gerstin, "Tangled Roots: Kalenda and Other Neo-African Dances in the Circum-Caribbean," *New West Indies Guide* 78 (2004), 5–41.

125. Quoted by Emery, 25.

126. George Washington Cable, "Creole Slave Songs," *Century Magazine* 31 (April, 1886).

127. Johnson, 37.

128. Dena J. Epstein, *Sinful Tunes and Spirituals: Black Folk Music to the Civil War* (Chicago and London: University of Illinois Press, 1977), 84–85.

CHAPTER 4

1. Eric Lott, *Love and Theft: Blackface Minstrelsy and the American Working Class* (New York: Oxford University Press, 1993).

2. See Marshall and Jean Stearns, *Jazz Dance: The Story of American Vernacular Dance* (New York: Da Capo Press, 1994), 23.

3. Ed. James, *Jig, Clog, and Breakdown Dancing Made Easy, with Sketches of Noted Jig Dancers* (New York: Self-Published, 1873), 1.

4. James, 11.

5. Charles Dickens, *The Works of Charles Dickens*, Vol. V (New York: Collier, ca. 1880s), 295.

6. Charles Rockwell, "Sketches of Foreign Travel and Life at Sea," *African Repository and Colonial Journal* 18 (September, 1842), 277.

7. Sir Robert Schomburgh, "Pictures of Barbados," *The Anglo American, A Journal of Literature, News Politics, the Drama, Fine Arts* 10 (October 23, 1847), 3.

8. Ibid.

9. Quoted by Stearns, 37.

10. See Stearns, 37, for a mention of acrobatic dancers from Sierra Leone. Men and women dancers from Tunisia and Morocco do the Pot Dance and Tray Dance in which the dancer executes acrobatic moves to fast music while balancing either a jug of water or a tray of crockery on the head.

11. Allen Parker, *Recollections of Slavery Times* (Worcester, Massachusetts: Charles W. Burbank, 1895), 67. For an online version, see http://docsouth.unc.edu/neh/parker/parker.html. Accessed 7/9/05.

12. William Cullen Bryant, Letter XI: "The Interior of South Carolina. A Corn-Shucking" in *Letters of a Traveller*, available at www.blackmask.com/thatway/books142c/letrav.htm. Accessed 7/6/05.

13. One great way to make comparisons is to see a demonstration by professional dancer Ira Bernstein. The web site *Ten Toe Percussion* contains thirteen 45-second excerpts from Bernstein's live performance at the Klein Carre Theatre in Amsterdam, The Netherlands. You can click on "English Clogging," "Irish Step Dancing," "Appalachian Flatfooting," "Soft Shoe," or "Jazz Tap" and visually absorb these related styles. Go to http://www.97watts.com/tentoepercussion/ and begin clicking. I accessed the site on 7/6/05.

14. James, 4.

15. Rita Ramsey, *Home Lessons in Tap Dance* (New York: Dutton, 1932) 16.

16. "Clogging History," *International Encyclopedia of Dance* (New York: Oxford University Press, 1998).

17. Mike Seeger, *Talking Feet: Buck, Flatfoot and Tap, Solo Southern Dance of the Appalachian, Piedmont and Blue Ridge Mountain Regions.* (Berkeley, California: North Atlantic Books, 1992), 22. Other dancers interviewed for Seeger's study made similar remarks. Jay Burris, for example, said, "The old-time flatfoot dancing is more on your heel and toe and flatfooted, keeping your feet close to the floor, not picking your feet up any more than three inches" (23). Biddie Reece described the style as "Kind of shuffling your feet on the floor and not raising them up" (58). In North Carolina and other places with significant Native American populations, the native people's dances influenced clogging and flatfooting, as well.

18. Constance Valis Hill, "Tap Dance in America: A Very Short History," 3. See document at www.nypl.org/research/lpa/dan/hines/TAPENCY2002cites.pdf.

19. See an online discussion by Caoimhim Mac Aoidh, an expert on the fiddle music of Donegal: http://www.standingstones.com/cmaoitm.html.

20. See Tyler Anbinder, *Five Points: The 19th-Century New York City Neighborhood that Invented Tap Dance, Stole Elections, and Became the World's Most Notorious Slum* (New York: The Free Press, 2001), 42–46.

21. See James W. Cook, *Common-Place* 4 (October 2003), parts I,II,III,IV, and V. The publica-

tion is accessible online at http://www.common-place.org/vol-04/no-01/cook/cook-2.shtml. Accessed on 7/6/05. Cook examines Pete Williams' dancing cellar in detail in a discussion based on period reading, and is well worth reading.

22. Charles Dickens, *American Notes and Pictures from Italy* (London: Chapman and Hall, 1842), 43.

23. Katherine Dunham, "The Negro Dance," in *The Negro Caravan*, eds. Sterling A. Brown, Arthur P. Davis, and Ulysses Lee (New York: Dryden Press, 1941), 997–998. Marian Winter adds, "The juba dance (simplified from *giouba*) was an African step dance which somewhat resembled a jig with elaborate variations, and occurs wherever the Negro settled, whether in the West Indies or South Carolina." See Marian Hannah Winter, "Juba and American Minstrelsy,' in *Chronicles of the American Dance*, ed. Paul Magriel (New York: Henry Holt and Company, 1948), 40. The name is also associated with a Haitian drum rhythm of Vodun and (according to Winter) a supernatural being in some African American folklore.

24. Julian Gerstin, "Tangled Roots: Kalenda and Other Neo-African Dances in the Circum-Caribbean," in *New West Indies Guide* 78 (2004), 7ff.

25. For more information on Davis, see Dale Cockrell, *Demons of Disorder: Early Blackface Minstrels and their World* (Cambridge, New York, and Melbourne: Cambridge University Press, 1997), 88. Also, Stephen Johnson quotes the *Theatrical Journal*, 27 March 1851, as referring to "Mr. and Mrs. Dwight, Negro Melodists and Juba Dancers," as well as *Era*, 23 November 1851, for reference to "Messrs. Busby and Brandon, Negro Melodists and Juba Dancers," and to "D Hodgson, the female Juba." See Stephen Johnson, "Juba's Dance: An Assessment of New Acquired Information," first published in *the Proceedings of the 26th Annual Conference of the Society for Dance History Scholars* (SDHS, 2003). The text of the presentation is also available at http://www.erin.uto ronto,ca/~sjohnson/juba/Microhistory/article2.html.

26. See Cook, part IV, 2. Cook says that Barnum deceived the sporting fraternity with false advertising that suggested that Juba was a white in blackface and fraudulently presented him as the much-admired Irish dancer John Diamond. When a *Sunday Flash* writer discovered the subterfuge, he wrote, "The boy is

fifteen or sixteen years of age; his name is "Juba," and to do him justice, he is a very fair dancer. He is of harmless and inoffensive disposition, and is not, I sincerely believe, aware of the meanness and audacity of the swindler to which he is presently a party" (quoted by Cook, 3).

27. Quoted by Cook, 3.

28. Quoted by Cook, 4.

29. See Cook, 4–5.

30. Texts of the reviews of Lane's dance in London that are quoted in this chapter have been taken from The Juba Project web site at http://www.erin.utoronto.ca/~sjohnson/juba/.

31. Lynne Fauley Emery, *Black Dance from 1619 to Today*, 2nd ed. (Princeton: Princeton Book Company, 1988), 96. I thank the Juba Project for calling this to my attention.

32. Johnson, 5.

33. Stearns, 172–176.

34. Quoted by Stearns, 175. See also www.bobhope.com for additional confirmation that Hope took dancing lesions from King Rastus Brown.

35. Stearns, 176.

36. Rusty E. Frank, *Tap! The Greatest Tap Dance Stars and their Stories, 1900–1955* (New York: Da Capo Press, 1994), 224.

37. Stearns, 174.

38. Frank, 224.

39. Frank, 225.

40. Frank, 225.

41. Stearns, 175.

CHAPTER 5

1. Constance Rourke, *American Humor* (New York: Harcourt, Brace, 1931), 98.

2. Eric Lott, *Love and Theft: Blackface Minstrelsy and the American Working Class* (New York and Oxford: Oxford University Press, 1993).

3. See Kheven Lee LaGrone, "From Minstrelsy to Gangsta Rap: The 'Nigger' as Commodity for Popular American Entertainment," *Journal of African American Men* 5 (Fall, 2000), 117.

4. See Stephanie Dunson, "The Minstrel in the Parlor: Nineteenth-Century Sheet Music and the Domestication of Blackface Minstrelsy," *ATQ* 16 (December 2002), 241–256.

5. Helene Magaret, "The Negro Fad," *Forum and Century* 87 (January 1932), 39.

6. Toll notes, for example, "In the nostalgic plantation songs Black

minstrels wrote, they expressed longing for the happy days of their childhood and for their departed family and friends. Unlike the white-written songs that stressed blacks' love for their masters and mistresses, Blacks' songs rarely even mentioned this love." See Toll's Introduction to the 1974 reprint of Ike Simond's *Old Slack's Reminiscence and Pocket History of the Color Profession from 1865 to 1891* by Bowling Green University Popular Press, xxv.

7. H. P. Gratton, "The Origin of the Christy's Minstrels," *The Theatre* (March, 1882). Quoted by Hans Nathan, *Dan Emmett and the Rise of Early Negro Minstrelsy* (Norman, Oklahoma: University of Oklahoma Press, 1962), 145.

8. Robert C. Toll, *Blacking Up: The Minstrel Show in Nineteenth Century America* (New York: Oxford University Press, 1974), 31.

9. Lott, 171.

10. Museum of the City of New York owns an oil painting of the 57th performance, entitled *Thomas D. Rice Performing his 'Jumping Jim Crow' routine at the American Theatre, Bowery, New York, November 23, 1833.* See the painting at http://www.cooper.edu/humanities/classes/coreclasses/hss4/whitch atham.html. I accessed this site on 8/22/05.

11. Carl Wittke, *Tambo and Bones: A History of the American Minstrel Stage* (Durham, North Carolina: Duke University Press, 1930), 73

12. Wittke, 60.

13. Simon Featherstone, "The Blackface Atlantic: Interpreting British Minstrelsy," *Journal of Victorian Culture* (Autumn 1998), 236.

14. See Richard Waterhouse, "The Minstrel Show and Australian Culture," *Journal of Popular Culture* 24 (Winter, 1990), 147–167. You can also see a thumbnail history of minstrelsy in Australia in "Minstrelsy in Australia: A Brief Overview" at www.nugrape.net/minstrel.htm. I accessed this site on 8/9/05.

15. Elizabeth Robins Pennell, "London at Play," *Century Illustrated Magazine* 54 (August, 1897), 572.

16. See "Banjo and Bones," *The Critic and Good Literature* 26 (June 28, 1884), 308.

17. *Putnam's Monthly*, February, 1854. Quoted by Nathan, 218.

18. Lott, 66–67.

19. Toll, 3–4.

20. A New York newspaper, for example, called for the closure of a

minstrel show at the Academy of Music in Chicago "on account of its obscenity." *New York Times* (November 29, 1866), 1.

21. Wittke, 20.

22. Toll, 27. For a longer account of correspondences between a number of important minstrels songs and English/European sources, see Nathan's Chapter 12, "Early Minstrel Tunes," in *Dan Emmett and the Rise of Early Negro Minstrelsy*, 159–188.

23. Nathan 205–207.

24. Nathan, 71, note 3.

25. Frances Kemble, *Journal of a Residence on a Georgia Plantation in 1838–1839* (New York: Harper & Brothers, 1864), 96.

26. See Toll, 198–199.

27. Tom Fletcher, *100 Years of the Negro in Show Business* (New York: Da Capo Press, 1984), xvii.

28. Fletcher, 7.

29. Toll, 199.

30. Fletcher, xviii.

31. Toll, 199.

32. Fletcher, 7–8.

33. Toll, 201.

34. Toll, 200.

35. Toll, 201.

36. Toll, 234.

37. "The Opposing 'Sluggers,'" *New York Times* (December 22, 1885), 2.

38. "Grand Opera House," *New York Times* (November 26, 1889), 4.

39. Conde Hamlin, "The American Stage," *St. Paul Pioneer Press*. Collected in *Current Literature* 8 (December, 1891), 611.

40. "Banjo and Bones," 308.

41. Wittke, 135.

42. For a fuller discussion of this issue, see David Krasner, "Parody and Double Consciousness in the Language of Early Black Musical Theatre," *African American Review* 29 (Summer, 1995).

43. See, for example, "A Minstrel Show in Trouble," *New York Times* (November 19, 1888), 8.

44. *New York Times* (December 11, 1888), 1.

45. *New York Times* (December 1, 1892), 5.

46. *New York Times* (December 19, 1893), 12.

47. See the *New York Times* on February 12, 1888, 3; November 20, 1887, 11; March 6, 1892, 11; and August 22, 1890, 5.

48. Mike Pearson, "'No Joke in Petticoats': British Polar Expeditions and Their Theatrical Presentations," *The Drama Review* 48 (Spring, 2004), 44.

49. See Featherstone, pp. 234–251.

50. Marshall and Jean Stearns, *Jazz Dance: The Story of American Vernacular Dance* (New York: Da Capo Press, 1994), 57.

51. Stearns, 57–58.

52. Thomas L. Morgan and William Barlow, *From Cakewalks to Concert Halls: An Illustrated History of African American Popular Music from 1895 to 1930* (Washington, D.C.: Elliott & Clark Publishing, 1992), 15.

53. Stearns, 51.

54. Fletcher, 61–62.

55. This statement by Arthur Marshall is quoted by Stearns on p. 50 of his *Jazz Dance*.

56. Toll, 216.

57. Toll, 216–217.

58. Toll, 218–219.

59. As Fletcher concisely writes, "The minstrels had their largest following in the south," 57.

60. Fletcher 57.

61. Toll, 234.

62. Fletcher, 58.

63. Wittke, 129.

64. "Under the Palmetto," *The Continental Monthly* 4 (August 1863), 200.

65. Brenda Dixon Gottschild, *Digging the Africanist Presence in American Performance Dance and Other Contexts* (Westport, Connecticut and London: Greenwood Press, 1996), 83.

66. For lavish pictures of scenes from *Shuffle Along*, see Robert Kimball and William Bolcom, *Reminiscing with Sissle and Blake* (New York: Viking Press, 1973), 84ff.

67. Thomas L. Riis, *Just Before Jazz: Black Musical Theater in New York, 1890 to 1915* (Washington, DC: Smithsonian Institution Press, 1989), 7.

68. Simond, 26.

69. James O. Horton, "Humor and the American Racial Imagination," *American Quarterly*, 45 (March 1993), 166–170.

70. Adam Gussow, "'Make My Getaway': The Blues Lives of Black Minstrels in W.C. Handy's 'Father of the Blues,'" *African American Review* 35 (Spring, 2001), 6–23.

71. Fletcher 58.

72. Toll, 226–227.

73. Fletcher, 62.

74. Simond, xvii.

75. Stearns, 50.

76. Stearns, 63.

77. *Lewiston Journal*, July 23, 1887. Reported in *the New York Times* (July 25, 1887), 5.

78. For examples of the broadsides, see Brooks McNamara, *Step Right Up* (Jackson: University Press of Mississippi, 1995), 27 and 39.

79. See Morgan and Barlow, 65; Stearns, 64; and Woll, 32.

80. Stearns, 64.

81. Robert Kimball and William Bolcom, *Reminiscing with Sissle and Blake* (New York: Viking Press, 1973), 43.

82. Quotes from Thompson and Markham are both from Stearns, 64.

83. Stearns, 78.

84. Riis, 148–149.

85. Stearns, 75.

86. Fletcher, 20.

87. Fletcher 22.

88. Stearns, 76.

89. Fletcher, 21, and Riis, 23.

CHAPTER 6

1. Rita Ramsey, *Home Lessons in Tap Dancing* (New York; E.P. Dutton, 1932); Rosalind Wade, *Tap Dancing in 12 Easy Lessons* (Philadelphia: David McKay Company: n.d.); *Tip Top Tapping: Simplified Lessons in Tap Dancing* (New York: Book-A-Mag Company, 1940).

2. Allen Woll, *Black Musical Theatre from Coontown to Dreamgirls* (Baton Rouge and London: Louisiana State University Press, 1989), 11–12.

3. See Tom Fletcher, *100 Years of the Negro in Show Business* (New York: Da Capo Press, 1984), 43; Thomas Morgan and William Barlow, *From Cakewalks to Concert Halls: An Illustrated History of African American Popular Music from 1895 to 1930* (Washington, D.C.: Elliott & Clark Publishing, 1992), 58; Thomas L. Riis, *Just Before Jazz: Black Musical Theater in New York, 1890 to 1915* (Washington, D.C.: Smithsonian Institution Press, 1989), 75–79.

4. Quoted by Riis, *Just Before Jazz*, 78.

5. Riis, *Just Before Jazz*, 77.

6. Constance Hill, *Brotherhood in Rhythm: The Jazz Tap Dancing of the Nicholas Brothers* (New York and Oxford: Oxford University Press, 2000), 22.

7. Marshall and Jean Stearns, *Jazz Dance: The Story of American Vernacular Dance* (New York: Da Capo Press, 1994), 119.

8. Morgan and Barlow, 21.

9. Will Marion Cook, "Clorindy, the Origin of the Cakewalk," *Theatre Arts* (September, 1947), 64–65.

10. Riis, *Just Before Jazz*, 80.

11. Reviewers sometimes commented on the disparity of quality between the skimpy script on the one hand and the superb song and dance on the other. See comments later in this chapter on *In Dahomey*

in London, for example. Three decades later, reviewers were making similar comments. Robert Martin, in reviewing *Shuffle Along of 1933*, said the piece was "at its best when dancing, at its worst when trying to tell a story."

12. Morgan and Barlow, 63.
13. Riis, *Just Before Jazz*, 80.
14. Fletcher, 105.
15. Fletcher, 123.
16. Fletcher 107
17. For the story of this scandal, see Walter Lord, *The Good Years: From 1900 to the First World War* (New York: Harper and Brothers, 1960), 105–114; illustration on 148m.
18. "Lady Middleton, 'Peeress,' and Others Write Letters," *New York Times*, August 24, 1913, SM5.
19. Riis, *Just Before Jazz*, 82.
20. Woll, 34.
21. Quoted in *The Music and Scripts of In Dahomey*, ed. Thomas Riis (Madison, Wisconsin: A-R Editions, Inc., 1996), xix.
22. Riis, *Music and Scripts*, xix-xx.
23. A script for the play, written by Paul Laurence Dunbar and Jesse Shipp, has been published by James V. Hatch and Ted Shine in their *Black Theatre U.S.A.: Plays by African Americans, the Early Period 1847–1938* (New York: The Free Press, 1996), 63–85.
24. Riis, *Just Before Jazz*, 91ff.
25. Woll, 38.
26. For a discussion of how Walker reversed the minstrel stereotype of the black dandy, see Barbara L. Webb, "The Black Dandyism of George Walker: A Case Study in Genealogical Method," *The Drama Review* 45 (Winter, 2001),7–24.
27. Riis, *Just Before Jazz*, 91–105.
28. Jeffrey P. Green, "*In Dahomey* in London in 1903," *The Black Perspective in Music*, Vol. 11 (Spring 1983), 23.
29. Both reviews quoted by Green, 24.
30. The London newspaper *The Era* (May 23, 1903).
31. *The Era*, June 27, 1903.
32. Quoted by Henry T. Sampson, *Blacks in Blackface: A Source Book on Early Black Musical Shows* (Metuchen, New Jersey: Scarecrow Press, 1980), 80.
33. The Cincinnati *Age*, March 18, 1909, 95.
34. Sampson, 71–72; Riis, *Just Before Jazz*, 125, 128, 129; Morgan and Barlow 41, 58–61.
35. Riis, *Just Before Jazz*, 174.
36. Stearns and Stearns, 127–128.
37. Morgan and Barlow, 79; Stearns, 128, 323; Fletcher, 193.
38. Stearns, 129.

39. *A "Tough Dance,"* December 9, 1902. American Mutoscope & Biograph Company. To see the moving film, go to http://memory.loc.gov/mbrs/varsmp/1894.mpg.
40. Jim Burris and Chris Smith, "Ballin' the Jack," 1913.
41. Stearns and Stearns, 125.
42. Robert Kimball and William Bolcom, *Reminiscing with Sissle and Blake* (New York: The Viking Press, 1973), 20.
43. Kenneth L. Kusmer, *A Ghetto Takes Shape: Black Cleveland, 1870–1930* (Urbana and Chicago: University of Illinois Press, 1978), 161–162.
44. For more information on the Harlem Renaissance, see http://www.nku.edu/~diesmanj/harlem_intro.html and http://dir.yahoo.com/Arts/Humanities/Literature/Periods_and_Movements/Harlem_Renaissance/.
45. Billy Strayhorn's "Take the 'A' Train" (1941) was itself a superb example of jazz.
46. This explanation is indebted to James Collier's *The Making of Jazz: A Comprehensive History* (Boston: Houghton Mifflin, 1978). See pages 4–6.
47. From sheet music by Howard Johnson and Cliff Hess, "The Wedding of the Shimmie and Jazz" (New York: Leo Feist, 1919).
48. Kimball and Bolcom, 13.
49. Alan Date, "'Shuffle Along' Full of Pep and Real Melody," *New York American* (May 22, 1921). The full text of the article can be seen in Kimball and Bolcom, 99.
50. Hill, 26.
51. Woll, 58.
52. Kimball and Bolcom, 106.
53. Woll, 72.
54. Stearns and Stearns, 134–135; Woll, 70.
55. Stearns and Stearns, 139.
56. Kimball and Bolcom, 148.
57. Ad for a performance at the Olympic Theatre in Chicago.
58. James Weldon Johnson, *Along This Way* (New York: Penguin, 1968), 201.
59. Stearns and Stearns, 144.
60. "'Liza' is Melodious," *New York Times*, November 28, 1922, 28.
61. Heywood Broun, *New York World*, November 28, 1922. Quoted by Stearns, 143.
62. Carole Marks and Diana Edkins, *The Power of Pride: Stylemakers and Rulebreakers of the Harlem Renaissance* (New York: Crown Publishers, 1999), 160.
63. Morgan and Barlow, 87; Stearns, 142.
64. "'Plantation Review' Lively," *New York Times* (July 18, 1922), 22.

65. "The Season's Runs," *New York Times* (June 24, 1923), xi.
66. Stearns and Stearns, 145.
67. Woll, 86.
68. Stearns and Stearns, 145.
69. Stearns and Stearns, 145.
70. Morgan and Barlow, 116.
71. "The Charleston," Sergei Marinoff School of Classic Dancing (Chicago, 1925), 1.
72. Woll, 89.
73. Hill, 27.
74. Filmed in 1931, this footage is available through the anthropological archives of the Smithsonian Institution. It was also one of the video clips offered in the exhibition *When the Spirit Moves: The Africanization of American Movement* by the National Afro-American Museum and Cultural Center, which opened in 1999.
75. Kimball and Bolcom, 158–190.
76. Ethel Waters, *His Eye is on the Sparrow* (Garden City, NY: Doubleday, 1951), 189.
77. Stearns, 106.
78. A. J. Piron, "I Wish I could Shimmy Like My Sister Kate" (New York: Clarence Williams Music Publishing Company, 1922).
79. Jimmy Lucas and Billy Frisch, "Minnie, Shimme For Me" (New York: Broadway Music Corporation, 1918).
80. Lyrics by Eugene West, music by Joe Gold and Edmund J. Porray. "Introduced by Sophie Tucker and Her Five Kings of Syncopation."
81. *Chronicle of the Twentieth Century*, ed. Clifton Daniel (Mount Kisco, New York: Chronicle Publications, 1982), 279.
82. Waters, 161.
83. "The Original Black Bottom Dance," Gus Horsley and Perry Bradford, 1926.
84. Stearns and Stearns, 111 and 197.
85. Elise Marcus, "More Low-Down Dancing," *The Dance* (January, 1928), 41.
86. *How to Dance: the Latest and Most Complete Instructions in Ballroom Dance Steps* (New York: Padell Book Company, 1937), 44.
87. Betty Lee, *Dancing: All the Latest Steps* (New York: Edward J. Clode, Inc., 1927), 289–300.
88. Ray Henderson, "Black Bottom" (New York: Harms, 1926).
89. Will Marion Cook, "Spirituals and Jazz," *New York Times*, December 26, 1926, x8.
90. Bruce Reynolds, *Paris with the Lid Lifted* (New York: A. L. Burt Company, 1927), 127.

91. "Madrid Yields to Jazz," *New York Times* (July 24, 1927), E6.

92. "Uses Phone to London for a Dancing Lesson," *New York Times* (Jan 21, 1927), 13.

93. "Dancing Masters Move to Purify Charleston," *New York Times* (May 15, 1926), 19.

94. "Dr. Straton Tells of Buying Drinks," *New York Times* (April 5, 1920), 17.

95. M. F. Ham, *Light on the Dance* (Anchorage, Kentucky, 1921).

96. See "Police Censor Dancing," *New York Times* (June 9, 1919), 14; "Move to Reform Dancing," *New York Times* (August 31, 1919), 13; "To Suppress 'Jazz' Dances," *New York Times* (February 4, 1920), 13; Display Ad 117, *New York Times* (July 27, 1919), 42.

97. Reynolds, 154.

98. Brenda Dixon Gottschild, *Waltzing in the Dark: African American Vaudeville and Race Politics in the Swing Era* (New York: St. Martin's Press, 2000), 31.

99. Herman "Skip" Mason, Jr. *African-American Entertainment in Atlanta* (Charleston: Arcadia, 1998), 35.

100. Marks and Edkins, 164.

101. "Plays of the Moment: 'Black Birds,' the Coloured Artists' Revue at the London 'Pav,'" *The Sketch* (October 13, 1926), 86–87.

102. "Wales at Negro Revue," *New York Times* (September 21, 1926), 33.

103. "Scores Collapse at Mills Funeral," *New York Times* (November 7, 1927), 25.

104. Stearns and Stearns, 181.

105. "The Dance: Negro Art Loses in Originality," *New York Times* (July 8, 1928), 98.

106. Robert Benchley in the *New Yorker* (October 18, 1930). Quoted by Stearns and Stearns, 156.

107. Brooks Atkinson, "The Play," *New York Times* (October 23, 1930), 40.

CHAPTER 7

1. Thomas Morgan and William Barlow, *From Cakewalks to Concert Halls: An Illustrated History of African American Popular Music from 1895 to 1930* (Washington, DC: Elliott & Clark, 1992), 53.

2. Cholly Atkins and Jacqui Malone, *Class Act: The Jazz Life of Choreographer Cholly Atkins* (New York: Columbia University Press, 2001), 127.

3. Marshall and Jean Stearns, *Jazz Dance: The Story of American Vernacular Dance* (New York: Da Capo Press, 1968), 294.

4. Tom Fletcher, *100 Years of the Negro in Show Business* (New York: Da Capo, 1984), 121.

5. Fletcher 122–123.

6. Fletcher, 165, 210.

7. Adagio was a smooth, lyrical dance style based on European movement vocabulary, including ballet moves.

8. Brenda Dixon Gottschild, *Waltzing in the Dark: African American Vaudeville and Race Politics in the Swing Era* (New York: St. Martin's Press, 2000), 141.

9. Mark S. Foster, "In the Face of 'Jim Crow': Prosperous Blacks and Vacations, Travel and Outdoor Leisure, 1890–1945," *Journal of Negro History* 84 (December 1999), 130–149. Foster also mentions Hotel Waddy in West Baden, Indiana; Crittendon Hotel and Pythian Bath House in Hot Springs, Arkansas; and Mt. Clemons Hotel and Mineral Baths in Mt. Clemons, Michigan.

10. Ethel Waters with Charles Samuels, *His Eye is on the Sparrow* (New York: Doubleday, 1951), 132.

11. Constance Valis Hill, *Brotherhood in Rhythm: The Jazz Tap Dancing of the Nicholas Brothers* (New York: Oxford, 2000), 122.

12. Hill, 141 and 173.

13. Peter Leslie, *A Hard Act to Follow: A Music Hall Review* (New York and London: Paddington Press Ltd., 1978), 11.

14. Waters, 207. Rusty E. Frank, *Tap! The Greatest Tap Dance Stars and their Stories, 1900–1955* (New York: Da Capo Press, 1990), 49.

15. Hill, 110 ff.

16. Gottschild, 156.

17. Frank, 222.

18. Atkins and Malone, 84–87.

19. Jim Haskins, *The Cotton Club* (New York: Hippocrene Books, 1994), 18.

20. Nadine George-Graves, *The Royalty of Negro Vaudeville: The Whitman Sisters and the Negotiation of Race, Gender, and Class in African American Theater, 1900–1940* (New York: St. Martin's Press, 2000), 12–19.

21. George-Graves, 19.

22. Stearns and Stearns, 86.

23. Waters, 93.

24. Waters, 82.

25. Stearns and Stearns, 86.

26. Stearns and Stearns, 90.

27. Stearns and Stearns, 90.

28. Stearns and Stearns, 91.

29. Frank, 121.

30. Frank, 122.

31. Frank, 43.

32. Stearns and Stearns, 88–91.

33. Stearns and Stearns, 89.

34. George-Graves, 23–25.

35. Jim Haskins and N.R. Mitgang, *Mr. Bojangles: The Biography of Bill Robinson* (New York: Morrow, 1988), 43–44.

36. Haskins and Mitgang, 62–83.

37. Frank, 122.

38. Stearns and Stearns, 87.

39. George-Graves, 101.

40. Joe Laurie, Jr., *Vaudeville: From the Honky-Tonks to the Palace* (New York: Holt, 1953), 203.

41. Thomas Riis, *Just Before Jazz: Black Musical Theater in New York, 1890–1915* (Washington: Smithsonian Institution Press, 1989), 171.

42. Morgan and Barlow, 83.

43. Morgan and Barlow, 84.

44. Jason L. Ellerbee, *African American Theaters in Georgia: Preserving an Entertainment Legacy* (Unpublished Thesis, College of Charleston, 2000), 13.

45. Gottschild, 52.

46. Waters, 172.

47. George-Graves, 99–100.

48. Gottschild, 23.

49. Gottschild 23–24.

50. Waters, 165–171.

51. Sammy Davis, Jr., Jane Boyar, and Burt Boyar, *Yes I Can: The Story of Sammy Davis, Jr.* (New York: Farrar, Straus & Giroux, 1965), 161.

52. Atkins and Malone, 106–112.

53. Gottschild, 30–31.

54. Frank, 25.

55. Haskins and Mitgang, 44.

56. Gottschild, 42.

57. Haskins and Mitgang, 50–53.

58. Haskins and Mitgang, 100.

59. Haskins and Mitgang, 162.

60. Haskins and Mitgang, 91.

61. Frank, 180.

62. Haskins and Mitgang, 215.

63. Haskins and Mitgang, 9.

64. Waters, 71.

65. Waters, 73.

66. Waters, 83.

67. Waters, 108–125.

68. Waters, 134.

69. Waters, 156.

70. Stearns and Stearns, 231.

71. Stearns and Stearns, 234.

72. Stearns and Stearns, 245.

73. Stearns and Stearns, 265–266.

74. Stearns and Stearns, 268–269.

75. Frank, 28.

76. Stearns and Stearns, 270.

77. Quoted by Gottschild, 61.

78. Haskins, 37.

79. Gottschild, 63.

80. Haskins, 57.

81. William Barlow, "Black Music on Radio During the Jazz Age," *African American Review*, Vol 29 (Summer, 1995), 325–328.

82. Haskins, 57.
83. Herman "Skip" Mason, Jr., *African-American Entertainment in Atlanta* (Charleston: Arcadia, 1998), 31.
84. Atkins and Malone, 55–58
85. Haskins, 44–46.
86. Hill, 70.
87. Frank, 70.
88. Haskins, 64.
89. Haskins, 104–106.
90. Hill, 41.
91. *Pie, Pie, Blackbird* (Warner Brothers, 1932), one reel. See Hill, 55ff, for a precise description of the performance and interpretive commentary.
92. Hill, 58–59.
93. Hill, 144.
94. Hill, 72.
95. Frank, 155.
96. Frank, 155.
97. Frank, 159–160.
98. Frank, 157.
99. Stearns and Stearns, 277.
100. Frank, 158.
101. Stearns and Stearns, 213.
102. Frank, 73.
103. See Arthur Murray, *Let's Dance* (Standard Brands, 1937), 26–27, which contains instructions for the Shag, Susie Q, and Truckin'; Arthur Murray, *Arthur Murray's Dance Book* (n.d., no pagination), which devotes four pages to the Shag, Truckin,' and the Big Apple.
104. Donald Bogle, *Toms, Coons, Mulattoes, Mammies, & Bucks: An Interpretive History of Blacks in American Films* (New York: Continuum, 1997), 49.
105. Haskins and Mitgang, 205.
106. Hill, 93.
107. Hill, 181–184.
108. Hill, 184.
109. Frank, 72.
110. Atkins and Malone, 98.
111. Atkins and Malone, 99.
112. Frank, 47.
113. Frank, 47.
114. Atkins and Malone, 122.
115. Stearns and Stearns, 305.
116. Stearns and Stearns, 308–309.
117. Waters, 175.
118. This description is by Brenda Dixon Gottschild, 67.
119. Frank, 125.

Chapter 8

1. John Roberts, "Introduction and Acknowledgements," *From Hucklebuck to Hip-Hop: Social dance in the African American Community in Philadelphia* (Philadelphia: Odunde, 1995), no page number.
2. Roberts, 41.
3. Roberts, 24.
4. Rusty Frank, *The Greatest Tap Dance Stars and their Stories, 1900–1955* (New York: Da Capo Press, 1990), 114.
5. Frank, 115.
6. Frank 128.
7. Frank, 131–133
8. Carol Martin, *Dance Marathons: Performing American Culture in the 1920s and 1930s* (Jackson: University Press of Mississippi, 1994), xx.
9. Don McDonagh, *Dance Fever* (New York: Random House, 1979), 62.
10. Martin, 28–29, 56.
11. Martin, 13.
12. Martin, 64; Marshall and Jean Stearns, *Jazz Dance: The Story of American Vernacular Dance* (New York: Da Capo, 1994), 315–316.
13. Brenda Dixon Gottschild, *Waltzing in the Dark: African American Vaudeville and Race Politics in the Swing Era* (New York: St. Martin's Press, 2000), 13.
14. "Swing Bands Put 23,400 in Frenzy," *New York Times* (May 30, 1938), 13.
15. McDonagh, 57.
16. See *Lindy Made Easy (with Charleston)* (Dance Guild, Inc., 1956), 35.
17. Stearns and Stearns 331.
18. You can see a segment of this routine at http://www.savoystyle.com/hellzapoppin.html, choreographed by Frankie Manning. Manning, a regular of the Savoy Ballroom, was a dazzling Lindy Hopper and brilliant choreographer.
19. To hear Manning giving a personal reminiscence of the Lindy Hop at the Savoy Ballroom, go to http://www.pbs.org/jazz/places/spaces_savoy_ballroom.htm. Here you can also listen to some of the music of the Chick Webb orchestra just as it was performed at the famous ballroom.
20. See Herman "Skip" Mason, Jr., *African-American Entertainment in Atlanta* (Charleston: Arcadia, 1998), 17, for a photo of a poster advertising the 1940 edition of the Whitman Sisters show.
21. Stearns and Stearns, 329.
22. Arthur Murray, *Arthur Murray's Dance Book* (New York: Arthur Murray, 1941), 6.
23. Lawrence Hostetler, *How to Do the Latest Dance Steps* (Reader Service, 1947), 36–38.
24. "Jitterbug Jumps from Low to High," *New York Times* (October 12, 1942), 13.
25. Maurice Waller and Anthony Calabrese, *Fats Waller* (New York: Schirmer Books, 1977), 31.
26. Roberts, 53.
27. Zora Neal Hurston, "Characteristics of Negro Expression," in *Hurston: Folklore, Memoirs, & Other Writings* (New York: The Library of America, 1995), 841.
28. Katrina Hazzard-Gordon traced the etymology of the word in her *Jookin': The Rise of Social Dance Formations in African-American Culture* (Philadelphia: Temple University Press, 1990), 79–81.
29. Hazzard-Gordon, 76.
30. Stearns and Stearns, 24.
31. Hazzard-Gordan, 76.
32. To hear some of the music of the Savoy Ballroom, along with recorded reminiscences, go to the web site http://www.pbs.org/jazz/places/spaces_savoy_ballroom.htm.
33. Stearns and Stearns, 330.
34. John Briggs, "The Savoy Era of Jazz Closes on Auctioneer's Brief Reprise," *New York Times* (October 1, 1958), 39.
35. Stearns and Stearns, 322.
36. John Martin, "The Dance: Social Style," *New York Times* (January 10, 1943), X5.
37. See "Big Apple," *Time* (Sept. 13, 1937).
38. See www.jitterbuzz.com/bwood.html for the details of Wood's interview with dance historian, teacher, and choreographer Lance Benishek.
39. See the Arthur Murray Dance Studios web site at http://www.dancetonight.com/amihistory.html.
40. "Topics of the Times," *New York Times* (August 18, 1937), 18.
41. Bosley Crowther, "From the 'Turkey Trot' to the 'Big Apple,'" *New York Times* (November 7, 1937), 150.
42. "The Biggest Apple," *Stage* (October, 1937), 63.
43. See Arthur Murray, *Let's Dance* (Standard Brands, 1937), and *Arthur Murray's Dance Book* (New York: Arthur Murray, 1938).
44. "'Big Apple' Teams Rewarded," *New York Times* (April 22, 1938), 34.
45. "Apple Growers Hold 'Big Apple' Contest," *New York Times* (April 15, 1938), 21.
46. "Gay Hotel parties Acclaim 1938 here," *New York Times* (January 1, 1938), 2. "Butlers and Maids Dance Big Apple," *New York Times* (January 13,1938), 23; "Big Apple to Roll into White House," *New York Times* (December 18, 1937), 4; "Roosevelts Plan Holiday Parties," *New York Times* (December 23, 1937), 18.
47. "'Big Apple' Leads to Stu-

dent Protest," *New York Times* (November 10, 1937), 22.

48. "Auto Thefts Laid to 6 Dancing Boys," *New York Times* (February 13, 1938), 28.

49. Michael Shore with Dick Clark, *The History of American Bandstand: It's Got a Great Beat and You Can Dance to It* (New York: Ballantine Books, 1985), 2–3.

50. Shore and Clark, 13. Dick Clark with Fred Bronson, *Dick Clark's American Bandstand* (New York: CollinsPublishers, 1997), 27.

51. Clark and Bronson, 34.

52. See Lichtman's comments on http://www.people.cornell.edu/pages/kp15/fifties_two.html.

53. Shore and Clark, 7.

54. Shore and Clark 12–13.

55. Jim Dawson, *The Twist: The Story of the Song and Dance that changed the World* (Boston and London: Faber & Faber, 1995), 41.

56. For some examples, see Shore and Clark, 15.

57. Clark and Bronson, 20.

58. Dawson, 17.

59. Roberts, 34.

60. Roberts, 36.

61. Roberts, 37.

62. Roberts, 37.

63. See http://www.people.cornell.edu/pages/kp15/fifties_two.html.

64. Dawson, 17.

65. Dawson, 17.

66. Dawson, 34.

67. Dawson, 16.

68. John A. Jackson, *American Bandstand: Dick Clark and the Making of a Rock 'n' Roll Empire* (New York and Oxford: Oxford University Press, 1997), 214.

69. Dawson, 33.

70. McDonagh, 94.

71. For instructions on how to do some of these dances, see the *Hullabaloo Discothèque Dance Book* (New York: Scholastic Book Services, 1966).

72. Kurt B. Reighley, *Looking for the Perfect Beat: The Art and Culture of the DJ* (New York: Simon & Schuster, 2000), 12.

73. Reighley, 12–13.

74. Jack Villari and Kathleen Sims Villari, *The Official Guide to Disco Dance Steps* (Secaucus, New Jersey: Chartwell Books, 1978), 15.

75. John-Manuel Andriote, *Hot Stuff: A Brief History of Disco* (New York: HarperCollins, 2001), 11.

76. Walter Hughes, "In the Empire of the Beat: Discipline and Disco." In *Microphone Fiends: Youth Music and Youth Culture*, ed Andrew Ross and Tricia Rose (New York: Routledge, 1994), 147–157.

77. Peter Shapiro, *Turn the Beat Around: The Secret History of Disco* (New York: Faber and Faber, 2005), 184.

78. Barry Walters, "Disco: The Longest Night—Sexual Freedom During the Disco Era," *The Advocate* (July 21, 1998). You can find the article on the Internet at http://www.highbeam.com/library/docfree.asp?DOCID=1G1:20944424&ctr-lInfo=Round18%3AMode18c%3ADocG%3AResult&ao=.

79. Tanangachi Mfuni, "History in a Harlem Man's Apartment," *New York Amsterdam News* (May 26, 2005), 5.

80. "Disco: Dancing Madly Backwards," 1–3. From Cornerstone Archives, at http://www.cornerstonemag.com/pages/show_page.asp?262.

81. "Disco: Dancing Madly Backwards," 3. The article cites *Disco Fever: The Beat, People, Places, Styles, Deejays, Groups* (New York: Signet, 1978), 5.

82. Martha Cooper, *Hip Hop Files: Photographs 1979–1984* (Cologne and Paris: From Here to Fame Publishing, 2004), 31.

83. Quoted by Cooper, 44.

84. Quoted by Cooper, 55.

85. Quoted by Cooper, 31.

86. Sally Banes, "To the Beat Y'All: Breaking Is Hard to Do." In *Writing Dancing in the Age of Postmodernism*, ed. Sally Banes (Hanover, New Jersey: University Press of New England, 1994), 121. The article was first published in the *Village Voice* on April 10, 1981.

87. Banes, 122.

88. Banes, 122.

89. Nelson George, *hip hop America* (New York: Viking, 1998), 15.

90. See Sally Banes, "Lock Steady." In *Writing Dancing in the Age of Postmodernism*, ed. Sally Banes (Hanover, New Jersey: University Press of New England, 1994), 134–135.

91. For demonstrations, see http://www.fantasticpoppers.com/videos.htm.

92. Chalfant and Tony Silver created the PBS documentary *Style Wars*. Two other early films about the dance and its culture are *Wild Style* and *Beat Street*.

93. Banes, "To the Beat Y'All," 124.

94. George, 22.

95. Cooper, 210.

96. Lisa J. Yarger, "'That's ... Where Stepping Came from': Afro-centricity and Beliefs about Stepping," *North Carolina Folklore Journal*, Vol. 47 (2000), 110.

97. Elizabeth C. Fine, *Soulstepping: African American Step Shows* (Urbana and Chicago: University of Illinois Press, 2003), 11–12.

98. Fine, 12–13.

99. Fine, 16–19.

100. Elizabeth C. Fine, "Stepping, Saluting, Cracking, and Freaking: The Cultural Politics of African-American Step Shows," *The Drama Review* 35 (Summer, 1991), 48.

101. Amy Davis, "'Deep in My Heart': Competition and the Function of Stepping in an African American Sorority," *North Carolina Folklore Journal* 43 (1996), 92.

102. Jacqui Malone, "Stepping: Regeneration Through Dance at Howard University." In *When the Spirit Moves: African American Dance in History and Art* (Wilberforce, Ohio: National Afro-American Museum and Cultural Center, 1999), 67.

103. Alicia J. Rouverol, "'Hot,' 'Cool,' and 'Getting Down': African American Style and Aesthetics in Stepping," *North Carolina Folklore Journal*, 43 (1996), 97.

104. Malone, 71.

105. Fine, *Soulstepping*, ix.

Bibliography

Abrahams, Roger. *Singing the Master: The Emergence of African American Culture in the Plantation South.* New York: Pantheon Books, 1992).

Aimes, Hubert H. "African Institutions in America," *Journal of American Folklore* 18 (January-March 1905), 15–32.

Ajayi, Omofolabo. *Yoruba Dance.* Trenton, New Jersey: Africa World Press, 1998.

Allen, William Francis, Lucy McKym Garrison, and Charles Pickard Ware. *Slave Songs of the United States.* Bedford, Massachusetts: Applewood Books, 1996.

_____. *Diary, 1863–1866 II.* Unpublished manuscript, State Historical Society of Wisconsin.

Anbinder, Tyler. *Five Points: The 19th-Century New York City Neighborhood That Invented Tap Dance, Stole Elections, and Became the World's Most Notorious Slum.* New York: The Free Press, 2001.

Anderson, Jack. "Enough Chitchat? Bring In da Tapping," *New York Times* (October 7, 1997), E5.

Anderson, Jervis. *This Was Harlem: 1900–1950.* New York: Farrar Straus Giroux, 1982.

Andrews, Kenneth. "Broadway, Our Literary Signpost," *The Bookman* 54 (September, 1921), 52–55.

Andriote, John-Manuel. *Hot Stuff: A Brief History of Disco.* New York: HarperCollins, 2001.

"Apple Growers Hold 'Big Apple' Contest," *New York Times* (April 15, 1938), 21.

Aptheker, Herbert. *American Negro Slave Revolts,* 6th ed. New York: International Publishers, 1993.

The Art of the Dogon. Home Vision Entertainment, 1988.

Asante, Kariamu Welsh. *African Dance: An Artistic, Historical, and Philosophical Inquiry.* Trenton, New Jersey: Africa World Press, 1996.

Atkins, Cholly, and Jacqui Malone. *Class Act: The Jazz Life of Choreographer Cholly Atkins.* New York: Columbia University Press, 2001.

Atkins, John. *A Voyage to Guinea, Brazil, and the West Indies.* London, 1735.

Atkinson, Brooks. "Bill Robinson Appears as the Guest Star of Lew Leslies "Blackbirds of 1933–1934" *New York Times* (December 4, 1933), 22.

Atkinson, J. Brooks. "The Play," *New York Times* (October 23, 1930) 40.

"Auto Thefts Laid to 6 Dancing Boys," *New York Times* (February 13, 1938), 28.

Avirett, James Battle. *The Old Plantation.* New York: F. T. Neely, 1901.

Baker, Jean-Claude, and Chris Chase. *Josephine: The Hungry Heart.* New York: Random House, 1993.

Ball, Edward. *Slaves in the Family.* New York: Ballantine Books, 1999.

Banes, Sally. *Writing Dancing in the Age of Postmodernism,* ed. Sally Banes. Hanover, New Jersey: University Press of New England, 1994.

"Banjo and Bones," *The Critic and Good Literature* 26 (June 28, 1884), 308–309.

Banks, Marry Ross. *Bright Days on the Old Plantation.* Boston: Lee and Shepherd, 1882.

Barlow, William. "Black Music on Radio During the Jazz Age," *African American Review,* Vol 29 (Summer, 1995), 325–328.

Barrow, David. "A Georgia Corn-Shucking," *Century Magazine* 24 (1882), 873–878.

Beadle's Dime Ball-Room Companion and Guide to Dancing (New York: Beadle and Company, 1868).

Benton, Celia M. "Corn Shuckings in Sampson County," *North Carolina Folklore Journal* 24 (1974), 131–139.

Berlin, Ira. *Many Thousands Gone: The First Two Centuries of Slavery in North America.* Cambridge and London: Harvard University Press, 1998.

"Big Apple," *Time* (Sept. 13, 1937), 34.

"'Big Apple' Leads to Student Protest," *New York Times* (November 10, 1937), 22.

"'Big Apple' Teams Rewarded," *New York Times* (April 22, 1938), 34.

"Big Apple to Roll into White House," *New York Times* (December 18, 1937), 4.

"The Biggest Apple," *Stage* (October, 1937), 63.

Blakely, Thomas D., Walter E. A. van Beek, and Dennis L. Thomson. *Religion in Africa.* Portsmouth, NH: Heinemann, 1994.

Blassingame, John W. *The Slave Community: Plantation Life in the Antebellum South.* New York and Oxford: Oxford University Press, 1972.

_____, ed. *Slave Testimony: Two Centuries of Letters, Speeches, Interviews, and Autobiographies.* Baton Rouge: Louisiana State University Press, 1977.

Blesh, Rudi, and Harriet Janis, *They All Played Ragtime.* New York: Knopf, 1950.

Bogle, Donald. *Toms, Coons, Mulattoes, Mammies, & Bucks: An Interpretive History of Blacks in American Films.* New York: Continuum, 1997.

Boston *Weekly News-Letter* (October 15–22, 1730), 1.

Briggs, John. "The Savoy Era of Jazz Closes on Auctioneer's Brief Reprise," *New York Times* (October 1, 1958), 39.

Brooks, Webster. "Connecticut, the Birthplace of Democracy in America," symposium presentation at The Africa Meeting House in Boston, July 24, 2004.

Bryant, William Cullen. Letter XI: "The Interior of South Carolina. A Corn-Shucking" in *Letters of a Traveller,* available at www.blackmask.com/thatway/books142c /letrav.htm. Accessed 7/6/05.

Buckman, Peter. *Let's Dance,* New York: Paddington, 1978.

Burwell, Letitia. *A Girl's Life in Virginia Before the War.* Dahlonega, Georgia: Crown Rights Book Company, 2003. Reprinted from 1895 edition by Frederick A. Stokes Company, New York.

"Butlers and Maids Dance Big Apple," *New York Times* (January 13,1938), 23.

Cable, George Washington. "Creole Slave Songs," *Century Magazine* 31 (April, 1886), 807–628.

_____. "The Dance in Place Congo," *Century Magazine* 31 (February, 1886), 517–532.

_____. "New Orleans," *St. Nicholas: An Illustrated Magazine for Young Folks* (November, 1893), 40–49.

Carney, Judith A. *Black Rice: The African Origins of Rice Cultivation in the Americas.* Cambridge and London: Harvard University Press, 2001.

Chenault, John Cabell. *Old Cane Springs: A Story of the War Between the States in Madison County, Kentucky,* rev. and suppl. Jonathan Truman Dorris. Louisville: The Standard Printing Company, 1937.

Chronicle of the Twentieth Century, ed. Clifton Daniel. Mount Kisco, New York: Chronicle Publications, 1982.

A Chronology of African American Military Service from the Colonial Era through the Antebellum Period. http://www.ufphq.com/aams.htm.

Clapp, Rev. Dexter. "Letter on the Religious Condition of Slaves," *Monthly Religious Magazine* (May, 1846), 206–208.

Clark, Dick, with Fred Bronson. *Dick Clark's American Bandstand.* New York: CollinsPublishers, 1997.

Cockrell, Dale. *Demons of Disorder: Early Blackface Minstrels and their World.* Cambridge, New York, and Melbourne: Cambridge University Press, 1997.

Coe, Robert. *Dance in America.* New York: E. P. Dutton, 1985.

Collier, James. *The Making of Jazz: A Comprehensive History.* Boston: Houghton Mifflin, 1978.

Colonial Albany Social History Project. http://www. nysm.nysed.gov/albany/population.html. Accessed June 12, 2005.

Connecticut State Library. "Connecticut's 'Black Governors.'" http://www.cslib.org/gov/blackgov.htm.

Connell, W. M. "A South Carolina 'Shouting,'" *The Illustrated American* (September 19, 1896), 395–396.

Cook, James W. *Common-Place* 4 (October 2003), parts I,II,III,IV, and V. The publication is accessible online at http://www.common-place.org/vol-04/no-01/cook/cook-2.shtml. Accessed on 7/6/05.

Cook, Will Marion. "Clorindy, the Origin of the Cakewalk," *Theatre Arts* (September, 1947), 64–65.

_____. "Spirituals and Jazz," *New York Times,* December 26, 1926, x8.

Cooper, James Fenimore. *Satanstoe.* New York: Burgess and Stringer, 1845.

Cooper, Martha. *Hip Hop Files: Photographs 1979–1984.* Cologne and Paris: From Here to Fame Publishing, 2004.

Courlander, Harold. *Negro Folk Music, U.S.A.* New York: Columbia University Press, 1963.

Crowther, Bosley. "From the 'Turkey Trot' to the 'Big Apple,'" *New York Times* (November 7, 1937), 150.

Dale, Alan. "'Shuffle Along' Full of Pep and Real Melody," *New York American* (May 22, 1921), 21.

"The Dance: Negro Art Loses in Originality," *New York Times* (July 8, 1928), 98.

"Dancing Masters Move to Purify Charleston," *New York Times* (May 15, 1926), 19.

Davis, Amy. "'Deep in My Heart': Competition and the Function of Stepping in an African American Sorority," *North Carolina Folklore Journal* 43 (1996), 92.

Davis, Sammy Jr., Jane Boyar, and Burt Boyar. *Yes I Can: The Story of Sammy Davis, Jr.* New York: Farrar, Straus & Giroux, 1965.

Dawson, Jim. *The Twist: The Story of the Song and Dance That Changed the World.* Boston and London: Faber & Faber, 1995.

Deagon, Kathleen, and Darcie MacMahon. *Fort Mose: Colonial America's Fortress of Freedom.* Gainesville: University Press of Florida, 1996.

DeCosmo, Janet L. "Junkanoo: The African Cultural Connection in Nassau, Bahamas," *The Western Journal of Black Studies* 27 (2003), 246–257.

DeFrantz, Thomas F. *Dancing Many Drums: Excavations in African American Dance.* Madison: University of Wisconsin Press, 2002.

Del Moral, Paulina. *Tribus Olvidadas de Coahuila* (Gobierno del Estado de Coahuila/Consejo Nacional Para La Cultura y las Artes, 1999).

Dickens, Charles. *American Notes and Pictures from Italy.* London: Chapman and Hall, 1842.

_____. *The Works of Charles Dickens,* Vol. V. New York: Collier, n.d., ca. 1880s.

Dirks, Robert. "Slaves' Holiday," *Natural History* 84 (December, 1975), 82–89.

"Disco: Dancing Madly Backwards." Cornerstone Archives, at http://www.cornerstonemag.com/pages/show_page.asp?262.

Display ad 117, *New York Times* (July 27, 1919), 42.

"Dr. Straton Tells of Buying Drinks," *New York Times* (April 5, 1920), 17.

Douglass, Frederick. *Life and Times of Frederick Douglass: His Early Life as a Slave, His Escape from Bondage, and His Complete History to the Present Time.* Hartford, Connecticut: Park Publishing Company, 1881.

Drewel, Henry John, and Margaret Drewel. *Gelede: Art and Female Power Among the Yoruba.* Bloomington: Indiana University Press, 1990.

Drewel, Margaret Thompson. *Yoruba Ritual: Performers, Play, Agency.* Bloomington: Indiana University Press, 1992.

DuBois, W.E.B. "Of the Faith of the Fathers," *Souls of Black Folks.* New York: Pocket, 2005.

Dunham, Katherine. "The Negro Dance. " In *The Negro Caravan,* eds. Sterling A. Brown, Arthur P. Davis, and Ulysses Lee. New York: Dryden Press, 1941.

Dunson, Stephanie. "The Minstrel in the Parlor: Nineteenth-Century Sheet Music and the Domestication of Blackface Minstrelsy," *ATQ* 16 (December 2002), 241–256.

Earle, Alice Morse. *Colonial Days in Old New York.* New York: Charles Scribner's Sons: 1896.

Edwards, Owen. "Going for the Gold," *Smithsonian* 36 (July, 2005), 20–23.

Eights, Dr. James. "Pinkster Festivities in Albany Sixty years Ago." In John Munsell, *Collections on the History of Albany,* vol. 2. Albany 1865. 323–327.

Ellerbee, Jason L. *African American Theaters in Georgia: Preserving an Entertainment Legacy.* Unpublished Thesis, College of Charleston, 2000.

Emery, Lynne. *Black Dance from 1619 to Today,* 2nd ed. Princeton: Princeton Book Company, 1988.

Epstein, Dena. *Sinful Tunes and Spirituals: Black Folk Music to the Civil War.* Urbana, Illinois: University of Illinois Press, 1977.

The Era, May 23, 1903.

Fabre, Genevieve. "Pinkster Festival, 1776–1811: An African-American Celebration." In *Feasts and Celebrations in North American Ethnic Communities,* ed. Ramon Guiterrez and Genevieve Fabre. Albuquerque: University of New Mexico Press: 1995. 13–28.

Faust, Drew Gilpin. "Slavery in the American Experience." In *Before Freedom Came: African-American Life in the Antebellum South,* ed. Edward D. C. Campbell, Jr. and Kym S. Rice. Charlottesville: University Press of Virginia, 1991.

Featherstone, Simon. "The Blackface Atlantic: Interpreting British Minstrelsy," *Journal of Victorian Culture* (Autumn 1998), 234–251.

Fenn, Elizabeth A. "'All Dance, Leap and Play': Jonkonnu, Slave Society, and Black Dance," *American Dance Festival 1988: The Black Tradition in American Modern Dance* (Durham, North Carolina: American Dance Festival, 1988). 9–10.

Fine, Elizabeth C. *Soulstepping: African American Step Shows*. Urbana and Chicago: University of Illinois Press, 2003.

____. "Stepping," *American Legacy* (Summer 2003), 19–22.

____. "Stepping, Saluting, Cracking, and Freaking: The Cultural Politics of African-American Step Shows," *The Drama Review* 35 (Summer, 1991), 39–59.

Fletcher, Tom. *100 Years of the Negro in Show Business*. New York: Da Capo Press, 1984.

Foster, Mark S. "In the Face of 'Jim Crow': Prosperous Blacks and Vacations, Travel and Outdoor Leisure, 1890–1945," *Journal of Negro History* 84 (December 1999), 130–149.

Frank, Rusty E. *Tap! The Greatest Tap Dance Stars and their Stories, 1900–1955*. New York: Da Capo Press, 1994.

Fredric, Francis. *Slave Life in Virginia and Kentucky*. London: Wertheim, McIntosh and Hunt, 1863. Reprinted in Abrahams, 239–242.

Garrison, Wendell Phillips. Letter to William Lloyd Garrison II, Dec. 2, 1868. Unpublished manuscript, Smith College Library.

"Gay Hotel parties Acclaim 1938 here," *New York Times* (January 1, 1938), 2.

George, Nelson. *Hip Hop America*. New York: Viking, 1998.

George-Graves, Nadine. *The Royalty of Negro Vaudeville: The Whitman Sisters and the Negotiation of Race, Gender, and Class in African American Theater, 1900–1940*. New York: St. Martin's Press, 2000.

Gerstin, Julian. "Tangled Roots: Kalenda and Other Neo-African Dances in the Circum-Caribbean," *New West Indies Guide* 78 (2004), 5–41.

Glass, Barbara, ed. *When the Spirit Moves: African American Dance in History and Art*. Wilberforce, Ohio: National Afro-American Museum and Cultural Center, 1999.

Goines, Leonard. Program for *Dance Black America*, April 21–24, 1983, presented by Brooklyn Academy of Music.

Gordon, Robert W. "The Negro Spiritual." In Augustine Smythe et.al., *The Carolina Low Country* (New York: Macmillan, 1931.

Gottschild, Brenda Dixon. *The Black Dancing Body: A Geography from Coon to Cool*. New York: Palgrave Macmillan, 2003.

____. *Digging the Africanist Presence in American Performance Dance and Other Contexts*. Westport, Connecticut and London: Greenwood Press, 1996.

____. *Waltzing in the Dark: African American Vaudeville and Race Politics in the Swing Era*. New York: St. Martin's Press, 2000.

"Grand Opera House," *New York Times* (November 26, 1889), 4.

Grant, Jane. "The Charleston Prances into Favor, *New York Times* (August 30, 1925), SM2.

Green, Doris. "Traditional Dance in Africa." In *African Dance: An Artistic, Historical, and Philosophical Inquiry*, ed. Kariamu Welsh Asante. Trenton, New Jersey: Africa World Press, Inc., 1996.

Green, Jeffrey P. "*In Dahomey* in London in 1903," *The Black Perspective in Music*, vol. 11 (Spring 1983), 22–40.

Gundersen, Edna. "Madonna Rekindles Her Inner Disco Diva," *USA Today* (November 15, 2005), 87.

Gussow, Adam. "'Make My Getaway': The Blues Lives of Black Minstrels in W.C. Handy's 'Father of the Blues,'" *African American Review* 35 (Spring, 2001), 6–23.

Hale, William Bayard. "A Study of Church Entertainments," *Forum* (January 1896), 570–577.

Ham, M. F. *Light on the Dance*. Anchorage, Kentucky, 1921.

Hamlin, Conde. "The American Stage," *St. Paul Pioneer Press*. Collected in *Current Literature* 8 (December 1891), 611.

Harland, Marion. *The Story of a Long Life*. New York and London: Harper and Brothers, Publishers, 1910.

Harnan, Terry. *African Rhythm, American Dance: A Biography of Katherine Dunham*. New York: Alfred A. Knopf, 1969.

Hartford Black History Project. "Emerging from the Shadows." http://www.hartford-hwp.com/HBHP/exhibit/03/1.html.

Haskins, Jim. *The Cotton Club*. New York: Hippocrene Books, 1994.

____, and N.R. Mitgang. *Mr. Bojangles: The Biography of Bill Robinson*. New York: Morrow, 1988.

Hatch, James V., and Ted Shine, eds. *Black Theatre U.S.A.: Plays by African Americans, the Early Period 1847–1938*. New York: The Free Press, 1996.

Hawes, Bess Lomax. *The Films of Bess Lomax Hawes*. Accompanies the four films Hawes made of African American dance. See text at http://media-generation.com/Films/Bess/master.pdf#search='the%20films%200f%20bessie%2010max%20hawes.'

Hazzard-Gordon, Katrina. *Jookin': The Rise of Social Dance Formations in African-American Culture*. Philadelphia: Temple University Press, 1990.

Henderson, Ray. "Black Bottom." New York: Harms, 1926.

Herskovits, Melville, and Frances Herskovits. *Rebel Destiny: Among the Bush Negroes of Dutch Guiana*. New York: McGraw Hill, 1934.

Higginson, Thomas Wentworth. *Army Life in a Black Regiment*. Boston: Houghton Mifflin, 1900.

Hill, Constance. *Brotherhood in Rhythm: The Jazz Tap Dancing of the Nicholas Brothers*. New York and Oxford: Oxford University Press, 2000.

Hill, Constance Valis. "Tap Dance in America: A Very Short History," 3. See document at *www.nypl.org/research/lpa/dan/hines/TAPENCY2002cites.pdf*.

Holloway, Joseph E. *Africanism in American Culture*. Bloomington: Indiana University Press, 1990.

Horsley, Gus, and Perry Bradford. "The Original Black Bottom Dance." 1926.

Horton, James O. "Humor and the American Racial Imagination," *American Quarterly* 45 (March 1993), 166–170.

Hostetler, Lawrence. *How to Do the Latest Dance Steps*. Reader Service, 1947.

How to Dance: The Latest and Most Complete Instructions in Ballroom Dance Steps. New York: Padell Book Company, 1937.

Hughes, Walter. "In the Empire of the Beat: Discipline and Disco." In *Microphone Fiends: Youth Music and Youth Culture*, ed Andrew Ross and Tricia Rose. New York: Routledge, 1994. 147–157.

Hullabaloo Discothèque Dance Book. New York: Scholastic Book Services, 1966.

Hurston, Zora Neal. "Characteristics of Negro Expression," in *Hurston: Folklore, Memoirs, & Other Writings* (New York: The Library of America, 1995.

International Encyclopedia of Dance. New York: Oxford University Press, 1998.

Jackson, Irene V. *More than Dancing: Essays on Afro-American Music and Musicians*. Westport, Connecticut: Greenwood Press, 1985.

Jackson, John A. *American Bandstand: Dick Clark and the Making of a Rock 'n' Roll Empire*. New York and Oxford: Oxford University Press, 1997.

Jacobs, Harriet. *Incidents in the Life of a Slave Girl, Written by Herself*. Cambridge: Harvard University Press, 1987.

James, Ed. *Jig, Clog, and Breakdown Dancing Made Easy, with Sketches of Noted Jig Dancers*. New York: 1873.

James, Wendy. "Reforming the Circle: Fragments of the Social History of a Vernacular African Dance Form," *Journal of African Cultural Studies* 13 (June, 2000), 140–152.

Jefferson, Margo. "'Noise' Taps a Historic Route to Joy," *New York Times* (November 26, 1995), H4.

"Jitterbug Jumps from Low to High," *New York Times* (October 12, 1942), 13.

Johnsing, Sam. "The Decadence of a Black Art," *Godey's Magazine* 134 (March 1897), 286–289.

Johnson, Charles, Patricia Smith, and the WGBH Series Research Team. *Africans in American: America's Journey through Slavery*. New York: Harcourt Brace, 1998.

Johnson, Howard, and Cliff Hess. "The Wedding of the Shimmie and Jazz." New York: Leo Feist, 1919.

Johnson, James Weldon. *Along This Way*. New York: Penguin, 1968.

_____. *The Book of American Negro Spirituals*. New York: Viking Press, 1925.

Johnson, Jerah. *Congo Square in New Orleans*. New Orleans: Louisiana Landmarks Society, 1995.

Johnson, Stephen. "Juba's Dance: An Assessment of New Acquired Information." *Proceedings of the 26th Annual Conference of the Society for Dance History Scholars* (SDHS, 2003).

Johnson, Walter. *Soul by Soul: Life Inside the Antebellum Slave Market*. Cambridge, MA: Harvard University Press, 1999.

Jones, G. William. *Black Cinema Treasures: Lost and Found*. Denton, Texas: University of North Texas Press, 1991.

The Juba Project web site. http://www.erin.utoronto.ca/~sjohnson/juba/.

Kemble, Fanny. *Journal of a Residence on a Georgian Plantation, 1838–39*. Athens, Georgia: University of Georgia Press, 1984.

Kendall, Elizabeth. "'Bring In da Noise' Steps Uptown, Feet First," *New York Times* (April 21, 1996), H7.

Kerr-Ritchie, Jeffrey. "Rehearsal for War: Black Militias in the Atlantic World," *Slavery & Abolition* 26 (April, 2005), 1–33.

Kimball, Robert, and William Bolcom, *Reminiscing with Sissle and Blake*. New York: Viking Press, 1973.

Kindem, Gorham. *Chuck Davis, Dancing Through West Africa*. Film Makers Library, 1987.

Knowles, Mark. *Tap Roots: The Early History of Tap Dancing*. Jefferson, North Carolina, and London: McFarland, 2002.

Kolchin, Peter. *American Slavery, 1619–1877*. New York: Hill and Wang, 1993.

Kopano, Baruti N. "Rap Music as an Extension of the Black Rhetorical Tradition: 'Keepin' It Real,'" *Western Journal of Black Studies* 26 (Winter 2002), 204–214.

Krasner, David. "Parody and Double Consciousness in the Language of Early Black Musical Theatre," *African American Review* 29 (Summer 1995), 309–317.

Kusmer, Kenneth L. *A Ghetto Takes Shape: Black Cleveland, 1870–1930*. Urbana and Chicago: University of Illinois Press, 1978.

Labat, Père. *Nouveau Voyage Aux Isles de l'Amerique*, trans. Anthony Bliss, vol. 2. The Hague, 1724.

"Lady Middleton, 'Peeress,' and Others Write Letters," *New York Times* (August 24, 1913), SM5.

LaGrone, Kheven Lee. "From Minstrelsy to Gangsta Rap: The 'Nigger' as Commodity for Popular American Entertainment," *Journal of African American Men* 5 (Fall, 2000), 117–131.

Laurie, Joe Jr. *Vaudeville: From the Honky-Tonks to the Palace*. New York: Holt, 1953.

Lee, Betty. *Dancing: All the Latest Steps*. New York: Edward J. Clode, Inc., 1927.

Leigh, Frances Butler. *Ten Years on a Georgia Plantation Since the War: Electronic Version*, 1st ed. (Library of Congress/Ameritech National Digital Library Competition, 1998). See http://docsouth.unc.edu/leigh/leigh.html.

Leslie, Peter. *A Hard Act to Follow: A Music Hall Review*. New York and London: Paddington Press Ltd., 1978.

Lhamon, W. T. Jr. *Raising Cain: Blackface Performance from Jim Crow to Hip Hop*. Cambridge and London: Harvard University Press, 1998.

Lindy Made Easy (with Charleston). Dance Guild, Inc., 1956.

"'Liza' Is Melodious," *New York Times* (November 28, 1922), 28.

Lomax, Alan. *Folk Song Style and Culture*. New Brunswick, New Jersey: Transaction Publishers, 1994.

Lomax, John, and Alan Lomax, *Folk Song, U.S.A.* New York: Duell, Sloan & Pearce, 1947.

Long, Edward. *This History of Jamaica*. London: T. Lowndes, 1774.

Lord, Walter. *The Good Years: From 1900 to the First World War*. New York: Harper and Brothers, 1960.

Lott, Eric. *Love and Theft: Blackface Minstrelsy and the American Working Class*. New York: Oxford University Press, 1993.

Lovisone, Carter. *The Disco Hustle*. New York: Sterling, 1979.

Lucas, Jimmy, and Billy Frisch. "Minnie, Shimme for Me." New York: Broadway Music Corporation, 1918.

Mack, Thomas L. "I'm Flying High." J. C. Groene & Co., Cincinnati, Ohio, 1886.

Mackenzie, Catherine. "Bermuda and Nassau Beckon," *New York Times* (December 29, 1935), xxi.

MacMillan, Dougald. "John Kuners," *Journal of American Folklore* 39 (January-March, 1926), 53–57.

"Madrid Yields to Jazz," *New York Times* (July 24, 1927), E6.

Magaret, Helene. "The Negro Fad," *Forum and Century* 87 (January 1932), 39–43.

Magriel, Paul (ed.). *Chronicles of the American Dance*. New York: Henry Holt and Company, 1948.

Making of a Mosaic: An Introduction to the Music and Dance of the Americas, National Dance Institute Artistic Supplement. n.d.

Marcus, Elise. "More Low-Down Dancing," *The Dance* (January, 1928), 41.

Marks, Carole, and Diana Edkins. *The Power of Pride: Stylemakers and Rulebreakers of the Harlem Renaissance*. New York: Crown Publishers, 1999.

Martin, Carol. *Dance Marathons: Performing American Culture in the 1920s and 1930s*. Jackson: University Press of Mississippi, 1994.

Martin, John. "The Dance: Social Style," *New York Times* (January 10, 1943), X5.

Mason, Herman "Skip" Jr. *African-American Entertainment in Atlanta*. Charleston: Arcadia, 1998.

Mather, Fred. *In the Louisiana Lowlands*, Chapter VI. Printed in *Forest and Stream: A Journal of Outdoor Life, Travel, Nature Study, and Shooting* 51 (October 29, 1898), 345–346.

Maxfield, Jane. "Millicent Matthie's Pitchy Patchy," *Arts & Activities* (January 1995), 31–33.

McDonagh, Don. *Dance Fever*. New York: Random House, 1979.

McElroy, Guy C. *Facing History: The Black Image in American Art 1710–1940*. San Francisco and Washington: Bedford Arts, Publishers, in association with The Corcoran Gallery of Art, 1990.

McIntosh County Shouters: Slave Songs from the Coast of Georgia. Smithsonian Folkways Recordings. Folkways F4344, 1984.

McKoy, Henry Bacon. *Wilmington, N.C.: Do you Remember When?* Greenville: Keys Printing, 1957.

McNamara, Brooks. *Step Right Up*. Jackson: University Press of Mississippi, 1995.

Mel Fisher Maritime Heritage Society Web Site. See http://melfisher.org/lastslaveships/slaveships.htm and http://www.melfisher.org/lastslaveships/intro.htm.

Memorial Hall Museum exhibit, *Turns of the Centuries*. See http://www.memorialhall.mass.edu/turns/index.jsp

Metropolitan Museum of Art. Website for *Genesis: Ideas of Origin in African Sculpture*, http://www.metmuseum.org/special/Genesis/origin_more.htm.

Mfuni, Tanangachi. "History in a Harlem Man's Apartment," *New York Amsterdam News* (May 26, 2005), 5.

"A Minstrel Show in Trouble," *New York Times* (November 19, 1888), 8.

Mook, Telfer. "Training Day in New England," *The New England Quarterly* 11 (December, 1938), 675–698.

Morgan, Thomas L., and William Barlow. *From Cakewalks to Concert Halls: An Illustrated History of African American Popular Music from 1895 to 1930*. Washington, D.C.: Elliott & Clark Publishing, 1992.

Moseley, "Irrepressible Conflict: Differences Between Northern and Southern Songs of the Civil War," *Journal of Popular Culture* 25 (Fall 1991), 45–56.

"Move to Reform Dancing," *New York Times* (August 31, 1919), 13.

Mulira, Jessie Gaston. "The Case of Voodoo in New Orleans." In *Africanisms in American Culture*, ed. Joseph E. Holloway. Bloomington: Indiana University Press, 1991.

Murray, Arthur. *Arthur Murray's Dance Book*. New York: Arthur Murray, 1938.

_____. *Arthur Murray's Dance Book* (n.d., no pagination).

_____. *Let's Dance*. Standard Brands, 1937.

Nadell, Bonnie, and John Small. *Break Dance: Electric Boogie, Egyptian, Moonwalk ... Do It!* Philadelphia: Running Press, 1984.

Nathan, Hans. *Dan Emmett and the Rise of Early Negro Minstrelsy*. Norman, Oklahoma: University of Oklahoma Press, 1962.

National Historic Landmarks web site page on Stono River Rebellion landmark. http://tps.cr.nps.gov/nhl/detail.cfm?ResourceId=1488&ResourceType=Site.

Nettl, Bruno. *Music in Primitive Culture*. Cambridge: Harvard University Press, 1972.

New York State Department of Economic Development, State Data Center. *Population of New York State by County, 1790 to 1990* (July 2000).

Nicholls, Robert W. "The Mocko Jumbie of the U.S. Virgin Islands: History and Antecedents," *African Arts* 32 (Autumn 1999), 48–61.

North Carolina Office of Archives and History in association with The University of North Carolina Press. *The Way We Lived in North Carolina*. http://www.waywelivednc.com/1770–1820/planters-slaves.htm. Accessed on 3/3/05.

Nunley, John W., and Judith Bettelheim, *Caribbean Festival Arts*. Seattle and London: St. Louis Art Museum and University of Washington Press, 1988.

"Old Times in Commack." *The Brooklyn Eagle* (April 4, 1908), 1.

"The Opposing 'Sluggers,'" *New York Times* (December 22, 1885), 2.

"Parade at Nassau," *New York Times* (December 26, 1937), 130.

Parker, Allen. *Recollections of Slavery Time*. Worcester, Massachusetts: Charles W. Burbank, 1895.

Parrish, Lydia. *Slave Songs of the Georgia Sea Islands*. Athens, Georgia: University of Georgia Press, 1992.

Payne, Bishop D. *Recollections of Seventy Years*, ed. C. S. Smith. Nashville, AME Sunday School Union, 1888.

Pearson, Mike. "'No Joke in Petticoats': British Polar Expeditions and Their Theatrical Presentations," *The Drama Review* 48 (Spring 2004), 44–59.

Pennell, Elizabeth Robins. "London at Play," *Century Illustrated Magazine* 54 (August 1897), 569–575.

Pern, Stephen. *Masked Dancers of West Africa: The Dogon*. Amsterdam: Time-Life Books, 1982.

Pie, Pie, Blackbird. Warner Brothers, 1932.

Piron, A. J. "I Wish I could Shimmy Like My Sister Kate." New York: Clarence Williams Music Publishing Company, 1922.

"Plans in the Island Colonies," *New York Times* (December 25, 1938), 116.

"Plantation Review Lively," *New York Times* (July 18, 1922), 22.

"Plays of the Moment: 'Black Birds,' the Coloured Artists' Revue at the London 'Pav,'" *The Sketch* (October 13, 1926), 86–87.

Pleat, Geraldine R., and Agnes N. Underwood. "Pinkster Ode, Albany, 1803," *New York Folklore Quarterly* 8 (1952), 31–45.

"Police Censor Dancing," *New York Times* (June 9, 1919), 14.

Pollitzer, William S. *The Gullah People and Their African Heritage*. Athens and London: University of Georgia Press, 1999.

"Population of New York State by County, 1790–1990." New York State Department of Economic Development, State Data Center, July, 2000.

Porter, Kenneth. Letter to Professor Beth Dillingham, 5 August 1969. Unpublished papers at the New York Public Library.

Potter, Everett. "Unmasking Jonkanoo," Americas 42 (1990), 14–17.

Pulse of the Planet, December 2, 2003, Program 3067.

Ramsey, Rita. *Home Lessons in Tap Dance*. New York: Dutton, 1932.

Reighley, Kurt B. *Looking for the Perfect Beat: The Art and Culture of the DJ*. New York: Simon & Schuster, 2000.

Reynolds, Bruce. *Paris with the Lid Lifted*. New York: A. L. Burt Company, 1927.

Reynolds, Sana. "The Human Need for Privacy: How Individualist and Collective Cultures Use Personal Space." Presentation at Association for Business Communication Conference, October 27–30, 2004.

Riis, Thomas L. *Just Before Jazz: Black Musical Theater*

in New York, 1890 to 1915. Washington, DC: Smithsonian Institution Press, 1989.

____, ed. *The Music and Scripts of* In Dahomey. Madison, Wisconsin: A-R Editions, 1996.

Roberts, John. *From Hucklebuck to Hip-Hop: Social Dance in the African American Community in Philadelphia.* Philadelphia: Odunde, 1995.

Rockwell, Charles. "Sketches of Foreign Travel and Life at Sea," *African Repository and Colonial Journal* 18 (September, 1842), 273–279.

"Roosevelts Plan Holiday Parties," *New York Times* (December 23, 1937), 18.

Rose, Phyllis. *Jazz Cleopatra: Josephine Baker in her Time.* New York: Vintage, 1989.

Rosenbaum, Art. *Shout Because You're Free: The African American Ring Shout Tradition in Coastal Georgia.* Athens, Georgia: University of Georgia Press, 1998.

Rourke, Constance. *American Humor.* New York: Harcourt, Brace, 1931.

Rouverol, Alicia J. "'Hot,' 'Cool,' and 'Getting Down': African American Style and Aesthetics in Stepping," *North Carolina Folklore Journal* 43 (1996), 96–108.

Sampson, Henry T. *Blacks in Blackface: A Source Book on Early Black Musical Shows.* Metuchen, New Jersey: Scarecrow Press, 1980.

"Satirical Character of the Virginians," *The Massachusetts Magazine or Monthly Museum* 4 (April, 1792), 242–244.

Schomburgh, Sir Robert. "Pictures of Barbados," *The Anglo American, A Journal of Literature, News Politics, the Drama, Fine Arts* 10 (October 23, 1847), 3–4.

Schultz, Christian. *Travels on an Inland Voyage through the States of New-York, Pennsylvania, Virginia, Ohio, Kentucky and Tennessee, and through the Territories of Indiana, Louisiana, Mississippi and New Orleans,* vol 2. New York: Isaac Riley, 1810. Facsimile edition.

"Scores Collapse at Mills Funeral," *New York Times* (November 7, 1927), 25.

"The Season's Runs," *New York Times* (June 24, 1923), xi.

Seeger, Mike. *Talking Feet: Buck, Flatfoot and Tap, Solo Southern Dance of the Appalachian, Piedmont and Blue Ridge Mountain Regions.* Berkeley, California: North Atlantic Books, 1992.

Sergei Marinoff School of Classic Dancing. *The Charleston.* Chicago, 1925.

Shapiro, Peter. *Turn the Beat Around: The Secret History of Disco.* New York: Faber and Faber, 2005.

Shelton, Jane De Forest. "The New England Negro: A Remnant," *Harper's New Monthly Magazine* 88 (March, 1894), 533–539.

Shore, Michael, with Dick Clark. *The History of American Bandstand: It's Got a Great Beat and You Can Dance to It.* New York: Ballantine Books, 1985.

Simond, Ike. *Old Slack's Reminiscence and Pocket History of the Color Profession from 1865 to 1891* by Bowling Green University Popular Press. N.D.

Singer, Barry. *Black and Blue: The Life and Lyrics of Andy Razaf.* New York: Schirmer, 1992.

Sloane, Sir Hans. *A Voyage to the Islands of Madera, Barbados, and Jamaica,* Vol. 1. London: B.M., 1707.

Sobel, Mechal, *The World They Made Together: Black and White Values in Eighteenth-Century Virginia.* Princeton: Princeton University Press, 1987.

"Society Women as Minstrels," *New York Times* (December 19, 1893), 12.

South Carolina Slave Laws Summary and Record. South Carolina Slave Laws Summary and Record. See http://www.slaveryinamerica.org/geography/slave_laws_SC.htm.

Spencer, John Michael. "Rhythm in Black Religion of the African Diaspora," *Journal of Religious Thought* 44 (Winter/Spring 1988), 67–82.

Stearns, Marshall, and Jean Stearns. *Jazz Dance: The Story of American Vernacular Dance.* New York: Da Capo Press, 1994.

Stuckey, Sterling. *Going Through the Storm: The Influence of African American Art in History.* New York: Oxford University Press, 1994.

____. *Slave Culture: Nationalist Theory and the Foundations of Black America.* Oxford University Press, 1988.

Sunkett, Mark. *Mandiani Drum and Dance: Djimbe Performance and Black Aesthetics from Africa to the New World.* Tempe, Arizona: White Cliffs Media, 1995.

"Swing Bands Put 23,400 in Frenzy," *New York Times* (May 30, 1938), 13.

Szwed, John F., and Morton Marks, "The Afro-American Transformation of European Set Dances and Dance Suites," *Dance Research Journal* 20 (Summer 1988), 29–36.

Taves, Ann. "Knowing Through the Body: Dissociative Religious Experience in the African- and British-American Methodist Traditions." *Journal of Religion* 73 (April 1993), 200–223.

Ten Toe Percussion web site. http://www.97watts.com/tentoepercussion/. I accessed the site on 7/6/05.

"They Did Not Need Burned Cork: Colored Girls Give a Lively Minstrel Show in Hempstead, L. I.," *New York Times* (February 15, 1894), 2.

Thornton, Rev. C. *An Inquiry Into the History of Slavery.* Washington, D.C.: William M. Morrison, 1841.

Thornton, John. *Africa and Africans in the Making of the Atlantic World, 1400–1680.* Cambridge: Cambridge University Press, 1992.

Thorpe, Edward. *Black Dance.* Woodstock, NY: Overlook Press, 1989.

Tip Top Tapping: Simplified Lessons in Tap Dancing. New York: Book-A-Mag Company, 1940.

"To Suppress 'Jazz' Dances," *New York Times* (February 4, 1920), 13.

"Topics of the Times," *New York Times* (August 18, 1937), 18.

"A Tough Dance," December 9, 1902. American Mutoscope & Biograph Company. http://memory.loc.gov/mbrs/varsmp/1894.mpg.

Towne, Laura. *Letters and Diary of Laura M. Towne,* ed. Rupert Sargent Holland. Cambridge: Riverside Press, 1912.

"Under the Palmetto," *The Continental Monthly* 4 (August 1863), 188–203.

"Uses Phone to London for a Dancing Lesson," *New York Times* (Jan 21, 1927), 13.

Van Valkenburgh, Franklin Butler. Franklin Butler *Grandpa's Letter to His Children: Being the Story of a Boy's Life in a Country Village from 1835 to 1847.* Available at http://www.navvf.org/grandpapa/g-papart18.html.

"Variety Shows: The War Their Opportunity," *New York Times* (April 9, 1876), 10.

Villari, Jack, and Kathleen Sims Villari. *The Official Guide to Disco Dance Steps.* Secaucus, New Jersey: Chartwell Books, 1978.

Wade, Rosalind. *Tap Dancing in 12 Easy Lessons* (Philadelphia: David McKay Company: n.d.).

"Wales at Negro Revue," *New York Times* (September 21, 1926), 33.

Wallace, Carol McD., Don McDonagh, Jean L. Druesedow, Laurence Libin, and Constance Old. *Dance: A Very Social History.* New York: Metropolitan Museum of Art and Rizzoli International Publications, 1986.

Waller, Maurice, and Anthony Calabrese. *Fats Waller*. New York: Schirmer Books, 1977.

Walser, Richard. "His Worship, the John Kuner," *North Carolina Folklore Journal* 47 (2000), 97–110.

Walters, Barry. "Disco: The Longest Night—Sexual Freedom During the Disco Era," *The Advocate* (July 21, 1998), 32–33.

Warren, Lee. *The Dance of Africa: An Introduction*. Englewood Cliffs, New Jersey: Prentice-Hall, 1972.

Waterhouse, Richard. "The Minstrel Show and Australian Culture," *Journal of Popular Culture* 24 (Winter 1990), 147–167.

Waters, Ethel. *His Eye Is on the Sparrow*. New York: Doubleday, 1951.

Watson, John. *Methodist Error or Friendly Advise to Those Methodists Who Indulge in Extravagant Religious Emotions and Bodily Exercises*. Trenton, New Jersey, 1819.

Webb, Barbara L. "The Black Dandyism of George Walker: A Case Study in Genealogical Method," *The Drama Review* 45 (Winter, 2001),7–24.

Welsch, Tricia. "Killing Them with Tap Shoes," Journal of Popular Film and Television 25 (January 1, 1998), 95–83.

Werthwein, Linda. "John Kooner—Revisited," *North Carolina Folklore Journal* 47 (2000), 111–118.

White, Shane. "'It Was a Proud Day': African Americans, Festivals, and Parades in the North, 1741–1834," *Journal of American History* 81 (1994), 13–50.

_____. "Pinkster: Afro-Dutch Syncretization in New York City and the Hudson Valley," *Journal of American Folklore* 102 (1989), 68–75.

_____, and Graham White. *Stylin': African American Expressive Culture from Its Beginnings to the Zoot Suit*. Ithaca and London: Cornell University Press, 1998.

Wikipedia. "National Underground Railroad Freed on Center." Photo of slave pen. http://en.wikipedia.org/wiki/National_Underground_Railroad_Freedom_Center#Slave_pen.

Williams-Myers, A. J. *The Long Hammering: Essays on the Forging of an African American Presence in the Hudson River Valley to the Early Twentieth Century*. Trenton, New Jersey: Africa World Press, 1994.

Wilson, Samuel. "Saint George and John Canoe," *Natural History* 12 (1991), 22–27.

Wittke, Carl. *Tambo and Bones: A History of the American Minstrel Stage*. Durham, North Carolina: Duke University Press, 1930.

Woll, Allen. *Black Musical Theatre from Coontown to Dreamgirls*. Baton Rouge and London: Louisiana State University Press, 1989.

Wood, Peter. "'Gimme de Kneebone Bent': African Body Language and the Evolution of American Dance Forms," in *The Black Tradition in American Modern Dance*. Durham: American Dance Festival, 1988.

_____, and Karen C. C. Dalton. *Winslow Homer's Images of Blacks: The Civil War and Reconstruction Years*. Austin: University of Texas Press, 1988.

Yarger, Lisa J. "'That's … Where Stepping Came from': Afrocentricity and Beliefs about Stepping," *North Carolina Folklore Journal* 47 (2000), 109–120.

Index